Mathematical Investigations in the Theory of
Value and Price
(1892)
Appreciation and Interest
(1896)

Mathematical Investigations in the Theory of Value and Price
(1892)
Appreciation and Interest
(1896)

BY

IRVING FISHER

REPRINTS OF ECONOMIC CLASSICS

Augustus M. Kelley, Bookseller
New York 1965

Reprinted 1965 by permission of Irving N. Fisher

Grateful acknowledgment is made to Yale University Library for the donation of its last copy of the rare 1892 edition.

Library of Congress Catalogue Card Number

65 - 19655

PRINTED IN THE UNITED STATES OF AMERICA
by SENTRY PRESS, NEW YORK, N. Y. 10019

MATHEMATICAL INVESTIGATIONS

IN THE

THEORY OF VALUE AND PRICES

BY

IRVING FISHER

*Professor of Political Economy in
Yale University*

NEW HAVEN

YALE UNIVERSITY PRESS

LONDON · HUMPHREY MILFORD · OXFORD UNIVERSITY PRESS

MCMXXV

First Model of Mechanism Pictured on Page 38, Constructed in 1893.

SECOND MODEL OF MECHANISM PICTURED ON PAGE 38, CONSTRUCTED IN 1925.

PREFACE
TO THIS REPRINT.

The following booklet is a photo-engraved reprint of my doctor's thesis, long since- out of print, and first published in the *Transactions* of the Connecticut Academy of Arts and Sciences, in 1892.

Twenty-five years later, in the midst of the World War, much to my surprise and pleasure, a French translation was made by Jacques Moret.*

Occasionally mathematical economists have suggested that the original American edition should be reprinted, one of them maintaining that "the book has become recognized as an economic classic and should be more available." So here it is, a third of a century after its first publication.

I cannot honestly recommend that it be read entire by anybody. But in my own classes I have, for many years, found use for pages 11-54 and pages 64-79. The book was written when I was more interested in mathematics than in economics. The vector analysis notation on page 81 was a tribute to J. Willard Gibbs, whose student I then was and who took a lively interest in the work.

The "Bibliography on Mathematico-Economic Writings" at the end was superseded years ago by my "Bibliography of Mathematical Economics" on pages 173-209 of Nathaniel T. Bacon's English translation of Cournot ("Researches into the Mathematical Principles of the Theory of Wealth") in the *Economic Classics Series,* edited by Professor W. J. Ashley and published by Macmillan in 1897.

The hydrostatic mechanism pictured on page 38 has been actually constructed—twice in fact. In 1893, the year after the thesis was published, my colleague, Professor Henry W. Farnam, generously defrayed the expense of constructing a model. This was used in my classes for many years. Eventually it wore out and was recently (1925) replaced by a second model somewhat improved and simplified. Photographs of both these models are reproduced herewith.

As I look back on this youthful production I take some satisfaction in finding that my treatment of so-called "marginal utility" and criticism of the then current notions of a "calculus of pleasure and pain" are in tune with modern psychology and that this fact has been favorably commented on by Professor Wesley C. Mitchell.

---

* *Recherches Mathématiques sur la Théorie de La Valeur et Des Prix.* M. Giard & É. Brière, Paris, 1917.

Preface to this Reprint.

The suggestion in this booklet that so-called "marginal utility" may be measurable statistically is now being followed up. Within a few months, I expect to publish the first attempt of this sort and to discuss its possible practical use in deciding on the proper rate of progression for an income tax.

IRVING FISHER.

Yale University, August, 1925.

[From Transactions of the Connecticut Academy, Vol. IX, July, 1892]

[The following memoir is in substance the writer's thesis for the degree of Ph.D. at Yale University, 1891.]

I. — MATHEMATICAL INVESTIGATIONS IN THE THEORY OF VALUE AND PRICES.

By Dr. IRVING FISHER.

[Read April 27, 1892.]

PREFACE.

John Stuart Mill* asserted that he had left nothing in the laws of value for any future economist to clear up. Until 1871 this statement doubtless had much the force of dogma. Even Jevons made preliminary obeisance before proceeding to break the ground afresh with the mathematical instrument. Jevons with characteristic candor expressly disclaimed finality ;† but few of his followers have realized with his clearness and honesty the need of further analysis along the lines which he laid down.

The truth is, most persons, not excepting professed economists, are satisfied with very hazy notions. How few scholars of the literary and historical type retain from their study of mechanics an adequate notion of force ! Muscular experience supplies a concrete and practical conception but gives no inkling of the complicated dependence on space, time, and mass. Only patient mathematical analysis can do that. This natural aversion to elaborate and intricate analysis exists in Economics and especially in the theory of value. The very foundations of the subject require new analysis and definition. The dependence of value on utility, disutility, and commodity, the equality of utilities, the ratio of utilities, the utility of a commodity as a function of the quantity of that commodity solely, or of that commodity and others conjointly, are subjects, the neglect of which is sure to leave value half understood, and the mastery of which claims, therefore, the first and most patient effort of the economi scientist.

These form the subject matter of the following memoir which is *a study by mathematical methods of the determination of value and prices.*

Much germane to the subject has been omitted because already elaborated by others. Cases of discontinuity belong to almost every step, to modify or extend the continuous case. But the application of this correction has been thoroughly worked out by Auspitz und Lieben. Multiple equilibrium and monopoly value are omitted for a similar reason.

The two books which have influenced me most are Jevons : " *Theory of Political Economy,*" and Auspitz und Lieben: " *Untersuch-*

---

* Pol. Econ., Bk. III, Ch. I, § 1.   † Pol. Econ., Pref. 3rd ed.

ungen ueber die Theorie des Preises." To the former I owe the idea of marginal utility and of mathematical treatment in general, to the latter the clear conception of the "symmetry" of supply and demand and the use of *rate of commodity* in place of absolute commodity, and to both many minor obligations.

The equations in Chapter IV, § 10, were found by me two years ago, when I had read no mathematical economist except Jevons. They were an appropriate extension of Jevons' determination of exchange of *two* commodities between *two* trading bodies to the exchange of *any number* of commodities between *any number* of traders and *were obtained as the interpretation of the mechanism* which I have described in Chapter IV. That is, the determinateness of the mechanism was expressed by writing as many equations as unknowns. These equations are essentially those of Walras in his *Éléments d'économie politique pure.* The only fundamental differences are that I use marginal utility throughout and treat it as a function of the quantities of commodity, whereas Professor Walras makes the quantity of each commodity a function of the prices. That similar results should be obtained independently and by separate paths is certainly an argument to be weighed by those skeptical of the mathematical method. It seemed best not to omit these analytical portions of Part I, both because they contribute to an understanding of the other portions of the work and because they were in a proper sense my own.

Three days after Part II was finished I received and saw for the first time Prof. Edgeworth's *Mathematical Psychics.* I was much interested to find a resemblance between his surface on page 21 and the total utility surfaces* described by me. The resemblance, however, does not extend far. It consists in the recognition that in an exchange, utility is a function of *both* commodities (not of one only as assumed by Jevons), the use of the surface referred to as an interpretation thereof and the single phrase (Math. Psych., p. 28) "and similarly for larger numbers in hyperspace" which connects with Part II, Ch. II, § 5.

There is one point, however, in which, as it seems to me, the writer of this very suggestive book has gone far astray. Mathe-

---

* His result, which translated into my notation is

$$\left(\frac{dU}{dA_1}\right)\left(\frac{dU}{dB_2}\right) - \left(\frac{dU}{dB_1}\right)\left(\frac{dU}{dA_2}\right) = 0,$$

becomes by transposition and division identical with part of the continuous proportion, Part I, Ch. IV, § 3.

matical economists have been taunted with the riddle : What is a unit of pleasure or utility ? Edgeworth, following the Physiological Psychologist Fechner, answers: "Just perceivable increments of pleasure are equatable" (p. 99). I have always felt that utility must be capable of a definition which shall connect it with its positive or objective commodity relations. A physicist would certainly err who defined the unit of force as the minimum sensible of muscular sensation. Prof. Edgeworth admits his perplexity : "It must be confessed that we are here leaving the *terra firma* of physical analogy " (p. 99). Yet he thinks it is "a principle on which we are agreed to act but for which it might be hard to give a reason ;" and again : [such equality] "it is contended, not without hesitation is appropriate to our subject."

This foisting of Psychology on Economics seems to me *in*appropriate and vicious. Others besides Prof. Edgeworth have done it. Gossen* and Jevons appeared to regard the "calculus of Pleasure and Pain"† as part of the profundity of their theory. They doubtless saw no escape from its use. The result has been that "mathematics" has been blamed for "restoring the metaphysical entities previously discarded."‡

These writers with Cournot,§ Menger,‖ and Marshall¶ appear to me to have contributed the most to the subject in hand. With the exceptions noted I have endeavored not to repeat them but to add a little to them, partly in the theory of the subject and partly in the mode of representing that theory. Readers to whom the subject is new will find the present memoir exceedingly condensed. In the attempt to be brief, the possible uses of the diagrams and mechanisms have been merely sketched, and elaborate explanations and illustrations have been omitted. I have assumed that my readers are already familiar with (say) Jevons, Walras, Menger or Wieser where illustrations and explanations regarding "final utility" abound. Much of Part II and Appendix I may not be thoroughly intelligible to those not familiar with higher geometrical analysis. These parts are made as brief as possible.

My especial thanks are due to Prof. Gibbs and Prof. Newton for valuable criticism.

IRVING FISHER.

Yale University, May, 1892.

---

* Menschlich Verhehr., *Braunschweig*, 1854.   † Jevons, p. 23, also pp. 8–9.
‡ Dr. Ingram.   § Théorie des Richesses, *Paris*, 1838.
‖ Volkswirthschaftslehre, *Wien*, 1871. ¶ Prin. of. Econ., *Macmillan*, 1890.

SYLLABUS.

APPENDIX I. Miscellaneous remarks on Part I.

Part I.—UTILITY OF EACH COMMODITY ASSUMED TO BE DEPENDENT ONLY ON THE QUANTITY OF THAT COMMODITY.

CHAPTER I.

UTILITY AS A QUANTITY.

§ 1.

THE laws of economics are framed to explain facts. The conception of utility has its origin in the facts of human preference or decision as observed in producing, consuming and exchanging goods and services.

To fix the idea of utility the economist should go no farther than is serviceable in explaining *economic* facts. It is not his province to build a theory of psychology. It is not necessary for him to take sides with those who wrangle to prove or disprove that pleasure and pain alone determine conduct. These disputants have so mangled the ideas of pleasure and pain that he who follows them and their circular arguments finds himself using the words in forced senses.

Jevons makes utility synonymous with pleasure. Cairnes* objects and claims that it leads to a circular definition of value. The circle is however at the very beginning and vitiates psychology not economics; the last dollar's worth of sugar (we are told) represents the same quantity of pleasurable feeling as the last dollar's worth of dentistry. This may be true as a mere empty definition, but we must beware of stating it, as a real "synthetic proposition,"† or of connecting it with the mathematics of sensations‡ as did Edgeworth.§

The plane of contact between psychology and economics is *desire*. It is difficult to see why so many theorists endeavor to obliterate the distinction between pleasure and desire.‖ No one ever denied that economic acts have the invariable antecedent, desire. Whether the necessary antecedent of desire is "pleasure" or whether independently of pleasure it may sometimes be "duty" or "fear" concerns a phenomenon in the second remove from the economic act of choice and is completely within the realm of psychology.

We content ourselves therefore with the following simple psycho-economic postulate:

Each individual acts as he desires.

---

* Pol. Econ., p. 21.   † Kant, Critique Pure Reason, Introduction.
‡ Ladd, Physiological Psychology, p. 361.   § See above (Preface).
‖ See Sidgwick, Methods of Ethics, Chap. IV.

§ 2.

The sense in which utility is a quantity is determined by three definitions:

(1) For a *given individual* at a *given time*, the utility of A units of one commodity or service (*a*) is equal to the utility of B units of another (*b*), if the individual has *no desire* for the one to the exclusion of the other.

A and B are here used as numbers. Thus if the first commodity is sugar and the second calico and if the individual prizes 2 pounds of sugar as much as 10 yards of calico, A is 2 and B is 10.

(2) For a given individual, at a given time, the utility of A units of (*a*) *exceeds* the utility of B units of (*b*) if the individual prefers (has a *desire* for) A to the exclusion of B rather than for B to the exclusion of A. In the same case the utility of B is said to be *less* than that of A.

The third definition will be given in § 4.

The two preceding definitions are exactly parallel to those of any other mathematical magnitude.

Thus: two forces are equal if at the same time they alone act on the same particle in opposite directions and *no* change of motion results. One is greater when additional motion is produced in its direction. Again : "two masses are equal which if moving with equal velocities along the same straight line in opposite directions and impinging on each other are reduced to rest by the collision."* Two geometrical magnitudes are equal if they can be made to coincide, etc., etc.

Just as coincidence is the test of equality and inequality of geometrical figures, and the tip of the scales the test of equality and inequality of weights, so is the desire of the individual, the test of the equality and inequality of utilities. It is to be noted that in each definition of equality the word "*no*" or some equivalent occurs. A standard mode of cancellation is thus designated.

§ 3.

Let us see how these definitions of utility apply to an act of purchase. An individual I enters a market with fixed prices to exchange some of a commodity (*a*) for another (*b*). We may suppose prices to be such that he gives one gallon of (*a*) and receives two bushels of (*b*), then a second gallon for two more bushels and so on

---

* Price, Calculus, vol. iii, p. 316.

until finally he has given **A** gallons and received B bushels. At what point does he stop?

Although the "exchange values" of **A** gallons of (*a*) and B bushels of (*b*) are equal, their *utilities* (to I) are not. He prefers B to the exclusion of **A**, for his act proves his preference (postulate). Therefore by definition (2) the utility of B exceeds that of **A**.

We may write:

$$\text{ut. of B} > \text{ut. of A.}$$

Why then did he cease to buy (*b*)? He sold exactly **A** gallons for B bushels. By stopping here he has shown his preference to buy no *more* (postulate). *Ergo* the utility of a small increment, say another bushel of (*b*) is less than the utility of the corresponding number of gallons of (*a*) (Def. 2). Likewise he prefers to buy no *less*. *Ergo* the utility of a small decrement, say one less bushel is greater than the gallons for buying it. Now by the mathematical principle of continuity, if the small increment or decrement be made infinitesimal *d*B, the two above *inequalities* become indistinguishable, and vanish in a common *equation*, viz:

$$\text{ut. of } d\text{B} = \text{ut. of } d\text{A}$$

*d*B and *d*A are here *exchangeable* increments. But the last increment *d*B is exchanged for *d*A at the same rate as **A** was exchanged for B; that is

$$\frac{\text{A}}{\text{B}} = \frac{d\text{A}}{d\text{B}}$$

where each ratio is the ratio of exchange or the price of B in terms of **A**.

or

$$\frac{\text{B}}{d\text{B}} = \frac{\text{A}}{d\text{A}}$$

multiplying this by the first equation, we have:

$$\frac{\text{ut. of } d\text{B}}{d\text{B}} \cdot \text{B} = \frac{\text{ut. of } d\text{A}}{d\text{A}} \cdot \text{A}$$

which may be written :*

$$\frac{d\text{U}}{d\text{B}} \cdot \text{B} = \frac{d\text{U}}{d\text{A}} \cdot \text{A.}$$

The differential coefficients here employed are called by Jevons "final degree of utility,"† and by Marshall "marginal utility."‡ Hence the equation just obtained may be expressed: *For a given*

---

* Cf. Jevons, Pol. Econ., p. 99.   † Jevons, Ibid., p. 51.

‡ Marshall, Prin. of Econ., Preface, p. xiv.

*purchaser at the time of purchase the quantity of the commodity
purchased multiplied by its marginal utility equals the like product
for the commodity sold.* Or again: for a given purchaser the utilities of A and B, though actually unequal *would be* equal if every
portion of A (and also of B) were rated at the same degree of utility
as the last infinitesimal. This hypothetical equality underlies, as
will subsequently appear, the notion of the equality of *values* of A
and B.

§ 4.

But the two definitions (1) and (2) do not fully determine the
sense in which utility is a quantity. To define when the " grades "
of two parts of a highway are equal or unequal (viz : when they
make equal or unequal angles with a horizontal), does not inform us
when one shall be *twice* as steep as the other. It does not oblige us
to measure the " grade " by the sine of the angle of elevation, or
by the tangent, or by the angle itself. If the two highways were
inclined at 10° and 20° respectively, the " grades " have a ratio of
1·97 if measured by sines, of 2·07 by tangents, and exactly 2 by
angles. For a long time philosophers could define and determine
when two bodies were equally or unequally hot. But not till the
middle of this century* did physicists attach a meaning to the phrase
" twice as hot."

It is here especially that exactitude has been hitherto lacking in
mathematical economics. Jevons freely confesses that " We can
seldom or never affirm that one pleasure is an exact multiple of
another."†

Now throughout Part I the assumption is made that the utility of
any one commodity (or service) depends on the quantity of that
commodity or service, but *is independent of the quantities of other
commodities and services.* This assumption is preliminary to the
definition we seek.

Our first problem is to find the ratio of two infinitesimal utilities.
If an individual I consumes 100 loaves of bread in a year the utility
of the last infinitesimal, or to fix our ideas, the utility of the last
loaf is (presumably) greater than what it would be if he consumed
150 loaves. What is their *ratio?* It is found by contrasting the
utilities of the 100th and 150th loaves with a third utility. This

---

* The first thermodynamic definition of one temperature as a multiple of
another was made by W. Thomson in 1848. See Maxwell, Theory of Heat, p.
155.

† p. 13.

third utility is that of oil (say) of which let B gallons be consumed by I during the year. Let β be that infinitesimal or small increment of B whose utility shall equal that of the 100th loaf. Now in substituting the hypothesis of 150 loaves *let us not permit our individual to alter B*, his consumption of oil.* The utility of the 150th loaf will be pronounced by him equal (say) to the utility of $\frac{1}{2}\ \beta$. Then the utility of the 150th loaf is said to be half the utility of the 100th.

That is, if :

	ut. of 100th loaf = ut. of β,	B being the total,
and	ut. of 150th loaf = ut. of $\beta/2$,	B being the total again,

the ratio is defined :

$$\frac{\text{ut. of 100th loaf}}{\text{ut. of 150th loaf}} = \frac{\beta}{\beta/2} = 2.$$

It is essential to observe that if the 100th loaf is twice as useful as the 150th when their ratio is defined as above in terms of increments of oil, it will also be twice as useful when the ratio is defined by any other commodity ; also that it matters not what total quantity (B) of oil or other commodity is employed.

This theorem may be thus stated:

Given (1)	ut. of 100th loaf = ut. of β,	B being total,
and (2)	ut. of 150th loaf = ut. of $\beta/2$,	B being total,
also (3)	ut. of 100th loaf = ut. of γ,	C being total,
To prove	ut. of 150th loaf = ut. of $\gamma/2$,	C being total,

where C is the quantity of another commodity (*c*) consumed by I in the same period and γ is such an increment of C that its utility shall equal that of the 100th loaf.

We may write from (1) and (3) :

ut. of 100th loaf = ut. of β = ut. of γ,
(100 loaves, B and C, being totals).

Now, if the first total (100 loaves) be changed to 150, B and C being unchanged, the above equation, dropping the first member, will still be true, viz :

ut. of β = ut. of γ,
(150 loaves, B and C, totals),

for, by our preliminary assumption these utilities are independent of the quantity of bread.

---

* As a matter of fact an individual who, if consuming 100 loaves of bread would consume B gallons of oil might, if consuming 150 loaves, use also *more* oil. But this fact in no wise hinders our inquiring how he would reckon utilities if he used the *same* amount.

Since β and γ are infinitesimal it follows from the mere mathematical principle of continuity that:

$$\text{ut. of } \beta/2 = \text{ut. of } \gamma/2,$$
$$(\text{B, C, totals}),$$

$\therefore$ by (2) $\text{ut. of 150th loaf} = \text{ut. of } \gamma/2,$

$$(\text{150 loaves, C, totals})$$ Q. E. D.

Hence our definition becomes :

$$\frac{\text{ut. of 100th loaf}}{\text{ut. of 150th loaf}} = \frac{\gamma}{\gamma/2} = 2.$$

Likewise :

$$\frac{\text{ut. of 100th loaf}}{\text{ut. of 150th loaf}} = \frac{\delta}{\delta/2} = 2,$$
$$\text{etc., etc.,}$$

all of which results harmonize.

Since C is any arbitrary quantity it follows that the definition of the above ratio is independent not only of the particular commodity employed as a means of comparison but also of the total quantity of that commodity.

It is to be noted here that if the utility of one commodity were dependent on the quantities of others, two applications of the definition would yield discordant results.*

We may state our definition in general terms as follows :

(3) The ratio of two infinitesimal utilities is measured by the *ratio of two infinitesimal increments of the same commodity* respectively equal in utility to the two utilities whose ratio is required, provided these increments are on the margin of equal finite quantities :

In general symbols this becomes :

$$\frac{\text{ut. of } d\text{A}}{\text{ut. of } d\text{B}} = n :—\text{if ut. of } d\text{A} = \text{ut. of } nd\text{M}$$

$$(\text{M total}),$$
$$\text{and ut. of } d\text{B} = \text{ut. of } d\text{M}$$
$$(\text{M also total}),$$

where n is any finite number, positive or negative, whole or fractional.

This definition applies not only to infinitesimal utilities of the same commodity (as of the 100th and 150th loaves of bread) but to those of different commodities or services.

---

* We shall afterward see how this affects our notions of utility (Part II, Ch. IV.

§ 5.

Definition (3) is perfectly analogous to other mathematical definitions. To define equality of forces does not fix their proportionality. This property is found in the additional definition: "The ratio of two forces is the ratio of their mass-accelerations." Before mechanics was a science, "*force*" stood for a "common sense" notion resolvable in the last analysis into a muscular sensation felt in pushing and pulling.* But to construct a positive science, force must be defined with respect to its connection with *space, time* and *mass.* So also, while utility has an original "common sense" meaning relating to feelings, when economics attempts to be a positive science, it must seek a definition which connects it with objective *commodity.*†

§ 6.

(**4**) *The marginal utility of a commodity* (as implied in § 3) *is the limiting ratio of the utility of the marginal increment to the magnitude of that increment.* Hence the ratio of two marginal utilities is the ratio of the utilities of two marginal increments divided by the ratio of these increments.

If the units of the commodity are small, the marginal utility is practically the utility of the last unit—for bread, of the last loaf, but if this loaf is sliced into 10 parts and these slices have different utilities, the marginal utility of bread is more nearly the utility of the last slice divided by $\frac{1}{10}$, and so on *ad infinitum.*

It is now an easy matter to find a unit of utility, the lack of which has been the reproach‡ of mathematical economists. The utility of the 100th loaf per year may be regarded as the unit of utility. Or in general:

---

* Spencer, First Principles, p. 169.

† Jevons, Marshall, Gossen, and Launhardt, omit indicating in any way what they mean by the ratio of utilities. Yet each of them embody the idea in their diagrams. Edgeworth (Math. Psych., p. 99) thinks "just perceivable increments [of pleasure] are equatable" and uses this "minimum sensible" as a unit in terms of which any pleasure is to be measured (in thought at least). His definition and mine show perhaps the very point of departure between psychology and economics. To measure a *sensation*, the minimum sensible is perhaps the only thinkable method (see Ladd, Physiological Psychology, p. 361). Here the phenomenon is subjective and so is its measure ; while in economics the phenomena are objective and likewise their measure.

‡ Dr. Ingram, Article: Pol. Econ., Ency. Brit., xix, 399.

(5) *The marginal utility of any arbitrarily chosen commodity on the margin of some arbitrarily chosen quantity of that commodity may serve as the unit of utility for a given individual at a given time.*

This unit may be named a *util.*

Any unit in mathematics is valuable only as a divisor for a second quantity and constant only in the sense that the quotient is constant, that is independent of a third quantity. If we should awaken to-morrow with every line in the universe doubled, we should never detect the change, if indeed such can be called a change, nor would it disturb our sciences or formulæ.

§ 7.

With these definitions it is now possible to give a meaning to Jevons' utility curve, whose abscissas represent the amounts of a commodity (say bread) which a given individual might consume during a given period and the ordinates, the utilities of the last (i. e. the least useful) loaf. For if corresponding to the abscissa 100 loaves an ordinate of arbitrary length (say one inch) be drawn to stand for the utility of the 100th loaf, we may use this as a unit (*util.*) For any other abscissa as 85 loaves whose marginal utility is (say) twice the former, the ordinate must be two inches, and so on. For any other commodity as oil the marginal utility of A gallons being contrasted with the utility of the 100th loaf of bread and this ratio being (say) three, an ordinate of three inches must be drawn. In all the curves thus constructed only one ordinate is arbitrarily selected, viz: that representing the utility of the 100th loaf.

§ 8.

Only differentials of utilities have hitherto been accounted for. To get the total utility of a given amount of bread we sum up the utilities for the separate loaves. Or in general:

(6) *The total utility of a given quantity of a commodity at a given time and for a given individual is the integral of the marginal utility times the differential of that commodity.*

That is:

$$\text{ut. of } (x) = \text{ut. } (dx_1) + \text{ut. } (dx_2) + \ldots + \text{ut. } (dx_n)$$

$$= \int_0^x \text{ut. } (dx)$$

$$= \int_0^x \frac{dU}{dx}\, dx.$$

(7) *The name* UTILITY-VALUE *of a commodity may be given to the product of the quantity of that commodity by its marginal utility* or

$$x \cdot \frac{dU}{dx}$$

The name is suggested from money-value which is quantity of commodity times its price.   (Cf. § 3).

(8) *The* GAIN *or consumer's rent is total utility minus utility value.* That is :

$$\text{Gain} = \int_0^x \frac{dU}{dx}\, dx - x \cdot \frac{Ud}{dx}$$

It is the actual total utility diminished by that total utility which the commodity would have if it were all rated at the same degree of utility as the last or least useful increment.

It is to be observed that total utility and gain are *not experiences in time* but the sum of increments of utility *substitutionally* successive.   The individual is to assign the marginal utility for the 90th loaf on the hypothesis that he were consuming 90 loaves per year, and then abandoning this supposition to substitute successively the hypothesis of 91 loves, 92, 93, etc., all for the same year.   That is, a number of mutually exclusive hypotheses *for the same period* are thought of.

<h2 style="text-align:center">§ 9.</h2>

The preceding definitions have been expressed relative to a particular instant of time.   This was because in actual life purchases are made by separate instantaneous acts.   But the important commodity-magnitudes in economics are "tons per year," "yards per day," etc., bought, sold, produced, consumed.   In order to make our definitions applicable to such quantities the element of time must be introduced.   Hence the following supposition :

During the given period of time (that is, the period for which commodity-magnitudes are considered) *the marginal utility to a given individual of a given commodity is the same at all instants at which he buys or consumes it or sells or produces it.*

This involves supposing that prices do not vary, for prices (as we shall see) are proportional to marginal utilities.

A housewife buys (say) 10 lbs. of sugar at 10 cts. per pound.   As she closes the bargain she roughly estimates that the last or tenth pound is about worth its price.   She did not stop at five pounds for she wanted a sixth more than the 10 cts. it cost her.   She may not buy sugar again for a fortnight.   When she does, we shall suppose the price to be the same, so that the last pound she then buys has the same utility as the last pound she previously bought. She may buy fifteen pounds. A fortnight later only five, all depending on her plans for using it. The whole yearly purchase may be 250 lbs. and we may write :

ut. (10th lb.) Jan. 1 = ut. (15th lb.) Jan. 15.

= ut. (5th lb.) Jan. 30.

= etc.

= ut. (250th lb.) for whole year.

Thus : *The marginal utility of a certain quantity of a commodity for a given period (say a year) is defined to be the marginal utility of that commodity on all occasions during that year at which it is bought or consumed, the sum of the individual purchases being the given yearly purchase and consumption.*

§ 10.

In the hypothetical case the marginal utility of 250 pounds per year equalled the marginal utility of 10 cts. In the same manner we may practically estimate the marginal utility of 200 pounds by supposing the price to be such that our housewife would buy 200 pounds. Thus a number of alternative suppositions are made *for the same period*. By means of these a utility curve can be constructed, one of the coördinates of which is the yearly consumption of sugar. To do this statistically is of course quite a different and more difficult though by no means hopeless proceeding.

Curves of this nature are the only ones to be here considered. But it is clear that there also exist utility curves for each time of purchase.* These would differ both from the "yearly" curve as well as from each other.

§ 11.

To meet a possible objection it must be pointed out that the use of a "yearly" utility curve assumes no nice calculation on the part of the individual as to his future income and receipts. He may even be and generally is totally ignorant of the number of pounds of butter he consumes per year. He creeps along from purchase to purchase and only at these individual acts does he estimate his needs and his abilities. Yet if he always completes his purchase with the same estimate of marginal utility as measured against other com-

---

* They would be the curves of Fleeming Jenkin : Graphic Representation of Supply and Demand.   Grant's Recess Studies, p. 151, *Edinburgh*, 1870.

modities, this must be the marginal utility for the year and the total yearly purchase is the quantity which bears this marginal utility. This marginal utility or "final" degree of utility of the commodity for the year is clearly not the utility of the last amount chronologically (that is Dec. 31), but the utility of the least useful part of any and each of the separate purchases.

§ 12.

It may further be objected that there is a fitful element in the problem which the above supposition ignores. We have supposed prices do not vary during the given period and also that the individual's utility-estimate does not vary. It may justly be claimed that not only do prices vary from day to day, but even if they did not, the individual's estimate of utility is fitful and, although at the instant he closes a bargain his estimate of utility must be regarded as corresponding to the given price, yet he is likely generally and certain sometimes to regret his action so that if he were to live the year over again he would act very differently.

This objection is a good illustration that a microscopic view often obscures the general broad facts. As a matter of fact the use of a period of time tends to eliminate those very sporadic elements objected to. First, though prices vary from hour to hour under the influence of excitement and changing rumors, and from season to season under causes meteorological and otherwise, yet these fluctuations are self-corrective. The general price through the year is the only price which is independent of sporadic and accidental influences. This general price is not the arithmetical mean of the daily prices but a mean defined as such that had it been the constant price during the period the amounts bought and sold would have been just what they actually are. Secondly, the individual caprice is self-corrective. If a man lays in too large a stock of provisions this week he will buy less next. The theory of probabilities therefore substantially harmonizes the theoretical and the actual. The apparently arbitrary suppositions regarding constancy of price, etc., may be looked upon as convenient definitions of an ideal average as just described.

One observation however must not be overlooked. Although accidental variations of price or choices of caprice afford both positive and negative errors and thus largely cancel each other, yet the effect on the *total utility* and the *gain* is always to diminish them. To buy too much or too little, to sell too cheap or too dear will be equally sure to diminish gain. Herein lies the virtue of insurance and the vice of gambling. Neither alters (directly) the amount of wealth. But insurance modifies and gambling intensifies its fluctuations. Hence the one increases the other decreases *gain*.

§ 13.

Again it may be objected to the foregoing definitions that the use of infinitesimals is inappropriate since an individual does not and cannot reckon infinitesimals. The same apparent objection attaches to any application of the calculus. We test forces by weights but cannot weigh infinitesimal masses nor do they probably exist; yet the theory of forces begins in infinitesimals. We apply fluxions to the varying density of the earth, though we know that if we actually take the infinitesimal ratio of mass to volume we shall generally get zero since matter is discontinuous. The pressure of a confined gas is due to collisions of its molecules against the containing vessel. As each molecule rebounds the change of momentum divided by the infinitesimal time is the pressure. Yet at any actual instant the value of this fluxion is quite illusory. But these facts do not militate against the use of fluxions for a thinkable theory of forces, density and gaseous pressure. In cases of discontinuity fluxions have important applications though infinitesimals may not exist. The rate of increase of population at a point in time is an important idea, but what does it mean? It is convenient to define it as infinitesimal increase of population divided by the infinitesimal time of that increase though we know that population increases discontinuously by the birth of whole individuals and not of infinitesimals.

1.

Practically we can find the *approximate* marginal utility of a commodity just as we *approximately* find the rate of increase of population by taking small increments in place of infinitesimals.

In actual fact inequality of utilities is the rule and absolutely equal utilities never exist. Instead of a curve of utility we should draw a belt (fig. 1) whose limits are ill-defined and whose width in general depends on the amount of antecedent attention which the individual has bestowed on the alternative amounts and modes of consumption.

§ 14.

Utility as defined in the preceding sections does not involve the economist in controversy as to the laws of the subjective states of pleasure and pain, the influence of their anticipation as connected with their probabilities,* the vexed questions whether they differ in quality as well as in intensity and duration,† whether duty can or cannot exist as a motive independently of pleasure,‡ etc.

It does not follow that these discussions have no meaning or importance. Doubtless pleasure and pain are connected with desire and doubtless they have an important biological and sociological function as registering "healthful" or "pathological" conditions.§ But the economist need not envelop his own science in the hazes of ethics, psychology, biology and metaphysics.

Perhaps utility is an unfortunate word to express the magnitude intended. Desirability‖ would be less misleading, and its opposite, undesirability is certainly preferable to dis-utility. "Utility" is the heritage of Bentham and his theory of pleasures and pains. For us his *word* is the more acceptable, the less it is entangled with his *theory.*

§ 15.

This chapter may be thus summarized:

Postulate : Each individual acts as he desires.

Definitions of utility.

(2) and **(1)**   ut. of A $\geqq$ ut. of B

if the given indiv. at the given time prefers A to B or neither.

(3) $\dfrac{\text{ut. of } d\text{A}}{\text{ut. of } d\text{B}} = n$

if ut. of dA$=$ut. of ndM (M total) and ut. of dB$=$ut. of dM (M also total).

(4) $\dfrac{d\text{U}}{d\text{A}} \equiv$ Marginal utility.

(5) $\dfrac{d\text{U}}{d\text{A}} \equiv$ Unit of utility (*util.*) (A being given).

---

* Jevons, p. 72.   † Jevons, p. 28, etc.

‡ Darwin, Descent Man, I, p. 76, Sidgwick, Methods Ethics, Ch. IV.

§ Marshall, Prin. of Econ., p. 181, Spencer, Data of Ethics, p. 79, L. Stephen, Science of Ethics, p. 366.

‖ Marshall, Prin. of Econ., p. 306.

(6) $$\int_0^A \frac{dU}{dA} \cdot dA \equiv \text{Total utility.}$$

(7) $$A \cdot \frac{dU}{dA} \equiv \text{Utility-value.}$$

(8) $$\int_0^A \frac{dU}{dA} \cdot dA - A \cdot \frac{dU}{dA} \equiv \text{Gain.}$$

Assumption : $$\frac{dU}{dA} \equiv \text{Function of A } only.$$

Corrollaries : From **(1)** and **(2)** and postulate, when B is exchanged for A

$$\frac{dU}{dB} \cdot B = \frac{dU}{dA} \cdot A.$$

From **(3)** and assumption, in the equation : ut. of dA/ut. of $dB = n$, the value of n is independent of the particular commodity and of its quantity M used in the definition.

CHAPTER II.

MECHANISM.

§ 1.

Scarcely a writer on economics omits to make some comparison between economics and mechanics. One speaks of a "rough correspondence" between the play of "economic forces" and mechanical equilibrium. Another compares uniformity of price to the level-seeking of water. Another (Jevons) compares his law of exchange to that of the lever. Another (Edgeworth) figures his economic "system" as that of connected lakes of various levels. Another compares society to a plastic mass such that a "pressure" in one region is dissipated in all "directions." In fact the economist borrows much of his vocabulary from mechanics. Instances are : Equilibrium, stability, elasticity, expansion, inflation, contraction, flow, efflux, force, pressure, resistance, reaction, distribution (price), levels, movement, friction.

The student of economics thinks in terms of mechanics far more than geometry, and a mechanical illustration corresponds more fully to his antecedent notions than a graphical one. Yet so far as I know, no one has undertaken a systematic representation in terms of mechanical interaction of that beautiful and intricate equilibrium which manifests itself on the "exchanges" of a great city but of which the causes and effects lie far outside.

§ 2.

In order to simplify our discussion the following preliminary suppositions* are made :

(1) A single isolated market large enough to prevent one man's *consciously* influencing prices.

(2) A given period, say a year.

(3) During this period the rate of production and consumption are equal and such that stocks left over from last year and stocks held over for next may have an influence which is unvarying or which is not a function of quantities produced and consumed during the year. Their influence is accounted for in the *form* of the curves to be employed just as is the influence of climate, population, political conditions, etc.

(4) Each individual in the market knows all prices, acts freely and independently and preserves the same characteristics during the period, so that the *forms* of his utility curves do not change.

(5) All articles considered are infinitely divisible and each man free to stop producing and consuming at any point.

(6) The marginal utility of consuming each commodity decreases as the amount consumed increases, and the marginal disutility of producing each commodity increases as the amount produced increases.

(7) As stated in Chapter I, § 4, the utility of each commodity is independent of the quantities of other commodities and likewise for disutility.

§ 3.

In fig. 2 let the curve MN be drawn with axes OE and OA. This curve is such that the shaded area represents any amount of the given commodity consumed by the given individual in the given period of time, and the ordinate (drawn downward) from O to R represents its marginal utility. The figure evidently interprets the fact that as the quantity of commodity increases its marginal utility decreases and *vice versa.*† OA indicates what the marginal utility would be if only an infinitesimal quantity of the commodity were consumed.

2.

Furthermore let a glass cistern (fig. 2) be formed having the figure OAMN for its front

---

* These are (essentially) those of Auspitz und Lieben.

† For the further properties of the curve MN and its relation to the curves of Jevons, Auspitz und Lieben and Fleeming Jenkin, see Appendix I, Division II.

face and a uniform thickness of unity so that the volume of liquid contained is always equal numerically to the area on the face. Hence the amount of liquid in the cistern may represent commodity and the distance of its surface from O, its marginal utility.

§ 4.

ONE COMMODITY (A)—ONE CONSUMER (I).

Let fig. 2 represent the utility cistern for I relative to A. Let us select as a unit of utility the marginal utility of money supposing this to be constant. Thus the cistern is (say) one inch in thickness; the number of cubic inches of water represents the number of units of the commodity (yards, gallons, or pounds, etc.) consumed by the individual during a given period (say a year) and the ordinate OR (in inches) represents the number of dollars at which the individual prizes the last yard or gallon (say) of the commodity.

Since the market is large enough to prevent any conscious influence on the price by the individual I, he acts with reference to a fixed price (p dollars). He will therefore consume such an amount of A that its marginal utility in dollars equals that of the price p, that is, the cistern will be filled till $OR = p$. This is evident, for if *less* should be consumed OR would be greater than p, that is, a little more commodity would be valued more highly than the dollars exchanged for it and so would be purchased, and if *more* should be consumed, reverse considerations hold.

If the price rises OR will increase and less be consumed but if it falls, more. If the price falls to zero as is the case for water and air the quantity consumed fills the whole cistern up to the horizontal axis. This volume is therefore the quantity of *maximum satisfaction*. If the price rises to OA the individual will cease consuming. This price is therefore the limiting *maximum price* at which he will buy.

The liquid contents of the cistern may be regarded as made up of successive horizontal infinitesimal layers each representing an increment of commodity. The height or distance of each layer from the origin represents the degree of utility of that layer. The last or top layer is on the *margin* of the whole and its vertical distance from the origin is the degree of utility of that marginal layer or increment of the commodity or briefly its marginal utility. Thus the margin of consumption has in the cistern an actual physical analogue.

§ 5.

ONE COMMODITY—ONE PRODUCER.

The definitions of utility in Chapter I apply also to negative utility or disutility. Corresponding to all that has been said relative to consumption are analagous remarks for production. 3. Thus we may construct a disutility curve and cistern (fig. 3) marginal disutility (O R) being measured upward from the origin. If utility be measured in money as in the last section, O A represents the minimum price at which the individual will produce the commodity, O R the current price and the shaded area (or the cubic contents behind it) the output.

The marginal disutility of production is here represented as decreasing as the amount of the product increases. This assumes a "law of diminishing returns." It is true that this law is seldom if ever rigorously true when applied to small amounts ; that is, the cost or disutility of producing the first unit is not less but greater than that of producing the second. But the marginal disutility continues to decrease only up to a certain point, after which it increases. This is usually true even of manufacturing. American bicycle factories are now running behind their orders. If they attempted to run their factories at a higher velocity the cost of the additional product would become greater than its price. In general at the actual rate at which a concern produces, the law of increase of disutility applies.

It would be possible by looping the curve MN near the bottom to make a cistern of such a form as to represent correctly both the law of decrease and increase, but as we are chiefly concerned with the point of equilibrium and as at equilibrium the law of increase usually applies such complicated curves are not here drawn.

If a producer has such a productive capacity as to *consciously* influence prices by a variation of his product, he may find his maximum gain by restricting his output even at a point where the law of decreasing disutility applies ; for if he should extend his production, his price might decrease faster than his cost.

These considerations together with the important one that in a productive enterprise the expenses are classified as "fixed" and "running," make many interesting cases of instability and indeterminateness and lead to the discussion of monopolies, combinations, rate wars, etc., etc. These each require special analysis. In the present memoir, however, attention is confined to those features of production which are strictly analogous to consumption. (See Appendix II, § 8.)

§ 6.

ONE COMMODITY—MANY CONSUMERS.

Let fig. 4 represent the utility cisterns for all individuals I, II, III, IV, . . . N, in the market and let utility be measured in money

4.

as before, the marginal utility of money being considered constant (say 1 util.).

The water in the connecting tubes (represented by oblique shading) does not stand for commodity.

The water will seek its own level. This is exactly what happens in the economic world and may be stated in the theorem: *A given amount of commodity to be consumed by a market during a given period will be so distributed among the individuals that the marginal utilities measured in money will be equal. Furthermore the marginal utility thus determined will be the price.*

This follows, for there can be but one price, and each individual will make his marginal utility equal to it, as shown in § 4.

If the stopper,* S, be pressed, more liquid (commodity) flows into the cisterns, there is an inevitable change in level and the price decreases. When it cheapens to 2, II begins to indulge. It is for the first time " within his reach."

It is to be noted that from the standpoint of a single individual the existence of the general price level is an unalterable fact and the amount which he consumes is accommodated to it, just as the general water level in several hundred cisterns may be said to determine

---

* A rubber compression ball would be used in practice. Throughout the descriptions, the mechanisms are those simplest to delineate and in many cases not those which might be actually employed.

the amount in any particular cistern. But, for the system as a whole, the price level is a consequence of the amount of commodity marketed. What appears as cause in relation to effect to an individual is effect in relation to cause for the whole market.

The quantities of commodity and the marginal utilities mutually limit and adjust themselves, subject to three conditions, (1) that due to the forms of cisterns, (2) that due to the total amount of commodity marketed, (3) uniformity of price, or of marginal utility.

§ 7.

ANALYTICAL.

The algebraic interpretation of the preceding mechanism or of the economic phenomena themselves is as follows :

Let $A_1, A_2, A_3, \ldots A_n$ be the (as yet unknown) quantities of the commodity consumed by I, II, III, ... N. Let

$$\frac{dU}{dA_1}, \quad \frac{dU}{dA_2}, \quad \ldots, \quad \frac{dU}{dA_n}$$

be their (unknown) marginal utilities. Then the three conditions mentioned in § 6 become :

(The unit of utility (util.) is that of the marginal dollar.)

(1)
$$\left\{ \begin{array}{l} \dfrac{dU}{dA_1} = F_1(A_1) \\[4pt] \dfrac{dU}{dA_2} = F_2(A_2) \\[4pt] \quad \ldots \\[4pt] \dfrac{dU}{dA_n} = F_n(A_n) \end{array} \right\} \begin{array}{l} n \text{ equations.} \\[8pt] 2\,n \text{ unknowns.} \end{array}$$

(2) $\quad \left\{ A_1 + A_2 + A_3 + \ldots + A_n = K \right\} \begin{array}{l} 1 \text{ equation.} \\ \text{no new unknowns.} \end{array}$

(Unit of utility is that of marginal dollar.)

(3) $\left\{ \dfrac{dU}{dA_1} = \dfrac{dU}{dA_2} = \dfrac{dU}{dA_3} = \ldots = \dfrac{dU}{dA_n} \right\} \begin{array}{l} n-1 \text{ independent equations} \\ \text{no new unknowns.} \end{array}$

Hence the number of equations is :

$$n + 1 + (n-1) = 2n$$

and of unknowns :

$$2n + 0 + 0 = 2n.$$

Therefore the numbers of equations and unknowns are equal and all quantities and utilities are determinate.

§ 8.

AGGREGATE COMMODITY.

Let C, fig. 4, be the *average* curve* of all the individual curves, I, II, III, ... N, and let the new cistern have a thickness equal to the sum of the thicknesses of the individual cisterns. Then as much water will be in the aggregate cistern as in all the others.* The water in the aggregate cistern may be regarded as a repetition of the contents of the individual cisterns. It represents no new commodity.

In cistern C it is almost too evident to require mention that an increased supply of this commodity (indicated by pressing the stopper) reduces the price while a diminished supply increases it. This fact is all that is usually exhibited in "demand curves" such as of Fleeming Jenkin.†

§ 9.

Fig. 5 and completely analogous explanations apply to production cisterns.

5.

* Formed as follows : Select *pts. of like price* on the individual curves, that is, pts. of like ordinates (as y_1, y_2, y_3, . . . y_n) and using the same ordinate for the new ordinate, take the average of their abscissas for the new abscissa and make the thickness of the new cistern equal to the sum of the thicknesses of all the individual cisterns. Then if in such a cistern liquid be allowed to flow to the level of the individual cisterns the amount of liquid contained in it will equal all that contained in the individual cisterns. For evidently the free surface of the water in the large cistern equals in area the total free surfaces in the small, and as such equality of horizontal infinitesimal layers or laminæ holds true at all successive levels, it holds true of the sums of the layers.

† The Graphic Representation of Supply and Demand. Grant's recess studies, p. 151.

§ 10.

The mechanism above described simply gives exactness to a common imagery in economics, such as "margin," "price levels," "planes" of demand (and supply) and : "a plentiful supply brings the commodity 'within reach' of consumers."

The notion of a cistern is also natural. Says Adam Smith : "The demand for food is limited by the capacity of a man's stomach." Not only is there a "limit," but the demand for food has varying intensities according to the degree in which the stomach is filled. The economic man is to be regarded as a number of cisterns or stomachs, each relative to a particular commodity.

CHAPTER III.

ONE CONSUMER (OR PRODUCER)—MANY COMMODITIES.

§ 1.

The next problem is that of the distribution of an individual's income over all the commodities in the market.

The income-spender considers not only the price of a given article in determining how much of that article he will take but also the relative advantages of using the same money for other things.

The manner in which this consideration affects the mechanism described in Chapter II is through the utility of money.*

In the last chapter, while the price varied in relation to the quantity of commodity, each individual's valuation or marginal utility of money was regarded as constant. This is nearly true *when only one commodity* is considered. In the present chapter, on the other hand, the individual valuation of money varies in relation to the quantity of money income, but the prices of all commodities are regarded as constant. This is nearly true when *only one individual* is considered.

---

* This sort of interaction, especially when extended to several consumers and several commodities (as in the next chapter), presented the most difficulties to the Auspitz und Lieben Analysis; on p. 63 in §16 they say : "Welche Aenderung eine Einzelkurve erleidet wenn sich die Vermögensverhältnisse des betreffenden Individuums ändert, lässt sich im allgemeinen nicht verfolgen. Wenn auch in der Regel die Ordinaten der kurven länger werden, wenn das Individuum wolhabender wird, so wird dies doch keineswegs gleichmässig der Fall sein, vollends nicht, wenn wir verschiedene Artikel betrachten."

§ 2.

Let the individual I distribute his income over the commodities
A, B, C, ... M.   Let the thickness of each cistern in fig. 6 be
proportional to the price of the commodity it contains.   Thus if A
bears a price of $2 per yard, B $1 per gallon and C $½ per pound, the
thickness of cistern B is 2, of B 1, and of C½.

6.

Let the unit of area on the front surface of each cistern represent
a unit of commodity, yards for A, gallons for B, etc.

Then the volume of liquid will evidently indicate the money value
of the commodity, for it equals the front area times the thickness,
that is, the quantity of commodity times its price.   Moreover the
sum of all the water will indicate the whole* income in dollars.
The unit of volume thus represents not a yard, gallon, pound, etc.,
but a *dollar's worth* in each case.   For A it would be ½ yard, for B
1 gallon, for C 2 lbs., etc.

Accordingly let the curves which limit the cisterns be so constructed that the ordinates shall represent marginal utility *per
dollar's worth* not per yard, gallon, etc.

§ 3.

The liquid will seek its own level corresponding to the economic
proposition : *A consumer will so arrange his consumption that the
marginal utility per dollar's worth of each commodity shall be the
same.*

---

* Saving is here regarded as a form of spending, the commodity purchased
being capital.   The analysis implies that the marginal utility of saving a dollar
equals the marginal utility of the dollar spent in other ways.   This would be
elaborated from another standpoint in a theory of distribution.   Cf. Launhardt ;
Volkswirthschaftslehre ; Böhm-Bawerk ; Kapital und Kapitalzins.

This follows because if the individual should vary his consumption from such a distribution, by expending an extra dollar on A he would divert that amount from another article or articles, say B. Then the level in the A cistern would be higher than in the B, which interpreted, is the dollar spent on A had less utility than if it had been devoted to B.

If the stopper be pressed, i. e. if the individual had had a larger income, the valuation of the last dollar's worth of each commodity decreases, or the marginal utility of money decreases. If it becomes at the maximum marginal utility of B he begins to spend on B. As it is in the figure he " cannot afford it."

The amount spent on any particular commodity depends on the general water level, i. e. the valuation of a dollar, while reversely the valuation of money depends on the total amount to be spent on all commodities.

Three conditions suffice to make the distribution determinate : (1) that due to the forms of the cisterns, (2) the condition that the total income equals a specified amount, (3) uniformity of marginal utility (per dollar's worth) of each commodity.

§ 4.

ANALYTICAL.

Let A, B, C, . . . M be the (unknown) quantities of various commodities consumed by I, and $\dfrac{dU}{dA}$, ... $\dfrac{dU}{dM}$ their (unknown) marginal utilities. Let p_a, p_b, . . . p_m be their (known) prices.

Then the above three conditions become :

(The unit of commodity is the *dollar's worth*.)

(1) $$\left\{ \begin{array}{l} \dfrac{dU}{dA} = F(A) \\[1mm] \dfrac{dU}{dB} = F(B) \\[1mm] \quad \cdot \quad \cdot \quad \cdot \\[1mm] \dfrac{dU}{dM} = F(M) \end{array} \right\} \begin{array}{l} m \text{ equations.} \\[2mm] 2m \text{ unknowns.} \end{array}$$

(2) $\left\{ Ap_a + Bp_b + \ldots + Mp_m = K \right.$ $\left\} \begin{array}{l} 1 \text{ equation.} \\ \text{no new unknowns.} \end{array} \right.$

(Unit of commodity is dollar's worth.)

$$(3) \qquad \left\{ \frac{dU}{dA} = \frac{dU}{dB} = \ldots = \frac{dU}{dM} \right\} \begin{array}{l} m-1 \text{ independent equation.} \\ \text{no new unknowns.} \end{array}$$

Number of equations $= m + 1 + m - 1 = 2m$.

" " unknowns $= 2m + 0 + 0 = 2m$.

Hence the system is determinate.

§ 5.

AGGREGATE INCOME.

Let I, fig. 6, be the average curve* of all the separate commodity curves A, B, C, . . . M, and let the new cistern have a thickness equal to the sum of the thicknesses of the original cisterns. Then the water in the resultant cistern equals the sum of that in the components.*

The liquid in the new cistern represents the money collectively considered and the ordinate the utility of the last dollar.

If this income increases, its marginal utility decreases and decreases in a law whose relation to the laws of utility for the separate commodities is shown by the relation of the resultant cistern to the components.

---

* In this case the average is not a simple arithmetical mean but a *weighted* average. Select *points of like utility* on the component curves, that is, points of equal ordinates. Average their abscissas, multiplying each by the ratio of the thickness of its cistern to that of the resultant cistern (viz : the sum of the thicknesses of the original cisterns). Thus if the thicknesses are p_a, p_b, . . . p_m and the abscissas x_a, x_b, . . . x_m, the resulting thickness and abscissa (P and X) are :

$$P = p_a + p_b + \ldots + p_m$$

$$X = \frac{x_a p_a + x_b p_b + \ldots + x_m p_m}{p_a + p_b + \ldots + p_m}$$

If in a cistern thus formed liquid enters to the level of the component cisterns, the liquid in the resultant cistern equals the total in the component. For the sum of the free surfaces in the component cisterns is

$$x_a p_a + x_b p_b + \ldots + x_m p_m$$

and the free surface in the resultant is

$$(p_a + p_b + \ldots + p_m) \cdot \left(\frac{x_a p_a + x_b p_b + \ldots + x_m p_m}{p_a + p_b + \ldots + p_m} \right)$$

Since these two expressions are equal and this equality holds of infinitesimal layers at the free surface and so successively at all levels it must hold of the sums of these layers.

§ 6.

An analogous discussion applies to fig. 7.   In place of a given income we must suppose a given amount of expenses to be met by the

7.

production of various commodities.*   It is at this point that an important distinction between production and consumption enters, viz: in civilized life men find it advantageous to consume *many* things but to produce *few*.   The discussion of this difference pertains to Part II.

CHAPTER IV.

M COMMODITIES—N CONSUMERS (OR PRODUCERS).

§ 1.

We have seen the laws of distribution of commodities from two points of view, by first restricting our discussion to one commodity among many consumers and afterward to one consumer among many commodities.   Our discussion is like a tourist's view of a great city, who glances up each east and west street while riding along the same avenue and then takes a "cross town" course and sees each avenue from a single street.   We are now to seek a bird's-eye view.

The variables and their variations which have been described are comparatively simple.   But the possible variations in the more general case are so complicated that they can scarcely be seen or described without the aid of a mechanism.

---

* Borrowing capital is to be here regarded as a form of producing.   The disutility of borrowing the last dollar equals the disutility of producing the last dollar's worth of goods.   See foot note to § 2.

§ 2.

First of all an analysis will serve to set the two preceding discussions in a common point of view.

In any purchase the last infinitesimal commodity bought has a utility equal to that of the money given, that is :

$$\text{ut. of } dA = \text{ut. of } dm$$

or :

$$\frac{dU}{dA} \, dA = \frac{dU}{dm} \cdot dm \qquad \text{(see Ch. I, § 3.)}$$

or :

$$\frac{dU}{dA} = \frac{dU}{dm} \cdot \frac{dm}{dA}$$

or :

$$\frac{dU}{dA} = \frac{dU}{dm} \cdot p_a$$

where p_a is the money price.

That is, the marginal utility of a commodity (per pound, yard, etc.) equals the marginal utility of money (per dollar) times the ratio of exchange of money for commodity :

This equation is fundamental. In our first discussion (one commodity, various consumers) the marginal utility of money was supposed constant so that

$$\frac{dU}{dA} \propto p_a$$

or the marginal utility of a commodity is measured by it price.

In the second discussion the other factor, the price, was supposed constant, and :

$$\frac{dU}{dA} \propto \frac{dU}{dm}$$

or the marginal utility is measured by the valuation of money.

§ 3.

In the present chapter we are restricted to neither of these special suppositions. For the individual I, we may write

$$\frac{dU}{dA_1} = \frac{dU}{dm_1} \cdot p_a$$

$$\frac{dU}{dB_1} = \frac{dU}{dm_1} \cdot p_b$$

$$\cdots\cdots\cdots\cdots$$

$$\frac{dU}{dM_1} = \frac{dU}{dm_1} \cdot p_m$$

whence, since the marginal utility of money to I is the same in each case,

$$\frac{d\mathrm{U}}{d\mathrm{A}_1} : \frac{d\mathrm{U}}{d\mathrm{B}_1} : \cdots \cdot \frac{d\mathrm{U}}{d\mathrm{M}_1} = p_a : p_b : \cdots \cdot p_m$$

Since this is true for every individual and the prices to all individuals are the same, we may write:

$$p_a : p_b : \cdots \cdot p_m = \frac{d\mathrm{U}}{d\mathrm{A}_1} : \frac{d\mathrm{U}}{d\mathrm{B}_1} : \cdots \cdot : \frac{d\mathrm{U}}{d\mathrm{M}_1}$$

$$= \frac{d\mathrm{U}}{d\mathrm{A}_2} : \frac{d\mathrm{U}}{d\mathrm{B}_2} : \cdots \cdot : \frac{d\mathrm{U}}{d\mathrm{M}_2}$$

$$= \cdots \cdots \cdots \cdots \cdots$$

$$= \frac{d\mathrm{U}}{d\mathrm{A}_n} : \frac{d\mathrm{U}}{d\mathrm{B}_n} : \cdots \cdot : \frac{d\mathrm{U}}{d\mathrm{M}_n}$$

These equations express in the most general way the theory of marginal utilities in relation to prices. This theory is not, as sometimes stated, "the marginal utilities to the same individual of all articles are equal," much less is it "the marginal utilities of the same article to all consumers are equal," but : *The marginal utilities of all articles consumed by a given individual are proportional to the marginal utilities of the same series of articles for each other consumer, and this uniform continuous ratio is the scale of prices of those articles.*

The idea of *equality* is inadequate and must be replaced by the idea of *proportionality.* The problem which confronts the individual must be figured as to so adjust his consumption of all commodities that the utilities of the last pound, yard, gallon, etc., shall bear the ratio which he finds their prices do, while the market as a whole must cause such prices to emerge as will enable each individual to solve this problem and at the same time just take off the supply.

§ 4.

This notion of a ratio is introduced into the following more complicated mechanism (fig. 8). Fig. 9 (an elevation of fig. 8) shows the various cisterns of various commodities for the individual I. The ordinates represent marginal utility *per unit of commodity.* It corresponds to fig. 6, except that in the latter the utility is *per dollar's worth* of commodity. The tops of the cisterns are no longer at· the same level. The cisterns are now to float like boats in a

8.

9.

tank* and free to move only vertically (being so constrained by a telescope arrangement beneath and not shown in the diagram).

A glance at fig. 8 or fig. 10 (a plan of fig. 8) will show that any right and left row of cisterns is relative to a single individual and corresponds to fig. 6 and that any front and back row is relative to a single commodity and corresponds to fig. 4.

The water in these cisterns must be subjected to two sets of conditions, first: the sum of all the contents of IA, IIA, IIIA, etc., shall be a given amount (viz: the whole of the commodity A consumed during the

10.

given period) with a like given sum for the B row, C row, etc., secondly: the sum of IA, IB, IC, etc., each multiplied by a coefficient (the price of A, of B, of C, etc.), shall be given (viz: the whole income of I during the period) with a like given sum for the II row, III row, etc.

---

* The level of water in each cistern is intended to be that of the level in the tank. The only constant cause which will make the levels different is the *difference* between the weight of the whole cistern and the weight of the water displaced by its walls (partly wood) which difference is slight, may be plus or minus, and is equal to the weight of the excess or deficit of water in the cistern above or below the outside level.

To realize these two sets of conditions each cistern is divided into two by a vertical partition of wood. The front compartments are all of unit thickness one inch (say). All front compartments belonging to the same front-and-back row are mutually connected by tubes (in the tank but not in connection with the water of the tank) thus fulfilling the first set of conditions.

The thickness of the back compartments is adjustable but is (as will soon appear) constrained to be always equal to the price, thus if the price of A is $1, of B $3 and C $1.20, the thickness of all cisterns in the A row will be 1, in the B row 3 and in the C row 1.2 (inches).

Since the thickness of the front compartment is unity, the contents of each back compartment equals the contents of the front multiplied by the number of inches of thickness of the back cistern, that is the back compartment contains a volume of water equal to the amount of the commodity multiplied by its price. It contains therefore the *money value* of the commodity. The double cistern represents the double light in which each commodity is commonly regarded—so many pounds, yards, etc. and so many dollar's worth.

All back compartments of the same right and left rows are mutually connected by tubes—that is the sum of their contents is given—thus fulfilling the second set of conditions.

The back compartments can change their thicknesses, as the walls at the right, left and bottom are of flexible leather; the back plane is kept parallel to the wood partition by two double " parallel rules" not diagramed.

There remains to be described the system of levers. The purpose of these levers is to keep the continuous ratio of marginal utilities, the same for all individuals and equal to the ratio of prices.

First there is a system of oblique* levers (F12, etc., fig. 9) connected by sliding pivots with the tops of the cisterns and having their lower extremities hinged to wooden floats F, the hinges being on the level of the water of the tank. These floats are free only to shift laterally. It is evident from the similar triangles FR1 and FR2 in fig. 9 that the ordinates of the two cisterns IA and IB are proportional to the distances of the A and B rods R and K from the hinge in the left float F. Likewise in the row behind, the ordinates are proportional to the same distances. Hence the four ordinates are proportional to each other and in general all the

---

* A convenient angle for each lever can be assured by a careful selection of commodity units. Thus if the marginal utility *per pound* gives inconvenient ordinates in the A row, reconstruct the cisterns in that row so that the ordinates are lengthened to represent marginal utility per ton or shortened for the ounce.

ordinates of the front row are proportional to those of the row next behind, also of the second row behind and so on. Remembering that each ordinate is a marginal utility we have:

$$\frac{d\mathrm{U}}{d\mathrm{A}_1} : \frac{d\mathrm{U}}{d\mathrm{B}_1} : \cdots = \frac{d\mathrm{U}}{d\mathrm{A}_2} : \frac{d\mathrm{U}}{d\mathrm{B}_2} : \cdots = \frac{d\mathrm{U}}{d\mathrm{A}_3} : \frac{d\mathrm{U}}{d\mathrm{B}_3} : \cdots = \cdots$$

which is the required condition that marginal utilities must be proportional (§3).

Secondly there are the horizontal levers (F34, etc., fig. 10) lying on the surface of the water in the tank. These relate to prices. The sliding pivots 3, 4, etc. are connected with rods RRR, which in turn are connected by vertical pins with the rear walls of the cisterns. A motion of one of these rods causes all back compartments in that row to expand or shrink in unison. The pivots 3, 4, etc. are so situated on these rods that if the levers F34, etc. should assume a right-and-left position along the dotted line FF, the back compartment of every cistern would be completely closed. Hence R3 equals the thickness of each back compartment in the A row, R4 the corresponding thickness in the B row and so on.

By the similar triangles FR3 and F34 in fig. 10, it is clear that the lines R3 and R4, and consequently the rear thickness in the A and B rows are proportional to the distances of the A and B rods R and R from the float F. But we have just seen that the ordinates of IA and IB are proportional to these same distances. Hence the thicknesses of the back compartments of the cisterns are proportional to the ordinates of those cisterns, that is to marginal utilities. Hence we are free to call the thickness of each back compartment, the money* price of the commodity to which that cistern relates.

---

* Money is here used solely as a measure of value. It is not one of the commodities in the market. The high or low price of commodities in terms of this money is dependent entirely on the amount of it at which we agree to rate the yearly consumption of the market, that is the amount of liquid originally in the back cisterns. We are so accustomed to regard money as the medium of exchange and therefore as a commodity that we may not observe that it is perfectly possible to have a measure of value which is not a commodity at all. Thus we might agree to call the consumption of the United States for a year $10,000,-000,000, and this agreement would immediately fix a measure of value, though the new dollar need have no equality to the gold or silver dollar. It would be easy to translate between such an arbitrary standard and any commodity standard. Thus if statistics showed that the consumption measured in gold dollars was $12,000,000,000, the agreed standard is at 120 compared with gold and by means of this factor we can reduce the prices of all commodities. In the mechanism the aggregate amount of liquid in the back cisterns corresponds to the $10,000,000,000. If we take it so and if the amount of liquid in the I row is given at $1,000, this means that (in whatever standard) the consumption of I is one-ten-millionth in value the aggregate consumption.

It is to be observed that the cisterns are free to move only *vertically*, the rods and rear cistern walls only *forward and backward*, the wooden floats can shift only sidewise *right and left* while the levers assume such positions as the mechanism compels.

§ 5.

Let given quantities of water be introduced into each front-and-back-row of front cisterns and into each right-and-left row of back cisterns. The system will attain a stable equilibrium and the level of water in each cistern will be that of the tank.

The front cisterns of a front-and-back row must have a uniform level on account of their mutual connection. The back cisterns of a right-and-left row must preserve a uniform level for a similar reason. The movable rear walls allow the pressure of the outside water in the tank to keep the back cisterns at the same level as the front. Without taking account of the levers the cisterns would thus all have the same level as the tank. But it would be possible to arrange their vertical positions and their rear thicknesses in many arbitrary ways. The levers simply specify or determine this arrangement.

§ 6.

It may be needful to restate carefully the magnitudes, their units and the conditions which determine them. The magnitudes are:

1. *The quantities of each commodity consumed by each individual during the year.* These are represented by the quantities of water in each front compartment.

2. *The given total quantities of each commodity consumed by the whole market*—represented by the fixed amount of water in each front and back row of front comparments and *registered on scales** A, B, C, at the rear of the tank. Each commodity-water may have a distinguishing color.

3. *The money paid for each commodity by each individual*—represented by the water in each back compartment.

4. *The total money income of each individual*—represented by the fixed amount of water in each right-and-left row of back compartments, and *registered on scales†* I, II, III, at the right of the tank.

---

* The stoppers A B, C regulate this amount of water. The stoppers are each directly connected with the pointers on the scales A, B, C, and so arranged that when the stopper is withdrawn so that the scale reads zero, the water entirely disappears from the cisterns.

† The stoppers I, II, III are also directly connected with pointers on the scales I, II, III.

5. *The marginal utility of each commodity to each individual* —represented by the ordinate of each cistern, i. e. by the distance from its top to the water level.

6. *The money price of each commodity* — represented (in any cistern in the same front-and-back-row) by the thickness of the back compartment, and *registered on scales** p_a, p_b, p_c at the rear. (The relation of price to marginal utility will recur.)

7. *The prices of commodities in terms of each other*—represented by the ratios of their ordinates.

8. *The marginal utility of money to each individual* — represented (in any cistern in the same right-and-left-row) by the ratio† of the ordinate of that cistern to the thickness of its back compartment and *registered on scales*‡ U I, U II, U III at the right.

11.

The units of these magnitudes are :

1. The unit of commodity is a *ton, yard, gallon,* etc., and is represented by (say) a *cubic inch* of water.

2. The unit of money is (say) a *dollar* and is represented by (say) a *cubic inch* of water.

3. The unit of price is one dollar per ton, yard, gallon, etc., and is represented by one inch.

4. The unit of marginal utility for each individual is the marginal utility of (say) 100 tons of A. It may be called a *util* and by a proper

---

* The rods RRR are each connected by a cord and pulley with the pointers of the scales p_a, p_b, p_c.

† This ratio is evidently the marginal utility of money ("valuation of money") because as seen in chapter IV, § 2,
$$\frac{dU}{dA} = \frac{dU}{dm} \cdot p_a$$

whence : $\frac{dU}{dm} = \frac{\dfrac{dU}{dA}}{p_a} = \frac{\text{ordinate of cistern}}{\text{thickness of its back compartment}}.$

‡ Fig. 11 (which views the outside of the right wall of the tank) shows the device by which this is accomplished. Evidently from the labels
$$\frac{x}{1} = \frac{\dfrac{dU}{dA}}{p_a} \text{ or } x = \frac{dU}{dm}.$$

The pointer obviously varies with x. It is so arranged as to register zero when $x = 0$.

adjustment of the breadth of each cistern may be represented by one *inch*. That is, if 100 cu. in. of water are put in each A cistern the ordinate must be one inch. This applies as well to the utility of money, so that the scale U at the left indicates the number of *utils* at which the individual values the last dollar of his income. It should, however, be noted that the variation of utils is only valuable in the same register, that is, for the same individual. There is no important meaning attached to the ratio of the scale readings U for two individuals. If that of I is 1 and of II 2 it means simply that II values his last dollar twice as much as his 100th ton of A, while I values his last dollar just as much as his 100th ton of A. It is interesting to observe that analogously the price registers are not to be compared, for while one indicates price per ton the other indicates price per yard, etc. Thus the mechanism is independent of any common measure of utility for different individuals and any common measure of prices for different commodities.

§ 7.

It will be observed that the numbers on the various registers are so connected that the product of the register of A by that of its price added to the like products for B, C, etc., will equal the sum of all the income registers.

Moreover if each cistern is provided with a graduation to show marginal utility, this number will be found to be the product of the number for price in its front-and-back row, by that for valuation of money in its right-and-left row.

§ 8.

The mechanism just described is the physical analogue of the ideal economic market. The elements which contribute to the determination of prices are represented each with its appropriate rôle and open to the scrutiny of the eye. We are thus enabled not only to obtain a clear and analytical *picture* of the interdependence of the many elements in the causation of prices, but also to employ the mechanism as an instrument of investigation and by it, study some complicated variations which could scarcely be successfully followed without its aid. Its chief uses may be briefly classified as follows :

1. Arrange the stoppers I, II, III, etc., so that the money incomes of I, II, III, are all equal. The differences of distribution of the commodities will depend on individual characteristics, that is, on

the character of the cisterns. If all the A cisterns are alike and also all B cisterns, all C cisterns, etc., then each commodity will be distributed in equal parts among the individuals.

2. Press stopper I. This amounts to increasing the income of I. It does not increase the amount of commodities in the market but gives a larger share to I. The total money value of the same aggregate commodities in the whole market has increased by the amount of liquid added by depressing the stopper.

The added water in the back cisterns of the I row will make the back compartments in this row fuller than the front. The back level will be temporarily above the water level of the tank and (as the cisterns will sink) the front level will be temporarily below. The effect of the former is to bulge out the movable rear wall in the I row, to extend the rods and to cause the same expansion in the back compartments of the II, III, etc. rows. This makes the back liquids in these rows lower and the front liquids higher than the tank level. Hence the front cisterns of the II, III, etc. rows pour part of their contents into the I row whose level as we have seen is below that of the tank.

In economic language to give a greater money value to one individual causes for him smaller marginal utilities (cisterns sink), a lower marginal utility of money, and increased consumption of commodities. For other individuals it increases marginal utilities (cisterns rise), decreases consumption, increases prices (back cisterns expand), and may increase or decrease their marginal utility of money-income according as marginal utilities (ordinates) increase faster than prices (back thicknesses) or the reverse.

So much for the effect on different individuals. Now as to the effect on the various commodities. Prices in general have risen but not necessarily all articles. Suppose article C is consumed little or not at all (cistern narrow) by the enriched individual I but is extensively used by those whose valuation of money has increased. Then since the valuation of money to II is equal to the quotient of the ordinate of IIC divided by the thickness of the back cistern of IIC, and since this ordinate has not lengthened by any appreciable loss of commodity C from II to I, the thickness must have lessened, that is, the price has been reduced.

Not only may there be such exceptional commodities but there may be exceptional individuals. Thus a man may be the principal consumer of just those commodities and those only whose price has fallen. His consumption will increase, his marginal utility of money decrease. He is benefited not injured by the increase of income of his neighbor I.

3. Press stopper I and raise III. I, II, III now represent a wealthy middle class and poor man respectively. We observe first that this change causes the poor man to relinquish entirely some things (luxuries) as C while decreasing his necessaries slightly; second that the rich man increases his luxuries enormously and his necessaries slightly, and thirdly that slight modifications will appear in the prices and hence in the middle-class consumption.

The nature of the effect on prices depends on the character of the cisterns of I and III, and on the magnitude of the changes in their incomes. In order that prices may not change, one condition (necessary but not sufficient) is that the amount of money income added to I must equal that taken from III, for if the amounts of commodities are not to change, nor their prices, their total values cannot. If all prices rise it proves a net increase of money income in the whole system.

If the increase of income of I equals the decrease of that of III, so that the total money value in the market is unchanged, and if furthermore all the cisterns of I and III have straight walls on the right and have their breadths* proportional, there will be no change in price. For if the cistern breadths of the III row are each, (say) half the corresponding ones in the I row, equilibrium will clearly be satisfied by shortening each ordinate of the I row by a uniform percentage (say 10%), and lengthening those of the III row by just twice the amount of shortening in the corresponding I ordinates. This will evidently cause the lengthening of the III ordinates to be uniform (say 15%). The ratio of marginal utilities has thus been preserved and hence the prices. Obviously the contents added to IA equals that taken from IIIA and equilibrium is reëstablished by a simple transfer from III to I. In this case there is no effect on II or any individual save I and III.

---

* The breadth of a cistern is evidently the differential of its area divided by the differential of the ordinate that is the *fluxion of commodity in reference to its marginal utility*. It is a magnitude important in the discussion of distribution of commodities. Involving as it does the second differential of utility it has no perfectly distinct recognition in popular language. A narrow cistern means that a slight reduction of its contents causes its ordinate to increase much, i. e. causes it to be greatly desired. The individual is very *sensitive* to a change in that commodity. He misses a little less of it and appreciates a little more. Reversely a broad cistern signifies that it is hard to satisfy the man by increase and hard to annoy him by decrease. These two sorts of cisterns may be called " sensitive " and " callous " (see Appendix I).

More generally in a redistribution of incomes without altering their aggregate, in order that no prices may change (1) no condition is necessary for those whose incomes have not changed; (2) for those whose incomes have changed the geometrical character of the cisterns must be such that a proportional shortening of the ordinates for each and every richer man will absorb in the. aggregate, the same additional commodity of each sort as is lost *in* the aggregate by the poorer through a proportional lengthening in the ordinates of each of them.

If the enriched man or men absorb·more of a given commodity than this requirement its price will rise, if less it will fall.

If the increase of income of I equals the decrease of III effects on prices must be compensatory. If one rises some other or others must fall. If IA is much broader than IIIA but IB is much narrower than IIIB, the price of A may rise and of B fall unless counteractions come from other commodities. For if we were to suppose prices unaltered, the cistern IA would absorb from IIIA so much and IB from IIIB so little that the ordinate of IIIA would be too long and of IIIB too short for equilibrium. In order to partially permit this lengthening and shortening there must be a corresponding lengthening and shortening in the whole A and B rows respectively and prices must be proportioned to these ordinates. In this case it is to be noted furthermore that a change in prices causes a change in the distribution of the income of II and all other individuals.

The marginal utility of money for I decreases, for III increases, and for II may slightly rise or fall, owing to the change of prices. With the breadths of the cisterns properly adapted to the changes in prices there may be no change* in the valuation of money for II.

---

* If the prices of only two commodities A and B change and AII and BII are straight walled, and if their breadths are inversely proportional to the difference of the squares of the old and the new prices, there will be no change in the valuation of money. For, let p and p' be the old and new prices, let x_a and x_b be the breadths (for II) of the A and B cisterns and let y_a, y_b and y_a', y_b' be their old and new ordinates. Since the marginal utility of money is not to change nor the prices of C, D, etc., their ordinates cannot and therefore their quantities (for II) cannot change. Hence the added expenditure (by II) on A must equal that taken from B, i. e. :

$$x_a y_a' p_a' - x_a y_a p_a = x_b y_b p_b - x_b y_b' p_b'.$$

But since the valuation of money is to be kept constant,

$$\frac{y_a'}{p_a'} = \frac{y_a}{p_a} = \frac{y_b}{p_b} = \frac{y_b'}{p_b'} = k.$$

If the price of A rises slightly and of B falls relatively more while the breadth of IIA is less than of IIB, the valuation of money to II will fall. For if not then the ordinates of IIA and IIB must change *pari passu* with the thickness of the back cisterns. The thickness and ordinate for IIA are, say each increased 10% and for IIB reduced 50%. There is clearly not room in IIA for all the money poured out of IIB. This surplus will spread over all A, B, C, etc., and reduce the ordinates and reduce the money valuation of II.

These artificially exact cases obviously stand for more general and approximate economic theorems. There are no such delicate adjustments in the actual world as here presented, but through ideal cases we study real tendencies.

4. Depress stopper A. The chief effect will be to lower the price of A. If it is a necessary* a relatively large share of the increase will go to the poor. It will probably occur that while the total money expenditure by the poor for this commodity will increase, that for the rich will *decrease.*† The marginal utility of money in general decreases especially for the poor man.

Most other commodities will rise in price if A decreases in price faster than it increases in quantity. For there will be a saving in the expenditure for A which must be made up elsewhere. But an exceptional commodity may fall in price. Thus if B happens to be extensively used (cisterns deep and broad) only by those who use A slightly, these persons will not save materially in the expenditure

---

Hence

$$x_a k p_a'^2 - x_a k p_a^2 = x_b k p_b^2 - x_b k p_b'^2.$$

Hence

$$x_a : x_b :: p_b^2 - p_b'^2 : p_a'^2 - p_a^2,$$

which is the condition required. More generally in order that the valuation of money to an individual shall not change, the cisterns of II must be so formed that when the money saved on some articles equals the extra spent on the others the ordinates may all change proportionally with the prices. If the ordinates increase more than this requirement or decrease less, the valuation of money will rise. In the reverse cases it will fall.

* A necessary may be defined as a commodity whose cistern is relatively deep and narrow. I. e. a very small quantity has a very great utility and a slight addition gives satisfaction very rapidly. A luxury has the reverse properties.

† When commodity *begins* to flow into a cistern its money value (the contents of the back cistern) increases in about the same rate as the commodity—it matters little how much the price (thickness) falls. Contrariwise when the cistern is nearly full a fall of price *decreases* the money value at about the same rate—the increase of commodity matters little. The dividing point is where the commodity increases at the same rate as the price decreases. These characters are more plainly shown in the diagrams of Auspitz und Lieben, p. 48, etc.

for A, but will be compelled to pour much money into C, D, etc. of which the prices have risen. This will cause a rise in their valuation of money and as the quantity of B does not decrease its price must.

Moreover there will be slight changes in all other quantities IB, IIC, etc. If (say) IIC decreases, it is due to one or both of two causes, a rise in price of C or a rise in valuation of money of II. In general the valuation of money will decrease. The decrease will be relatively great for the poor as compared with the rich, but (as just seen) will not necessarily decrease for all persons.

If A is a "luxury" the fall in its price will be small relatively to the foregoing case. Most of the increase of A will go to the rich. The total amount of money spent on it will probably *increase* which will in general decrease the price of other articles. Exceptions can be found analogous to that in the former case. The valuation of money will in general decrease, most perhaps for the middle class and more for the rich than the poor, but not necessarily for all.

5. The cases just discussed assume that the additional production of A is such that the incomes of I, II, III, etc. are not disturbed. To represent the case in which I *produces all* of A, after depressing A a given amount, slowly depress I until the *difference of income* as registered on the I scale shall equal the final reading on the A scale multiplied by the price of A *minus* the former A by its former price.

The chief change to any one article will be in the price of A which will decrease. The chief change to any one person will be to I whose income is increased (especially if the commodity is a luxury), whose expenditure for most other articles will increase though not necessarily for all, and whose valuation of money will decrease, owing both to an increase of income and to a decrease in price of other articles consequent on the withdrawal of money from them to be spent on A. Only exceptional articles will increase in price if their chief consumers sufficiently *decrease* their expenditure for A.

But it may be that the increase of A will so greatly depress the price that the value of the total will *decrease.* This is generally true of necessaries. The producer I will lose income, that is stopper I must be raised instead of depressed. His valuation of money will increase doubly, owing to the contraction of his income and the rise in price of other articles. The money* return to such a benefactor

---

* Monopoly price is not treated here. It is interesting to note that the Dutch East India Co. used to destroy a part of their spices to prevent a great fall of price. The same thing has been done by the Japanese in silk-worm eggs.

is therefore not even roughly proportioned to his benefaction. If the exact shares among I, II, III, etc. in the old and new production of A are known, the proper combination of stopper-positions may be made and the reactions, now exceedingly complicated, may be watched.

6. Depress each stopper A, B, C, etc. There will be a general fall in prices. But it will not be true that if the quantity of each commodity is doubled its price will be halved, and the price of one commodity in terms of another unaltered as Mill* apparently thought, for the ratios of exchange are not the ratios of the contents of the cisterns but of their ordinates. Nor will the ratios of distribution of commodities remain the same. If however all cisterns in each front and back row are geometrically similar and their filled portions also similar (a most unreal condition), the ratios of distribution of commodities will be unaffected† and if furthermore *all* cisterns are similar, the ratios of prices will be unaltered.‡

In the actual world aside from differences in the shapes of cisterns there are more important differences in the way in which they are filled. Those for necessaries are relatively full as compared with those for luxuries and those for the rich as compared with those for the poor. Hence the effect of a proportionate increase of production in all commodities will depress the price of necessaries much more than of luxuries.

The effects on the valuation or marginal utility of money will be more complicated. If we suppose the depression of the stoppers to begin when they are far extended, the effects may be roughly described as follows. At first the valuation of money *increases* since the prices decrease faster§ than the marginal utilities, reaches a maximum (which is different for each individual and depends on the initial distribution), and *decreases* when the decrease of ordinates is faster than that of the thickness of the back cisterns. These

---

* Pol. Econ., Bk. III, Ch. XIV, § 2.

† For proportional increase of the contents of the cisterns in the same front and back row will reduce their ordinates proportionally and shrink the back compartments alike, thus restoring equilibrium.

‡ For in addition to the above consideration the reduction of ordinates in all rows will be alike.

§ Because when a cistern is relatively empty, a rise in the surface of its contents diminishes the long ordinate by only a slight percentage but very materially contracts the back compartment.

changes in the valuation of money are of course subject to the condition that each income measured in money remains the same.

7. Depress all income stoppers proportionally, i. e. increase all incomes in the same ratio. Then will all prices increase and the valuation of money decrease exactly in this ratio. There will be no change in the distribution of commodities. There is merely a depreciated standard of money. Formerly the whole marketed commodity was valued at a given number of dollars, now this number is increased.

We have seen under number 1, that an increase in the money income of a single individual without an increase in commodities is a benefit to him, but such an increase when universal is beneficial to no one.

8. Remove cistern IA and replace it with a shallower one, i. e. suppose a change in the taste of I for A, making the article less attractive.

It is as if we raise the bottom of the original cistern IA. More of A will flow to other consumers and more of I's money will flow to the purchase of other commodities. A will fall in price, most other articles will rise. I's valuation of money will fall. For those who consume A extensively the valuation of money will fall. For others it may rise.

If all of the I cisterns grow shallower there will be a fall in the valuation of money for I, but either prices will not change or their changes must be compensatory, for the quantities of commodities have not been altered nor their aggregate value. If all of the I row cisterns change so as to admit of a uniform percentage shortening of ordinates without any commodity flowing out of any cistern, no commodity *will* flow out, no prices will change and there will be no change whatsoever in the distribution of commodities nor in the valuation of money to other people. If one cistern shortens more than this requirement, the effects will be analogous to those just described for a single cistern.

If all the cisterns of the A row are made shallower the price of A will decrease.* That of other articles will in general increase. In order that the distribution of commodities may not change, the A cisterns must be so changed as to admit of a shortening of ordin-

---

* Otherwise while the A ordinates shorten and their ratio to other ordinates lessens, the back cisterns would have a relatively too great thickness compared with the other thicknesses.

ates in a uniform percentage without loss or gain of commodity.   In this case the price of A will decrease while that of all other articles will increase exactly alike.*   The valuation of money will be reduced since the ordinate of a B cistern (say) has not changed while its back thickness has increased.   The changes just considered may be brought about if A suddenly goes out of fashion.

Perfectly analogous changes occur if a cistern or cisterns become narrower.   The individual is then more keenly "sensitive" to changes of quantities.   This change may occur through a discovery by which a little of the commodity is made to "go farther" than before.

Reverse changes occur if cisterns are broadened or deepened.

§ 9.

It is impossible to combine all the A cisterns into a single demand cistern for A as was done in Ch. II or to combine all the I cisterns into an income cistern as in Ch. III, for we can no longer overlook the influence of other commodities and other individuals.   The analysis therefore which treats of but one commodity at a time and constructs a demand curve for it is a superficial one for it does not reach all the independent variables.

§ 10.   ANALYTICAL.

Suppose there are n individuals and m commodities in our given isolated market during the given period and suppose the amounts of the commodities A, B, C, etc., are given K_a, K_b, K_c, etc., and the given incomes of I, II, III, etc. are K_1, K_2, K_3, etc.   Then the condition that the commodity-sums are given is:

$$
\left.
\begin{aligned}
A_1 + A_2 + A_3 + \ldots \ldots \ldots + A_n &= K_a \\
B_1 + B_2 + B_3 + \ldots \ldots \ldots + B_n &= K_b \\
C_1 + C_2 + C_3 + \ldots \ldots \ldots + C_n &= K_c \\
\text{-----------------------------} \\
\text{-----------------------------} \\
M_1 + M_2 + M_3 + \ldots \ldots \ldots + M_n &= K_m
\end{aligned}
\right\}
\begin{aligned}
&m \text{ equations.} \\
&mn \text{ unknowns.}
\end{aligned}
$$

---

* For their mutual ratios cannot change since the ordinates to which they are proportional do not.

The condition that the incomes are given is:

$$
\left.
\begin{aligned}
&A_1 \cdot p_a + B_1 \cdot p_b + \ldots \ldots + M_1 \cdot p_m = K_1 \\
&A_2 \cdot p_a + B_2 \cdot p_b + \ldots \ldots + M_2 \cdot p_m = K_2 \\
&\text{--- --- --- --- --- --- --- --- --- ---} \\
&A_n \cdot p_a + B_n \cdot p_b + \ldots \ldots + M_n \cdot p_m = K_n
\end{aligned}
\right\}
\begin{aligned}
&n \text{ equations.} \\
&m \text{ new unknowns} \\
&\quad \text{(prices).}
\end{aligned}
$$

The utility functions (the cistern-forms) are:

$$
\left.
\begin{aligned}
&\frac{d\,U}{d A_1} = F(A_1); \; \frac{d\,U}{d B_1} = F(B_1); \ldots \ldots ; \; \frac{d\,U}{d M_1} = F(M_1) \\
&\frac{d\,U}{d A_2} = F(A_2); \; \frac{d\,U}{d B_2} = F(B_2); \ldots \ldots ; \; \frac{d\,U}{d M_2} = F(M_2) \\
&\text{--- --- --- --- --- --- --- --- --- --- --- ---} \\
&\frac{d\,U}{d A_n} = F(A_n); \; \frac{d\,U}{d B_n} = F(B_n); \ldots \ldots ; \; \frac{d\,U}{d M_n} = F(M_n)
\end{aligned}
\right\}
\begin{aligned}
&mn \text{ equations.} \\
&mn \text{ new} \\
&\text{unknowns} \\
&\text{(marg. ut.).}
\end{aligned}
$$

The principle of proportion is:

$$
\left.
\begin{aligned}
&\frac{d\,U}{d A_1} : \frac{d\,U}{d B_1} : \frac{d\,U}{d C_1} \ldots : \frac{d\,U}{d M_1} = \\
&\frac{d\,U}{d A_2} : \frac{d\,U}{d B_2} : \ldots \ldots : \frac{d\,U}{d M_2} = \\
&\text{--- --- --- --- --- --- ---} = \\
&\frac{d\,U}{d A_n} : \frac{d\,U}{d B_n} : \ldots \ldots : \frac{d\,U}{d M_n} = p_a : p_b : p_c : \ldots : p_m
\end{aligned}
\right\}
\begin{aligned}
&n\,(m-1) \\
&\text{independent} \\
&\text{equations.} \\
&\text{no new} \\
&\text{unknowns.}
\end{aligned}
$$

Total number of equations: $m + n + mn + n\,(m-1) = 2mn + m$

"   "   unknowns $mn + m + mn + 0 = 2mn + m$

Therefore all magnitudes are determinate and the number of these magnitudes as well as the number of the equations is twice the number of commodities times the number of individuals plus the number of commodities.

The valuation of money for each individual can be found from the equations:

$$
\frac{d\,U}{d m_1} = \frac{\dfrac{d\,U}{d A_1}}{p_a} \text{ (Ch. IV, § 2.)}
$$

$$
\frac{d\,U}{d m_2} = \text{etc.}
$$

§ 11

For production the treatment is precisely parallel to the foregoing (figs. 12, 13).

12.

13.

CHAPTER V.

PRODUCTION AND CONSUMPTION COMBINED.

§ 1.

Hitherto it has been assumed that the quantities of commodities and incomes (or expenditures) have been *given*. But these quantities have themselves been determined by economic causes. Jevons[*] arranges the sequence as follows:

> " Cost of production determines supply,
> Supply determines final degree of utility,
> Final degree of utility determines value."

[*] Pol. Econ., Ch. IV, p. 165.

This represents the chronological order but only part of the causation. Cost of production is not the sole determinator of supply. Production is prophetic. When prices are steady the certain future price is an unquestionable regulator of supply. Auspitz und Lieben appear to me to deserve much credit for showing how all these facts harmonize. Price, production, and consumption are determined by *the equality of marginal utility and marginal cost of production.** Their clear exposition of this theory not only exhibits the "fundamental symmetry of supply and demand," but reconciles in a captivating manner the old one-sided and seemingly contradictory theories of value making them fall in place as opposite facets of the same gem. It is discouraging to find the old fight still going on. Dietzel† attempts to play the peacemaker by the makeshift of dividing the field between the contesting theories.

The apparent conflict grows out of an inadequate conception of mathematical *determinateness*. As the quantity of any commodity increases its marginal utility to consumers decreases while its marginal disutility to producers increases. If the latter exceeds the former the price which consumers will give is less than what producers will accept. Production is contracted and the utility and disutility approach each other. If the quantity is too small the machinery acts in the reverse way. The equilibrium though always miscalculated is constantly sought and its more delicate and rapid deflections are corrected by a special functionary, the speculator.

§ 2.

It is assumed that the rate of production during the given period is exactly equal to the rate of consumption. This is asserting an ideal equilibrium.

The expenses of transportation and retailing are included in "production."

The principle of proportion previously explained is now extended. The marginal utilities of consuming and the marginal disutilities of producing are in the same continuous ratio for each individual—the ratio of prices.

§ 3.

As the simplest case of combining production and consumption, suppose an individual to consume himself just that quantity of a given commodity which he produces.

---

* Auspitz und Lieben, § 5, p. 17.

† Die Klassische Werttheorie und die Theorie vom Grenznutzen. Conrad's Jahrbuch, 20.

14.

In Fig. 14 the stoppers* or pistons S and S′ which regulate the quantities in the cisterns for production and consumption, respectively, are so connected as to move together, keeping the quantities in the two cisterns equal. Furthermore the water pressure on them from the tank keeps the level of all three liquids the same—that in the tank and those in the two cisterns. The lever keeps the marginal utility equal to the marginal disutility, for its pivot is a fixed one and is placed midway between the axes of ordinates. The resulting determinate equilibrium is subject to three sets of conditions :

(1) The quantity consumed equals that produced—a condition provided for by the duplicate pistons.

(2) There must be a relation between the quantity produced and its marginal disutility and between the quantity consumed and its marginal utility—the character of the cisterns.

(3) Marginal utility and disutility are equal—the lever.

§ 4. ANALYTICAL.

If A_π and A_κ be the quantities of A produced and consumed, respectively, the conditions of equilibrium are :

$$A_\pi = A_\kappa \left. \begin{array}{l} \text{1 equation.} \\ \text{2 unknowns.} \end{array} \right\}$$

$$\left. \begin{array}{l} \dfrac{dU}{dA_\pi} = F(A_\pi) \\[2mm] \dfrac{dU}{dA_\kappa} = F(A_\kappa) \end{array} \right\} \begin{array}{l} \text{2 equations.} \\ \text{2 new unknowns.} \end{array}$$

$$\dfrac{dU}{dA_\pi} = -\dfrac{dU}{dA_\kappa} \left. \begin{array}{l} \text{1 equation.} \\ \text{no new unknown.} \end{array} \right\}$$

No. equations : $1+2+1=4$.
No. unknowns : $2+2+0=4$.

---

* In practice a more intricate frictionless bellows would be used.

§ 5.

In the more general case there are *n* individuals and *m* commodities.

15.

Fig. 15 simply connects fig. 9 and fig. 12 by a series of new levers
like that in fig. 14, so that for each individual the ordinates of the
production cistern and its consumption cistern shall be equal. There
are also analogous horizontal levers (fig. 16) to keep the price for

16.

consumers equal to that for producers. The stoppers are all duplicate
as in fig. 14 for each commodity. Moreover there are analogous
duplicate pistons to keep each individual's incomes and expenditures
equal.

The industrial machinery is now seen to be self-regulative. There
is no arbitrary assignment of incomes or of commodities. The only

changes possible are effected by change in the *forms* of the cisterns or by changing their *number*, that is by changing the " cost" of production or the utility of consumption, or by changing the population (which changes, we may remark, go together). By making the cisterns removable and replaceable the effects of varied conditions can be studied as in the preceding chapter.

However, this equilibrium is indeterminate in one respect. Unlike the former it does not fix the unit of value. The sum of the income-cistern-contents is arbitrary. If all duplicate income-and-expenditure-pistons are simultaneously depressed so as to increase all incomes proportionately, the equilibrium will not be upset nor will the distribution of commodities be affected. The rear cisterns will simply dilate in uniform* ratio. The money standard has alone changed.

This may be remedied by making *the thicknesses of all back cisterns for the commodity A equal to unity.* A thus becomes the standard of value, and henceforth all prices are in terms of this commodity. This is what is done in the actual world.

§ 6. ANALYTICAL.

$$
\left.
\begin{aligned}
A_{\pi,1} + A_{\pi,2} + \ldots + A_{\pi,n} &= A_{\kappa,1} + A_{\kappa,2} + \ldots + A_{\kappa,n} \\
B_{\pi,1} + B_{\pi,2} + \ldots + B_{\pi,n} &= B_{\kappa,1} + B_{\kappa,2} + \ldots + B_{\kappa,n} \\
\text{- -} & \\
M_{\pi,1} + M_{\pi,2} + \ldots + M_{\pi,n} &= M_{\kappa,1} + M_{\kappa,2} + \ldots + M_{\kappa,n}
\end{aligned}
\right\}
\begin{array}{l} m \text{ equations.} \\ 2mn \text{ unknowns.} \end{array}
$$

$$
\left.
\begin{aligned}
A_{\pi,1} \cdot p_a + \ldots + M_{\pi,1} \cdot p_m &= A_{\kappa,1} \cdot p_a + \ldots + M_{\kappa,1} \cdot p_m \\
\text{- -} & \\
A_{\pi,n} \cdot p_a + \ldots + M_{\pi,n} \cdot p_m &= A_{\kappa,n} \cdot p_a + \ldots + M_{\kappa,n} \cdot p_m
\end{aligned}
\right\}
\begin{array}{l} (n-1) \text{ inde-} \\ \text{pendent equa-} \\ \text{tions.} \\ m \text{ new un-} \\ \text{knowns (prices).} \end{array}
$$

$$
\left.
\begin{aligned}
\frac{dU}{dA_{\pi,1}} &= F(A_{\pi,1}) ; \ldots ; & \frac{dU}{dM_{\pi,1}} &= F(M_{\pi,1}) \\
\frac{dU}{dA_{\kappa,1}} &= F(A_{\kappa,1}) ; \ldots ; & \frac{dU}{dM_{\kappa,1}} &= F(M_{\kappa,1}) \\
\text{- - - - - - - - - - - - - - - -} & \\
\frac{dU}{dA_{\pi,n}} &= F(A_{\pi,n}) ; \ldots ; & \frac{dU}{dM_{\pi,n}} &= F(M_{\pi,n}) \\
\frac{dU}{dA_{\kappa,n}} &= F(A_{\kappa,n}) ; \ldots ; & \frac{dU}{dM_{\kappa,n}} &= F(M_{\kappa,n})
\end{aligned}
\right\}
\begin{array}{l} 2mn \text{ equations.} \\ 2 mn \text{ new un-} \\ \text{knowns} \\ \text{(marg. ut.).} \end{array}
$$

---

*Cf. Ch. IV, §8, number 7.

$$\left.\begin{array}{l}
\dfrac{d\mathrm{U}}{d\mathrm{A}_{\pi,1}} : \dfrac{d\mathrm{U}}{d\mathrm{B}_{\pi,1}} : \cdots : \dfrac{d\mathrm{U}}{d\mathrm{M}_{\pi,1}} : \dfrac{d\mathrm{U}}{d\mathrm{A}_{\kappa,1}} : \dfrac{d\mathrm{U}}{d\mathrm{B}_{\kappa,1}} : \cdots : \dfrac{d\mathrm{U}}{d\mathrm{M}_{\kappa,1}} = \\[2ex]
\dfrac{d\mathrm{U}}{d\mathrm{A}_{\pi,2}} : \dfrac{d\mathrm{U}}{d\mathrm{B}_{\pi,2}} : \cdots : \dfrac{d\mathrm{U}}{d\mathrm{M}_{\pi,2}} : \dfrac{d\mathrm{U}}{d\mathrm{A}_{\kappa,2}} : \dfrac{d\mathrm{U}}{d\mathrm{B}_{\kappa,2}} : \cdots : \dfrac{d\mathrm{U}}{d\mathrm{M}_{\kappa,2}} = \\[1ex]
\text{---} = \\[1ex]
\dfrac{d\mathrm{U}}{d\mathrm{A}_{\pi,n}} : \dfrac{d\mathrm{U}}{d\mathrm{B}_{\pi,n}} : \cdots : \dfrac{d\mathrm{U}}{d\mathrm{M}_{\pi,n}} : \dfrac{d\mathrm{U}}{d\mathrm{A}_{\kappa,n}} : \dfrac{d\mathrm{U}}{d\mathrm{B}_{\kappa,n}} : \cdots : \dfrac{d\mathrm{U}}{d\mathrm{M}_{\kappa,n}} = \\[1ex]
-p_a : -p_b : \cdots : -p_m : +p_a : +p_b : \cdots : +p_m
\end{array}\right\} \begin{array}{l} (2m-1)\,n \\ \text{indepen-} \\ \text{dent} \\ \text{equations.} \\ \text{no new} \\ \text{unknowns.} \end{array}$$

No. equations: $m + (n-1) + 2mn + (2m-1)\,n = 4mn + m - 1$

No. unknowns: $2mn + m + 2mn + 0 \qquad = 4mn + m.$

There are just one too few equations. It may not be evident at first why the second set does not contain n independent equations instead of $(n-1)$. The point is that any one of these equations can be derived from the others together with the equations of the first set. Thus multiply the equations of the first set by $p_a, p_b, \ldots p_m$ respectively and add the resulting equations arranging as follows:

$$\left.\begin{array}{l}
\mathrm{A}_{\pi,1} \cdot p_a + \mathrm{B}_{\pi,1} \cdot p_b + \ldots + \mathrm{M}_{\pi,1} \cdot p_m + \\
+\, \mathrm{A}_{\pi,2} \cdot p_a + \mathrm{B}_{\pi,2} \cdot p_b + \ldots + \mathrm{M}_{\pi,2} \cdot p_m + \\
+ \text{-----------------------------} \\
+\, \mathrm{A}_{\pi,n} \cdot p_a + \mathrm{B}_{\pi,n} \cdot p_b + \ldots + \mathrm{M}_{\pi,n} \cdot p_m
\end{array}\right\} =$$

$$\left\{\begin{array}{l}
\mathrm{A}_{\kappa,1} \cdot p_a + \mathrm{B}_{\kappa,1} \cdot p_b + \ldots + \mathrm{M}_{\kappa,1} \cdot p_m + \\
+\, \mathrm{A}_{\kappa,2} \cdot p_a + \mathrm{B}_{\kappa,2} \cdot p_b + \ldots + \mathrm{M}_{\kappa,2} \cdot p_m + \\
\text{-----------------------------} \\
+\, \mathrm{A}_{\kappa,n} \cdot p_a + \mathrm{B}_{\kappa,n} \cdot p_b + \ldots + \mathrm{M}_{\kappa,n} \cdot p_m.
\end{array}\right.$$

Subtracting from this equation the sum of all but the first (say) of the second set, our result is:

$$\mathrm{A}_{\pi,1} \cdot p_a + \mathrm{B}_{\pi,1} \cdot p_b + \ldots + \mathrm{M}_{\pi,1} \cdot p_m =$$
$$\mathrm{A}_{\kappa,1} \cdot p_a + \mathrm{B}_{\kappa,1} \cdot p_b + \ldots + \mathrm{M}_{\kappa,1} \cdot p_m$$

which is the first equation of the second set. This equation is therefore dependent on the others, or there is one less independent equation than appears at first glance. Hence we need one more equation. We may let:

$$p_a = 1.$$

This makes A the standard of value (cf. § 5).

No such limitation applies to the equations in Chapter IV.

CHAPTER VI.

THE COMPONENT PROCESSES OF PRODUCTION.

§ 1.

Without dwelling on the economic applications of the mechanism just described we hasten on to the description of a more complicated mechanism.

Production usually consists of a number of successive processes. The last of these is retailing. Let us group all other processes under the head of production. The price for production and consumption are no longer equal.

Hitherto we have had two sets of cisterns, the production set and the consumption set. Separate now, these sets far enough to introduce a third set for exchange or retailing as in fig. 17.

17.

The exchange set is a series of double cisterns each related to a particular commodity, and a particular person. Consider the cistern IA_e for instance (the sub-letter for exchange or retailing). In the front compartment is the quantity of A which I *buys and sells* or transfers from producer to consumer. The back compartment contains the money pay for doing it.

These exchange cisterns are connected with each other and with the *production* set by levers *precisely as if they were so many new commodities produced.*

So also the rods maintain a constant money rate for exchange; instead, however, of the former simple relation between the producers and consumers there is now the following that the sum of the ordinates of $A\,I_\pi$, and $A\,I_\epsilon$, equals the ordinate of AI_κ, and likewise for II, III, etc., also that the thickness of the back cisterns of A_π plus that of A_ϵ equals that of A_κ. These results are effected by parallel rulers, those for the former purpose being represented in fig. 17.

The new machinery required for the exchange process consists then (1) of triplicate pistons* which necessitate that the same quantity of A shall be produced, exchanged, and consumed ; (2) the additional rods and levers (horizontal and inclined) to make the marginal disutilities of producing and exchanging proportional to the recompense and which also maintain a constant price for exchanging the same thing ; and (3) the special contrivance to add the marginal disutilities of producing and exchanging for any individual so as to equal that of consuming, and also equate the sum of the prices of producing and exchanging to that of consuming.

§ 2. ANALYTICAL.

$$A_{\pi,1}+\ldots+A_{\pi,n}=A_{\epsilon,1}+\ldots+A_{\epsilon,n}=A_{\kappa,1}+\ldots+A_{\kappa,n}$$

$$M_{\pi,1}+\ldots+M_{\pi,n}=M_{\epsilon,1}+\ldots+M_{\epsilon,n}=M_{\kappa,1}+\ldots+M_{\kappa,n}$$

$2\,m$ equations. $3\,mn$ unknowns.

$$A_{\pi,1}\,p_{a,\pi}+\ldots+M_{\pi,1}\,p_{m,\pi}+A_{\epsilon,1}\,p_{a,\epsilon}+\ldots+M_{\epsilon,1}\,p_{m,\epsilon}=A_{\kappa,1}\,p_{a,\kappa}+\ldots+M_{\kappa,1}\,p_{m,\kappa}$$

$$A_{\pi,n}\,p_{a,\pi}+\ldots+M_{\pi,n}\,p_{m,\pi}+A_{\epsilon,n}\,p_{a,\epsilon}+\ldots+M_{\epsilon,n}\,p_{m,\epsilon}=A_{\kappa,n}\,p_{a,\kappa}+\ldots+M_{\kappa,n}\,p_{m,\kappa}$$

$n-1$ independent equations. $3\,m$ new unknowns (prices).

$$\frac{dU}{dA_{\pi,1}}=F(A_{\pi,1})\,;\,\ldots;\,\frac{dU}{dM_{\pi,1}}=F(M_{\pi,1})$$
$$\frac{dU}{dA_{\epsilon,1}}=F(A_{\epsilon,1})\,;\,\ldots;\,\frac{dU}{dM_{\epsilon,1}}=F(M_{\epsilon,1})$$
$$\frac{dU}{dA_{\kappa,1}}=F(A_{\kappa,1})\,;\,\ldots;\,\frac{dU}{dM_{\kappa,1}}=F(M_{\kappa,1})$$

$$\frac{dU}{dA_{\pi,n}}=F(A_{\pi,n})\,;\,\ldots;\,\frac{dU}{dM_{\pi,n}}=F(M_{\pi,n})$$
$$\frac{dU}{dA_{\epsilon,n}}=F(A_{\epsilon,n})\,;\,\ldots;\,\frac{dU}{dM_{\epsilon,n}}=F(M_{\epsilon,n})$$
$$\frac{dU}{dA_{\kappa,n}}=F(A_{\kappa,n})\,;\,\ldots;\,\frac{dU}{dM_{\kappa,n}}=F(M_{\kappa,n})$$

$3\,mn$ equations. $3\,mn$ new unknowns (marg. ut.).

---

* The income and expenditure-pistons are merely duplicate as before.

$$\left.\begin{aligned}
&\frac{d\mathrm{U}}{d\mathrm{A}_{\pi,\,1}}\cdots:\frac{d\mathrm{U}}{d\mathrm{M}_{\pi,\,1}}:\frac{d\mathrm{U}}{d\mathrm{A}_{\epsilon,\,1}}\cdots:\frac{d\mathrm{U}}{d\mathrm{M}_{\epsilon,\,1}}:\frac{d\mathrm{U}}{d\mathrm{A}_{\kappa,\,1}}\cdots:\frac{d\mathrm{U}}{d\mathrm{M}_{\kappa,\,1}}=\\
&\frac{d\mathrm{U}}{d\mathrm{A}_{\pi,\,2}}\cdots:\frac{d\mathrm{U}}{d\mathrm{M}_{\pi,\,2}}:\frac{d\mathrm{U}}{d\mathrm{A}_{\epsilon,\,2}}\cdots:\frac{d\mathrm{U}}{d\mathrm{M}_{\epsilon,\,2}}:\frac{d\mathrm{U}}{d\mathrm{A}_{\kappa,\,2}}\cdots:\frac{d\mathrm{U}}{d\mathrm{M}_{\kappa,\,2}}=\\
&\text{---}=\\
&\frac{d\mathrm{U}}{d\mathrm{A}_{\pi,\,n}}\cdots:\frac{d\mathrm{U}}{d\mathrm{M}_{\pi,\,n}}:\frac{d\mathrm{U}}{d\mathrm{A}_{\epsilon,\,n}}\cdots:\frac{d\mathrm{U}}{d\mathrm{M}_{\epsilon,\,n}}:\frac{d\mathrm{U}}{d\mathrm{A}_{\kappa,\,n}}\cdots:\frac{d\mathrm{U}}{d\mathrm{M}_{\kappa,\,n}}=\\
&p_{a,\,\pi}\ \cdots:p_{m,\,\pi}\ :p_{a,\,\epsilon}\ \cdots:p_{m,\,\epsilon}:-p_{a,\,\kappa}\cdots:-p_{m,\,\kappa}
\end{aligned}\right\}\begin{aligned}&n(3m-1)\\&\text{independ-}\\&\text{ent equa-}\\&\text{tions.}\\&\text{no new}\\&\text{un-}\\&\text{knowns.}\end{aligned}$$

$$\left.\begin{aligned}
p_{a,\,\pi}+p_{a,\,\epsilon}=p_{a,\,\kappa}\\
\text{----------------}\\
p_{m,\,\pi}+p_{m,\,\epsilon}=p_{m,\,\kappa}
\end{aligned}\right\}\begin{aligned}&m\text{ equations.}\\[1.2em]&\text{no new unknowns.}\end{aligned}$$

No. equations: $2m\ +(n-1)+3mn+n(3m-1)+m=6mn+3m-1$.
No. unknowns: $3mn+3m\ \ +3mn+0\ \ \ \ \ \ +0\ =6mn+3m$.

The second set apparently contains n equations instead of $n-1$ as above recorded. But, by multiplication of the first line of the first set, we have:

$$(\mathrm{A}_{\pi,1}+\ldots+\mathrm{A}_{\pi,n})\ p_{a,\pi}=(\mathrm{A}_{\kappa,1}+\ldots+\mathrm{A}_{\kappa,n})\ p_{a,\pi}$$
$$(\mathrm{A}_{\epsilon,1}+\ldots+\mathrm{A}_{\epsilon,n})\ p_{a,\epsilon}=(\mathrm{A}_{\kappa,1}+\ldots+\mathrm{A}_{\kappa,n})\ p_{a,\epsilon}$$

adding and remembering that $p_{a,\kappa}=p_{a,\pi}+p_{a,\epsilon}$ we get:

$$\mathrm{A}_{\pi,\,1}\cdot p_{a,\,\pi}+\ldots+\mathrm{A}_{\pi,n}\cdot p_{a,\,\pi}+\mathrm{A}_{\epsilon,\,1}\cdot p_{a,\,\epsilon}+\ldots+\mathrm{A}_{\epsilon,\,n}\cdot p_{a,\,\epsilon}=$$
$$\mathrm{A}_{\kappa,1}\cdot\ p_{a,\,\kappa}+\ldots+\mathrm{A}_{\kappa,n}\cdot p_{a,\,\kappa}$$

Writing the similar equations from the second, third, etc. lines of the first set and adding we get (rearranging terms):

$$\left.\begin{aligned}
&\mathrm{A}_{\pi,\,1}\cdot p_{a,\,\pi}+\ldots+\mathrm{M}_{\pi,\,1}\cdot p_{m,\,\pi}+\mathrm{A}_{\epsilon,\,1}\cdot p_{a,\,\epsilon}+\ldots+\mathrm{M}_{\epsilon,\,1}\cdot p_{m,\,\epsilon}+\\
&+\mathrm{A}_{\pi,\,2}\cdot p_{a,\,\pi}+\ldots+\mathrm{M}_{\pi,\,2}\cdot p_{m,\,\pi}+\text{---------------------}\\
&\text{--- -------------------------------------}\\
&+\mathrm{A}_{\pi,\,n}\cdot\ p_{a,\,\pi}+\text{--------------------------}+\mathrm{M}_{\epsilon,\,n}\cdot p_{m,\,\epsilon}
\end{aligned}\right\}=$$

$$\left\{\begin{aligned}
&\mathrm{A}_{\kappa,\,1}\cdot\ p_{a,\,\kappa}+\ldots+\mathrm{M}_{\kappa,\,1}\cdot\ p_{m,\,\kappa}+\\
&+\mathrm{A}_{\kappa,\,2}\cdot\ p_{a,\,\kappa}+\text{-----------------}\\
&\text{-----------------------------------}\\
&+\mathrm{A}_{\kappa,\,n}\cdot\ p_{a,\,\kappa}+\ldots+\mathrm{M}_{\kappa,\,n}\cdot\ p_{m,\,\kappa}
\end{aligned}\right.$$

If from this equation the sum of all but one of the second set be subtracted the result will evidently be the remaining one.

We are therefore at liberty to write

$$p_{a,\kappa}=1$$

to determine a standard of value.

§ 3.

An analogous mechanism and discussion applies to the separation of production into retailing, wholesaling, transportation and even the various technical processes distinctive of the production of each commodity. In making worsted for instance there are some 16 processes having this sort of dependence.

The reactions and equilibrium in the real world are still more complicated than those here presented. Not only is there equilibrium in one market as New York city, but a mutual dependence of various markets. The rate of transportation determines in part the amount of dependence and the amount of communication determines in part the rate of transportation. As Cournot* says, " * * le système économique est un ensemble dont toutes les parties se tiennent et réagissent les unes sur les autres."

End of Part I.

---

* Principes mathématiques, Ch. XI, p. 146.

Part II.—Utility of one commodity a function of the quantities of all commodities.

CHAPTER I.

TWO COMMODITIES.

§ 1.

Hitherto it has been assumed that the utility of a commodity is a function of the quantity of that commodity alone. It is true that it depends upon that quantity more than any other and the analysis of Part I is a necessary first approximation. In astronomy the attraction of the sun on the earth is first studied alone to determine the earth's motion; next the moon's influence is admitted, then the occasional "perturbations" due to planets and comets. Absolute accuracy is never attained for the earth's motion is a function of the mass and position of every body in the universe.

So also the utility of the 100th lb. of butter (100 lbs. per year) depends mostly on that 100 lbs. It would not be perceptibly influenced by a change in the quantity of clothing, but it would be perceptibly reduced if the amount of *bread* consumed were reduced from 300 loaves to 200, for bread and butter go together.

It is needful here to distinguish carefully between two ways in which the quantity of one commodity can affect the utility of others. Even under the supposition of Part I, a change in the price of clothes effected a change in the individual valuation of money and so changed the quantity of bread consumed and so in turn changed the marginal utility and price of bread. But under our new supposition, a change in the price of butter directly changes the utility of the *same quantity* of bread. In the first case marginal utility of bread can change only after a change in its *quantity*. In the second the marginal utility of the *same* amount of bread changes; the first contemplates a variation in the quantity of water in a cistern, the second contemplates a variation in the cistern wall itself.

In Part I we assumed: $\dfrac{d\,U}{dA_1} = F(A_1)$; but now we must write:
$$\frac{d\,U}{dA_1} = F(A_1,\ B_1,\ C_1,\ \ldots\ M_1).$$

§ 2.

It will be seen that this sort of dependence of particular commodities is very common. Articles are bought with reference to each other, oil with reference to the number of lamps used, bed linen to the number of beds, bureaus to the quantity of clothes to be stored, carpets to the amount of floor rented or built, bookcases to the number of books owned; the demand for steel rails is connected with that for railroad ties, that for locomotives with that for cars, etc.

Again in production, the "peculiar cases of value" of which Mill* speaks and which Jevons† treats come under the same head; coke and coal gas; mutton and wool; beef, hides, and tallow, etc.

The cases above instanced are cases of "completing"‡ articles. Under the head of "competing"‡ articles, come, mineral oil and other oils, various "qualities" of any article as meats, grades of flour, etc., while under production almost every two articles are competing. A man in one business does not wish to meddle with another or, otherwise expressed, the marginal disutility of producing 1,000 tons per year of coal is increased if the producer attempts to run a paper mill or trade in jewelry.

§ 3.

Introducing this new dependence of utilities, it is seen that, if the cisterns contain at one point of equilibrium the proper amount of water and have as ordinates the proper marginal utilities, as soon as any income or commodity stopper is pressed, not only does the water redistribute but the shapes of the cisterns change. If the quantity of bread is increased, the cisterns for biscuit may shrink and those for butter widen. That is the ordinate (marginal utility) for the *same quantity* of biscuit decreases, and of butter increases. The general effect is to keep the ratio of marginal utilities of bread and biscuit and so also their prices nearly constant, while the cheapening of bread may directly increase the marginal utility and price of butter irrespective of its quantity.

§ 4.

The essential quality of substitutes or competing articles is that the marginal utilities or the prices of the quantities actually produced and consumed tend to maintain a constant ratio. We may

---

* Bk. III, Ch. XVI.   † Page 197.

‡ Auspitz und Lieben, p. 170.

define *perfect substitutes as such that this ratio is absolutely constant.*
The essential attribute of completing articles is that the ratio of
the *quantities* actually produced and consumed tends to be constant
(as many shoe-strings as shoes for instance, irrespective of cost).
We may define *perfect completing articles as such that this ratio is
absolutely constant.*

If we suppose each set of competing and completing articles to
be "perfect," it is possible to arrange the cisterns so that the change
of form of some cisterns as due to change in the contents of other
cisterns shall be small or nothing. Thus if four grades of flour be
"perfect" competing, so that their marginal utilities are always in
the ratio 8, 9, 11, 17, we may form a joint cistern for individual I
whose contents shall be "flour," the quality unspecified. Each
cubic unit of liquid shall represent equivalent quantities of each
grade, i. e. $\frac{1}{8}$ barrel of the first quality, $\frac{1}{9}$ of the second, $\frac{1}{11}$ of the
third or $\frac{1}{17}$ of the fourth, while the ordinate shall represent the *common utility* of any one of these equivalent quantities.

If four completing articles as the parts of a coat, sleeves, pockets,
buttons, and coat proper are always produced and consumed in numbers proportional respectively to 2, 4, 3 and 1, we may form a joint
cistern for individual I whose contents shall be "coats," parts un-
distinguished.

With such combinations as these, the cistern analysis of Part I
will represent the economic relations fairly well and almost perfectly if the deviations from equilibrium are not followed too far.

But few articles are absolutely perfect representatives of either
the competing or the completing group, and a member of one group
may also belong to another. Thus butter is completing to bread
and biscuit, and although a cheapening of bread directly increases
the utility of butter it indirectly increases it by decreasing the use
of biscuit.

It is readily seen that the interrelations of the shapes of the cisterns—if we now treat each quality of meat, etc. and each part of a
utensil as a separate commodity—are too complicated even to be
mentally representable without some new mode of analysis.

§ 5.

The former analysis is incomplete, not incorrect. All the interdependence described in Part I exists, but there also exist other
connections between the shapes of the cisterns which could not be
mechanically exhibited. For any one position of equilibrium the

cistern mechanism may represent accurately the quantities, utilities, and prices, but the shape of each cistern is a function of the whole state of equilibrium and differs as soon as that differs. However in general the interdependence in the shapes of the cisterns is very slight. That is, the utility of a commodity usually varies so much more under a variation in the quantity of that commodity than under variations of other commodities that the relations discussed in Part I may be regarded as good first approximations. Especially is this true if the interdependent commodities are grouped as in § 4, so as to eliminate all the really important influences of commodities on each other.* It will subsequently appear that the analysis of Part II is also incomplete and so will it ever be. Neither economics nor any other science can expect an exhaustive analysis.

§ 6.

Recurring to the definitions of utility as a quantity (Part I, Ch. 1), it will be noted that the third definition which indicated the ratio of two utilities was based on the assumption that the utility of each commodity was independent of the quantity of any other commodity. This assumption was necessary to prove that two applications of def. (3) led to harmonious results (Part I, Ch. I, § 4). To abandon this assumption as we have now done is to forego the use of that third definition. At the close of Part II a further discussion of "utility as a quantity" will be given. At present we content ourselves by assuming the marginal utility of a given amount of some one article as our unit of utility. Of course if we should use some other marginal utility as a unit, the measurements will not now agree. This, however, is no calamity. It will presently appear that the meaning of the phrase " one utility is twice another " is of no real importance for the subject in hand.

§ 7.

Confine attention first to two commodities (*a*) and (*b*) consumed by one individual. Let this individual first arrange his *whole* consumption combination to suit himself. Then in order to *partially* analyze this equilibrium of choice let us metaphorically experiment on him

---

* Marshall, Prin. Econ., Math. note xii, p. 756, says: "Prof. Edgeworth's plan of representing U and V as general functions of *x* and *y* [see preface to this memoir] has great attractions to the mathematician; but it seems less adapted to express the every day facts of economic life than of regarding, as Jevons did, the marginal utilities of apples as functions of *x* [the quantity of apples] simply."

as follows.   He is directed to alter this consumption combination
by arranging his quantities A and B of the two selected commodities
(*a*) and (*b*) in all possible ways, but without changing the quantities
C, D, etc. of other commodities.   The marginal utility of each will
vary not only in relation to its own quantity but also the quantity
of the other commodity.   Thus,

$$\frac{d\,U}{dA_1} = F(A_1,\,B_1)$$

$$\frac{d\,U}{dB_1} = F(B_1,\,A_1)$$

These may be regarded as derivatives with respect to A and B of

$$U_1 = \varphi(A_1,\,B_1)$$

where U_1 is the total utility to I of the consumption combination
A_1 and B_1.

   In fig. 18 let the abscissa OX represent the quantities B_1 of (*b*) and
the ordinates (OY) the quantities A_1 of (*a*).

Any point P by its co-ordinates represents
a possible combination of quantities A_1
and B_1 consumed by I.   By varying point
P all possible combinations of A_1 and B_1
are represented.   At P erect a perpendicular to the plane of the page whose
length shall represent the marginal utility
of A_1 for the combination, that is, the
degree of utility of a small addition of
A_1, (B_1 *remaining the same*).   If P as-
sumes all possible positions, the locus of the extremity of this perpendicular will be a surface.

   Again at P erect a different perpendicular for the marginal utility
of B_1; its extremity will generate another surface.   The first *surface* takes the place of a utility *curve* for (*a*), the second for (*b*).
These two surfaces may be regarded as the derivative surfaces
(with respect to the variation of A_1 and of B_1), from a primitive
whose ordinate (perpendicular at P), is the *total utility* of the combination of A_1 and B_1 represented by the point P.   This surface is
usually convex like a dome with a single maximum part, but it need
not always be.   There may be two maxima as will presently appear.
In such a case it cannot be everywhere convex.

   If a plane be drawn tangent to this last surface at a point over P,
the slope of the plane parallel to the A direction will be the ordinate

of the first derived surface ; i. e., will be the marginal utility of A_1, while the right and left slope will be the marginal utility of B_1 or the ordinate of the second derivative surface. The primitive surface thus supplies a convenient way of uniting in thought the two marginal utilities. Its absolute height* above the plane of the paper is of no consequence ; it may be lowered or heightened without disturbing tangential directions or affecting its two derivatives.

§ 8.

The three surfaces thus constructed need not extend indefinitely over the plane. They may approach vertical plane or cylindrical asymptotes so that for some points in the plane there may be no surface vertically over or under.

Mathematically the total utility and marginal utilities at these points are *imaginary.* Economically it is impossible that the individual should consume quantities of (*a*) and (*b*) indicated by the coordinates of such points.† Those parts of the plane where such points are may be called "empty."

§ 9.

If (fig. 18) the point P moves vertically (up and down on the page) the extremity of the perpendicular for the total utility describes one of Auspitz und Lieben's curves for A_1, it being understood however that the quantities of other commodities do not change.‡

The perpendicular for the marginal utility of A_1 generates in the first derivative surface a Jevonian§ curve of utility for A_1 it being understood that B_1, C_1, etc. are constant. *This curve will usually descend but it may not and cannot in certain regions if the surface is derived* from a primitive with two maxima, or any concave primitive. The other perpendicular, however, traces a curve which has never been used, viz : one which shows the relation between the quantities A_1 and the marginal utility of B, *while* B_1 *remains constant.* This curve will in general descend or ascend according as the articles (*a*) and (*b*) are competing or completing. For instance,

---

* It is in fact the arbitrary constant of integration.

† This "asymptote" and "imaginary" interpretation appears to cover the class of difficulties which led Marshall to say his curves failed to have meaning at points at which the individual could not live.

‡ It is rather, then, an "Elementarkurve" of a "Lebensgenusskurve" there being an "anfangsordinate."

§ Jevons' curve is evidently the derivative of Auspitz und Lieben's. See table Appendix I, Division II, § 2.

suppose (*a*) and (*b*) are two brands of flour. If I consumes during the period X units of one brand and 20 units of the other his desire for a 21st unit of the latter will depend on how much he has of the former (how large X is). If he has much of the first kind his desire is small.

A similar pair of curves may be found by moving P horizontally.

If the supposition in Part I were true the two strange curves (viz: connecting marginal utilities of *A* and B with quantities of *B* and A, respectively), would reduce to straight lines parallel to the plane of the paper.

§ 10.

The relations indicated by these three surfaces are really all included in one of them—the primitive. Consequently, to avoid troublesome transitions from one mode of representation to another we shall hereafter confine ourselves to this primitive surface.

Consider horizontal sections of this surface, that is sections parallel to the plane of the A and B axes. Each section forms a curve which may be called an *indifference curve*. It is the locus of points representing all consumption-combinations of A and B which have a given total utility. In fig. 18 the attached number to each curve represents the amount of this utility. They in general form a family of concentric curves vanishing finally at the point M of maximum satisfaction. M is the point at which the individual would arrange his consumption-combination of A and B if they cost nothing. There may be two or more maxima. For competing articles these maxima may lie in the axes (fig. 19), for one may prefer not to consume both.

19.

The ordinates may of course have any units of length. Suppose this unit to be indefinitely reduced from an inch to a millimeter, etc. Then our surface becomes a layer. Its thickness may be figured as a *density* (rather than an ordinate), distributed over the plane of the paper as electricity over a conductor. Each indifference curve is the locus of points where the density (formerly ordinate), is a given amount. This idea of density will be henceforth used though the necessity for its use does not come till the next chapter.

Fig. 20 shows the curves for competing articles and fig. 22 for completing. For "perfect" substitutes the curves (fig. 21) reduce to parallel straight lines whose intercepts on the A and B axes are inversely proportional to the fixed ratio of their marginal utilities.

The point M is indeterminate on the line 99. "Lehigh" and

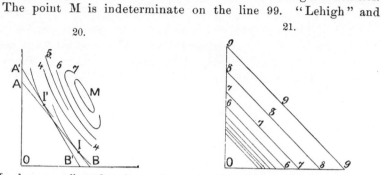

20.

21.

"Lackawanna" anthracite coal are nearly perfect substitutes. If it cost nothing the individual would indifferently consume the quan-

22.

23.

tity O9 (vertical) of one or O9 (horizontal) of the other or any combination of the two on the straight line 99 inclined in this case at 45°.

For perfect completing articles the whole family of curves reduces to a straight line passing through the origin (fig. 23). Let us regard a pair of shoes as two distinct commodities : right shoes and left shoes. For any point in the line OM (fig. 23), the desire for right shoes vanishes as long as no new left shoes are admitted, and yet the desire for a new pair may exist. The idea of marginal utility for right shoes has no application though that for pairs of shoes has.

§ 11.

There are endless points of view from which the primitive and its derivatives may be approached and made to yield the economic relations we seek.* Descriptions will be confined chiefly to the

---

* For instance we might take curves corresponding to the sections of the derivative surfaces at various heights, or curves orthogonal to the indifference curves (these will be again referred to), or curves representing the locus of points at which the marginal utilities of the two commodities have a given ratio.

indifference curves, the tangents and normals to which play an important rôle.

When our individual fixed his whole consumption combination to suit himself, let us suppose that he spent $25 per year on the two articles (*a* and *b*) under consideration. We may metaphorically compel him, while not altering in the least his purchases of other articles and hence having the same $25 to spend on (*a*) and (*b*), to contemplate spending it in a different way. If the price of (*a*) is $0.25 and of (*b*) is $0.50, the two simplest methods of spending his $25 is to spend it all on (*a*) and purchase 100 units, or to spend all on (*b*) and purchase 50 units.

In fig. 18 lay off OA = 100 units and OB = 50 units. Then *any point on the straight line AB will represent a consumption combination of A and B purchasable for $25.* * AB may be called a *partial income line.* Our individual is therefore left free only to select his combination somewhere on this line. The combination 5 or 5 present equal inducements but not as great as 6 or 6 on an arc of greater utility, nor there as much as at I. He will select his combination in such a manner as to obtain the maximum total utility, which is evidently at the point I *where AB is tangent to an indifference curve.*† At this point " he gets the most for his money."

His selection I is of course just what it was before we began our analysis. But we have advanced one step. We have partially analyzed this equilibrium, that is we see the equilibrium for A and B while the prices and quantities of other articles remain the same. It is as if a pendulum free to swing in any vertical plane is found at rest and a scientist attempts to analyze its equilibrium. He forthwith confines its motion to a single plane and discusses its equilibrium there. The analogy suggested may be extended. The principle underlying the equilibrium of a pendulum or any mechanical equilibrium (as of a mill pond or of a suspension bridge) is: that configuration will be assumed which will minimize the potential. So also the supreme principle in economic equilibrium is: that arrangement will be assumed which will maximize utility‡.

---

* Proof: Equation of AB is $\dfrac{y}{OA} + \dfrac{x}{OB} = 1$ where x and y are the co-ordinates of any point on AB. This becomes $y \cdot \dfrac{25}{OA} + x \cdot \dfrac{25}{OB} = 25$; that is, x times its price + y times its price equals $25.

† When AB is tangent to two indifference curves that one will be selected which has the greater utility.

‡ See interesting remarks, Edgeworth : Mathematical Psychics. Also in his address as Pres. section Econ. Sci. and Statistics Brit. Asso., *Nature*, Sept. 19, 1889, p. 496.

§ 12.

Since OA and OB represent quantities A and B of commodities (*a*) and (*b*) purchasable for the same sum ($25), they are inversely proportional to the prices of (*a*) and (*b*).

If prices remain the same but the individual grows richer and the sum he can afford to spend on (*a*) and (*b*) is no longer $25 but $50, the line AB simply recedes twice as far remaining parallel to itself. As it changes, its varying point of tangency follows a tortuous line the locus of all points at which the individual would arrange his combination of A and B at the given prices.

If the price of (*a*) increases, OA relatively diminishes and a new point of tangency is found. If the articles are completing (fig. 22) a change of price will not cause the tangent line to very greatly alter the proportion of consumption of the articles for it will merely change the position of I to (say) I, and it is clear that the coördinates of I' have nearly the same ratio as those of I; if substitutes (fig. 20) a slight relative change in price will cause an enormous change in the proportions used (I and I'). This was found to be the case in 1889 when a copper syndicate attempted to raise the price of copper. Hardly any article exists which has not some substitute. This sort of dependence keeps manufacturers watchful. It is because of this dependence that some " useful " articles go out of use.

§ 13.

Fig. 24 represents two " grades " of the same commodity, as brown and granulated sugar. The superior grade is laid off on the B (horizontal) axis, and the inferior on the A (vertical) axis. The point of maximum satisfaction is in or near the B axis. If the individual is poor and can afford to spend little on the article he will buy the poorer quality. The line AB is tangent to an indifference curve in or near the A axis at I. If he grows richer the line AB recedes from the origin and he purchases the combination I' containing considerably more of B; he uses this superior quality on Sun-

da (say) while consuming A on week days. If he grows richer changes the position to I" using none of A or only a little.

The inclination of the line AB is such that OA > OB that is A is cheaper than B, for OA and OB are the quantites of A and B purchasable for the same money. If the prices of A and B were equal so that OA = OB, it would not be tangent to an indifference curve unless on the B axis and A would go out of use.

Moreover it is evident that a slight variation in the relative prices of A and B will change greatly the position of I for a poor man but will not change materially that of I″ for a rich man.

If the poor consumers predominate the line AB will follow the general trend of the curves near the origin. If the rich consumers predominate the line AB will become steeper (as in the dotted positions). That is the two prices of the two qualities separate widely.

This interprets the fact that in a rich market like New York City a slight difference in quality will make an enormous divergence in price while in some country towns different grades either do not exist or sell for nearly the same price. In the country districts of " the west " all cuts of beef sell for the same price (about 10 cts. per lb.). In the cities of the west two or three qualities are commonly distinguished, while in New York a grocer will enumerate over a dozen prices in the same beef varying from 10 to 25 cts. per lb.

§ 14.

In fig. 25 if the individual III attempts to change the position of

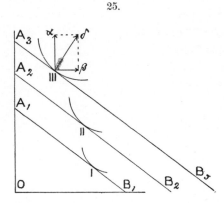

25.

III he may do so in many different " *directions.*" If he changes in the direction III α, he will increase his consumption of A without altering that of B or if toward B, III β, without altering A, if in any intermediate direction, III δ, he will increase both A and B and in the ratios of the components of that direction (III α and III β). The direction of maximum increase of utility is perpendicular to the indifference curve.* We may figure III δ as a *force.* If III were in any other position the force would evidently have a component along the line $A_3 B_3$ and would move III back to the position of equilibrium III.

---

* For between two infinitesimally distant indifference curves the shortest route is on their perpendicular.

We may call the perpendicular direction III δ the "maximum direction." It has the important property that its components III α and III β are proportional to the marginal utilities of A and B. This follows from a theorem* of vector calculus or thus: III α and III β are inversely proportional to OA_3 and OB_3, that is directly proportional to the prices of A and B and therefore proportional to their marginal utilities.†

§ 15.

If (fig. 25) the separate curve systems of all individuals I, II, etc. are drawn, and the lines AB drawn in each case, they will be parallel. For the prices are uniform among all individuals and OA and OB in each case are inversely as the prices.

Since the normals to these lines will also be parallel, this theorem may be stated: *The " maximum directions " of all are alike.*

§ 16.

These methods apply to the comparison of any *two* commodities and afford a means of graphically representing statistical relations connecting the demands for two articles so far as the variations in the quantities of other articles can be eliminated.

The same principles apply to the production of two articles. Hides and tallow are completing articles from a producer's standpoint. Likewise coke and coal gas, mutton and wool, and in general any article and its " secondary product."

On the other hand most articles are competing or substitutes from a producer's point of view. The difficulty of producing cloth is greatly increased if the same individual produces books. This is the root of the principle of division of labor and leads to that important contrast between production and. consumption once before alluded to. This and other contrasts will be mentioned in Appendix II, § 8. Marshall and others are fond of using the expression " fundamental symmetry of supply and demand." This notion must be supplemented by that of a " fundamental asymmetry." As social organization progresses each man (and each community or nation) tends to become producer of *fewer* things but consumer of *more.*

---

* Gibbs, Vector Analysis, §§ 50–53.

† For by similar triangles: $\dfrac{\text{III } \alpha}{\text{III } \beta} = \dfrac{\delta\beta}{\text{III } \beta} = \dfrac{OB_3}{OA_3} = \dfrac{p_a}{p_b}.$

Fig. 26 shows the usual sort of indifference production curves.

 26.   B is here laid off to the left and A downward ; the line AB is the locus of production combinations of A and B which can be sold for the same money, say $1,000. The point of tangency* I is the point at which the individual can produce the required $1,000 worth of A and B with the minimum disutility. The curves are such that the points of tangency will be generally at or near the axes, especially if the amount of production is large i. e. if the line AB is far from the origin. If B becomes cheaper (OB longer) the point of tangency will change but slowly until presently there are two points of tangency and if B becomes still cheaper the individual will change his profession suddenly from the position I to a position in or near the A axis.

The numbers on the indifference curves for production increase indefinitely negatively. There is usually no maximum or minimum point.

§ 17.

Finally an article consumed may be competing or completing to another produced. A blacksmith finds small utility in dumb bells; the production of horseshoes " competes " with the consumption of dumb-bells.

The relations between competing articles and completing articles are not always so simple, for articles may be competing at some combinations and completing at others. Statistical inquiries along these lines might be made with profit, and have apparently attracted little attention.†

CHAPTER II.

THREE OR MORE COMMODITIES.

§ 1.

The foregoing methods extend very readily to three dimensions. Suppose the whole market to attain equilibrium. As before, let us as it were, freeze this equilibrium except for three commodities A, B, and C. Then as before, we obtain a fixed sum of money disposable

---

* The tangency must be such that the curve is on that side of the straight line toward the origin. The other kind of tangency represents an unstable equilibrium.   † See Jevons, p. 135.

for the purchase of A, B, and C, by each individual. Construct three mutually perpendicular axes (OA, OB, OC,) in space. Conceive this space to be filled with matter whose density distribution is the total utility for A, B, and C, relative to a particular individual I. There may be "empty" portions of space. The locus of points representing combinations of A, B, and C, possessing a given utility will be an indifference *surface.* All such loci will form a "family" of concentric surfaces like the coats of an onion around one or more points of maxima.

Lay off on the A axis OA, equal to as many units of A as can be bought for the sum of money disposable by I for the purchase of A, B, and C. Lay off OB and OC similarly defined. Draw the plane A B C. This is the locus* of all consumption-combinations of A, B, and C, purchasable with the given sum of money. It is a "partial income plane." Its point of tangency with an indifference surface will mark the chosen combination. A *normal* at this point indicates the "maximum direction" and its A, B, and C components are the marginal utilities, proportional to the prices of A, B, and C.

§ 2.

The utility distributions may be very complicated. If the three articles are substitutes like oats, corn, and rye, the indifference surfaces may be almost plane and will allow but little change in the orientation of the partial income plane, while each slight change shifts the point of tangency greatly (cf. fig. 20 for two dimensions). If they are completing articles as cuffs, collars, and ties the indifference surfaces are arranged like concentric cocoons directed toward the origin (cf. fig. 22 for two dimensions).

But the three articles may be more intricately related in utility. Of tea, coffee and sugar, the first two are substitutes while the last is completing to both. If this triple completing and competing relation of articles were "perfect," the utility distribution would reduce to a plane passing through the origin and cutting between the "sugar" and "tea" axes, also between the "sugar" and "coffee" axes. Several characteristics of such an ideal utility dependence would exist. If the triple dependence is not "perfect" the plane referred to swells out into a flat disk or rather a "family" of concentric disks. The triple variation of prices and its effects on the

---

*For its equa. is $\dfrac{A}{OA} + \dfrac{B}{OB} + \dfrac{C}{OC} = 1$, whence: $A \cdot \dfrac{50}{OA} + B \cdot \dfrac{50}{OB} + C \cdot \dfrac{50}{OC} = 50$ or $A p_a + B p_b + C p_c = 50$.

relative amounts of the three articles (that is on the position of the point of contact) can readily be discerned by its aid. Far more complicated cases are supposable and exist in reality.

§ 3.

If we suppose for an instant that there are but three commodities in the market, the preceding analysis yields a complete account of the equilibrium in that market.

To sketch this briefly let us suppose the space to be filled with a utility density for I, another superposed but different distribution for II, and so on. Let us include production. If one man should be both a consumer and producer of the same article, the *net* consumption or production is now to be taken, and the total utility or disutility of this net amount is the density. The planes before referred to as partial income planes may now be called "total income and expenditure planes," and they *must each pass through the origin**

27.

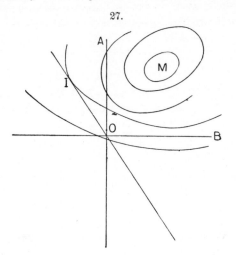

(OI, fig. 27 for two dimensions). Since the "maximum directions" (normal to their planes) are parallel, these planes *must all coincide*. The point in this plane selected by I will be that of tangency to an indifference surface for I. Likewise for II, III, etc. Such points

---

* For since income balances expenditure, if A_1, B_1, C_1, represent the (net) amounts consumed or produced by I, those consumed being treated as positive, and those produced as negative, the whole money value must be zero : i. e.

$$A \cdot p_a + B \cdot p_b + C \cdot p_c = 0,$$

which is the equation of a plane passing through the origin.

could be found whatever the position of the plane. But the plane must assume *such an orientation that the center of gravity of these points shall be the origin.* That is the algebraic sum of all the A coördinates consumed must equal the sum produced. Likewise the algebraic sum of the B and C coördinates must each be zero.

Hence with the geometrical analysis just described the equilibrium for a market of three commodities is determined when :

(1) All individuals' combinations lie in a common plane through the origin (each individual's sales and purchases cancel).

(2) Each individual's combination is at the point where this plane is tangent to an indifference surface for that individual (the point of maximum net utility).

(3) The points in the plane are so distributed as to make the origin their centre of gravity (the production and consumption of each commodity balance).

Whence it follows geometrically that the " maximum directions " are parallel, their components (marginal utilities) proportional as between different individuals and that this proportion is that of the orientation of the plane (the ratio of prices).

§ 4.

When this equilibrium is attained, let us, through the point of tangency I, representing the consumption combination for I, pass a section parallel to the plane of the A and B axes. The section of this plane with the total income plane gives a straight line which is none other than the partial income line of Ch. I, § 11 and its section with the indifference surfaces gives back the indifference curves of Ch. I, § 10.

§ 5.

We have temporarily assumed only three commodities for we have only three dimensions wherewith to represent them. A complete presentation of the interdependence of utilities would require m dimensions, for the utility of any one commodity A, is subject to m independent variations according to a change in any one of the m commodities, though (in general) the change of the quantity A itself is most important.

There is a curious glamour over "the fourth dimension." The popular interest is all to prove that it "exists." Its origin historically and its present usefulness is in the interpretation of a fourth independent variation, i. e. in representing just such relations as now concern us. It seems unfortunate that only mathematicians should be acquainted with this fact.

§ 6.

In this m dimensional space make m mutually perpendicular axes for the commodities A, B, C, . . . M. Fill the space with a total utility density. Pass an $m-1$ flat* through the origin giving it the proper orientation in view of the prices. The indifference loci will be $(m-1)$ spaces (curved). The point of tangency of the $(m-1)$ flat with an $(m-1)$ indifference locus will indicate the *total* consumption and production combination for an individual. A normal to the $(m-1)$ flat and $(m-1)$ indifference locus at their tangency shows his "maximum direction" and its components the marginal utilities of all articles.

These ideas are not so unfamiliar as they appear. This space is simply the "economic world" in which we live. We often speak of spending an income in this or that "direction," to express the relative amounts of commodities. When one speaks of the "point" which a consumer or producer reaches, the use of the word is a natural attempt to group in thought m different magnitudes. This is accomplished by regarding them as coördinates of a "point" in the "economic world." It is an application to economics of those ideas of "multiple algebra" which have added† so to the beauty and simplicity of geometry and mathematical physics.

§ 7.

These conceptions will tend to a more compact comprehension of the nature of economic equilibrium. In order to have equilibrium in the whole system including production :

(1) The utility distribution must be given for each individual.

(2) The "maximum directions" must be alike among all individuals and between production and consumption.

(3) The origin must be the centre of gravity of all the individual points : that is the sum of all A coördinates for consumption must equal the sum for production and likewise for B, C, etc.

(4) The common income and expenditure flat must pass through the origin : that is the money values of each man's production and consumption must cancel.

---

*I. e. a Euclidean space of $(m-1)$ dimensions related to the m-dimensional space as a plane is to our space.

† See J. W. Gibbs, Multiple Algebra, Proceedings *Amer. Asso. Adv. Sci.*, vol. xxxv.

§ 8.

By passing sections successively through the point I, we may narrow the discussion to as few variables as we choose. We may thus select any *three* and discuss them as before in real space (cf. § 4).

§ 9. ANALYTICAL.

For those familiar with multiple algebra, that is with the quaternion analysis of Hamilton, the " ausdehnungslehre " of Grassman, or the vector analysis of Prof. J. Willard Gibbs, the foregoing geometrical simplification will lead to a striking analytical simplification.*

Let I, II, . . . N, be vectors to the points I, II, . . . N from the origin. Let U_1, U_2, etc., represent the total utility at the points I, II, etc. Let $\triangledown U_1$, $\triangledown U_2$, etc., be vectors to represent in magnitude and direction the maximum rate of increase of utility at the points I, II, etc. (i. e. in the "maximum directions").

The conditions of equilibrium expressed in § 7 become :

(1) $\triangledown U_1 = F(I)$; $\triangledown U_2 = F(II)$; . . . $\triangledown U_n = F(N)$

(2) $\triangledown U_1 \propto \triangledown U_2 \propto \triangledown U_3 \propto$ . . . $\propto \triangledown U_n$

(3) $I + II + III +$ . . . $+ N = 0$

(4) $I . \triangledown U_1 = II . \triangledown U_2 =$ . . . $= N . \triangledown U_n = 0$

The first equation represents the several utility distributions. The second means that the "maximum directions" are alike ; the third that the amount of each commodity produced and consumed cancel, and the fourth that for each individual the values of production and consumption cancel.†

---

* See J. W. Gibbs' Vector Analysis, p. 16, § 50.

† The scalar equations which the preceding vector equations replace can readily be deduced from them. Let a, b, c, etc., be unit vectors along the A, B, C, etc. axes. Multiply $\triangledown U_1 = F(I)$ by a, b, c, etc. respectively. We obtain m equations of the form $\triangledown U_1 . a = F(I) . a$ or:

$$\frac{dU}{dA_1} = F(A_1, B_1, C_1, \ldots M_1).$$

Likewise m scalar equations are contained in $\triangledown U_2 = F(II)$, etc.

Again from (2) since $\triangledown U_1 \propto \triangledown U_2$,

$$\triangledown U_1 . a : \triangledown U_1 . b = \triangledown U_2 . a : \triangledown U_2 . b \text{ or:}$$

$$\frac{dU}{dA_1} : \frac{dU}{dB_1} = \frac{dU}{dA_2} : \frac{dU}{dB_2}.$$

Likewise for C_1, D_1, . . . M_1. Likewise for $\triangledown U_3$, etc.

Again (3) yields $I . a + II . a + III . a +$ . . . $+ N . a = 0$ or

$$A_1 + A_2 + A_3 + \ldots + A_n = 0.$$

Likewise for B, C, . . . M, making m equations.

§ 10.

It is seen that analytically the treatment of interdependent commodities differ from that of independent commodities only in this, that the equations which represent the functions have more letters ; i. e. we have

$$\frac{d\,U}{dA_1} = F(A_1, B_1 \ldots N_1) \text{ instead of } = F(A_1).$$

All other equations are just as in Part I. In fact these function equations are, so to speak, the residuary formulæ ; they contain all the unanalyzed conditions of the problem.

The marginal utilities are (as in Part I) in a continuous ratio which is the ratio of prices. Yet there are some peculiar cases which could not occur under the suppositions of Part I, viz : those cases arising when the marginal utility of one or more articles has no meaning.

If two articles are perfect completing articles, as gun and trigger, there is no such quantity as the marginal utility of triggers alone. There is, however, a marginal utility of a combined gun and trigger. Now there are separate marginal disutilities for producing the gun and trigger. How are all these quantities to be introduced into our continuous proportion of marginal utilities ?

Suppose for a moment there were *no* difficulty of this sort. The proportion for each individual would be just as before (Part I, Ch. IV, § 10) and might be expressed as follows [G&g for gun T&t for trigger] :

$$-\frac{p_g}{\dfrac{dU}{dG_\pi}} = -\frac{p_t}{\dfrac{dU}{dT_\pi}} = \left\{ \frac{p_g}{\dfrac{{}^*dU}{dG_\kappa}} \right\} = \left\{ \frac{p_t}{\dfrac{{}^*dU}{dT_\kappa}} \right\} =$$

$$\left\{ \frac{\dfrac{p_g}{{}^*dU}{dG_\kappa} + \dfrac{p_t}{{}^*dU}{dT_\kappa}} \right\} = \frac{p_g + p_t}{\dfrac{dU}{d(G\&T)_\kappa}}$$

Finally: It is clear that

$$I = Aa + Bb + \ldots + Mm \text{ and } \nabla U_1 = \frac{dU}{dA_1}a + \frac{dU}{dB_1}b + \ldots + \frac{dU}{dM_1}m.$$

Substituting these values in $I . \nabla U_1 = 0$ we have after performing the multiplication and remembering that $a . a = 1$ and $a . b = a . c = \ldots = b . c = \ldots = 0$,

$$A_1\frac{dU}{dA_1} + B_1\frac{dU}{dB_1} + \ldots + M_1\frac{dU}{dM_1} = 0$$

or since prices are proportional to marginal utilities:

$$A_1\,p_a + B_1\,p_b + \ldots M_1\,p_m = 0.$$

Likewise for II, III, etc. making *n* equations.

Conversely we could derive the vector equations from the scalar.

The last two members of this equation are new and require a word of explanation. The next to the last is an obvious consequence of the principles of composition and division. Its denominator represents the marginal utility of Gun and Trigger combined and is written $\dfrac{d\,U}{d(\text{G\&T})_{\kappa}}$ in the last member.

But the quantities which are starred are those which can under our supposition no longer be said to exist. Hence all members of the equation containing a star drop out and we have left the first, second and last members. In other words, if two articles are perfectly completing their *joint* marginal utility is in the ratio to their *joint* price as the marginal disutility of producing either article is to its price (negatively) or as every other marginal utility is to its price.

In like manner if two articles are perfect completing articles from the producer's standpoint, as beef-hides and beef-meat, their joint marginal disutility is to their joint price as the marginal utility of either is to its price (negatively) or as any marginal utility is to its price.

If two articles are such that they are perfect completing both as to production and consumption and in the same ratios, they not only have no separate utilities or disutilities but they can have no separate prices. Thus, the head, limbs, tail and other parts of a horse are produced together and consumed (used) together; they have no separate price.

It is impossible for articles to exist which are perfect completing articles both for consumption and production but are produced in one ratio and consumed in another.

Suppose two articles are such that the production of one is perfectly completing to the consumption of the other. Suppose, for instance, that the production of a ton of iron involves the consumption of a ton of coal, and that the consumption of the ton of coal also implies the production of a ton of iron. The iron producer in this case could not be said to have utility for more coal so long as he does not produce more iron, nor can he be said to have disutility of producing more iron without consuming more coal. What utilities or disutilities then does he have? He may be said to have a joint marginal disutility of producing iron and consuming coal. This "joint" disutility is to the *difference* of the prices of iron and coal as the marginal utility of any commodity to him is to its price.

Like principles apply to three or more perfectly completing articles. As long as articles are not *perfectly* completing there is no need for the substitution of joint utilities for single ones. As a matter of fact the number of really *perfectly* completing articles is relatively small.

If two articles are " perfect " substitutes for consumption and the ratio of their marginal utilities is the same for all consumers, while from a producer's standpoint they are not " perfect" substitutes, the consumers fix the ratio of their prices (viz: that of their marg. ut.) and the producers produce quantities accordingly. But the quantities of each consumed by different individuals is entirely indeterminate. Thus the milk from each cow may be regarded as a separate commodity. The consumer is indifferent to which milk he drinks, and purely accidental causes determine how much of each he gets ; the producer, however, milks determinate amounts from each cow.

If two articles are perfect substitutes both for production and consumption and the ratio of their marginal utilities and of their marginal disutilities are all alike their prices will have this ratio, but the *relative* quantities of each produced and consumed is entirely indeterminate ; (e. g. the colors in the binding of a book).

If two articles are perfect substitutes and the ratio of their marginal utility of the first to the second is for every consumer greater than the ratio of their marginal disutilities to all producers, the first commodity alone will be produced and consumed and its price will be determined as for any commodity.

In general if two articles are perfect substitutes, but the ratio of their marginal utilities and the ratio of their marginal disutilities is different for different individuals, those to whom the ratio of marginal utilities of the first to the second is greater than the ratio of their prices will consume only the first, those whose utility ratio is less than the price ratio will consume only the second, those whose disutility ratio is greater than the price ratio will produce only the second ; those for whom it is less, only the first.* In this case the price of each article is determined just as usual, but for each individual who does not consume or produce one or the other, its marginal utility or disutility simply fails to have meaning and drops out of the equations ; just as in Part I, occasionally a cistern may be entirely out of the tank water.

---

* If some producers and consumers should have their utility or disutility ratio identical with the price ratio the relative amounts produced and consumed are indeterminate to the extent of this coincidence.

CHAPTER III.

MECHANICAL ANALOGIES.

§ 1.

For each individual situated in the "economic world," suppose a vector drawn along each axis to indicate the marginal utility in that "direction." The marginal utility of consuming (a) is a vector positive along the A axis, the marginal disutility of producing (a) (or the disutility of paying money for a) is an *equal* vector in the opposite direction. In like manner the marginal utilities and disutilities along all axes are equal and opposite.

This corresponds to the mechanical equilibrium of a particle the condition of which is that the component forces along all perpendicular axes should be equal and opposite.

Moreover we may combine all the marginal utilities and obtain a vector whose direction signifies the direction in which an individual would most increase his utility. The disutility vector which indicates the direction in which an individual would most increase the disutility of producing. These two vectors are (by evident geometry) equal and opposite.

The above is completely analogous to the laws of composition and resolution of forces.

If marginal utilities and disutilities are thus in equilibrium "gain" must be a maximum. This is the mere application of the calculus and corresponds exactly to the physical application of the calculus which shows that at equilibrium the balancing of forces implies that energy is a maximum. Now energy is force times space, just as gain is marginal utility times commodity.

§ 2.

In Mechanics.			*In Economics.*
A particle	corresponds to		An individual.
Space	"	"	Commodity.
Force	"	"	Marg. ut. or disutility.
Work	"	"	Disutility.
Energy	"	"	Utility.

Work or Energy = force × space.	Disut. or Ut. = marg. ut. × commod.
Force is a vector (directed in space).	Marg. ut. is a vector (directed in com.)
Forces are added by vector addition.	Marg. ut. are added by vector addition.
("parallelogram of forces.")	(parallelogram of marg. ut.)
Work and Energy are scalars.	Disut. and ut. are scalars.

The *total work* done by a particle in moving from the origin to a given position is the integral of the *resisting forces* along all space axes (resisting forces are those directed toward the origin) multiplied by the distances moved along those axes.

The *total disutility* suffered by an individual in assuming a given position in the "economic world" is the integral of the *marg. disut.* along all commod. axes (marg. disut. are directed toward the origin) multiplied by the distances moved along those axes.

The " *total energy*" (the work done *upon* the particle) may be defined as the like integral with respect to *impelling forces.*

The *total utility* enjoyed by the individual is the like integral with respect to *marg. utilities.*

The *net energy* of the particle may be defined as the " total energy" less the " total work."

The net ut. or *gain* of the individual is the " total utility " less the " total disutility."

Equilibrium will be where net energy is maximum ; or equilibrium will be where the impel. and resist. forces along each axis will be equal.

Equilibrium will be where gain is maximum ; or equilibrium will be where the marg. ut. and marg. disut. along each axis will be equal.

(If " total energy " be subtracted from " total work" instead of vice versa the difference is "*potential*" and is minimum).

(If "total ut." be subtracted from "total disut." instead of vice versa the difference may be called "*loss*" and is minimum).

CHAPTER IV.

UTILITY AS A QUANTITY.

§ 1.

In Part I, Chap. I, Utility was defined with reference to a single ·individual. In order to study prices and distribution it is not necessary to give any meaning to the ratio of two men's utilities. Jevons apparently did not observe this. Auspitz und Lieben did. So did George Darwin.*

§ 2.

It would doubtless be of service in ethical investigations and possibly in certain economic problems to determine how to compare the utilities of two individuals. It is not incumbent on us to do this. When it is done the comparison will doubtless be by objective standards. If persons alike in most respects show to each other their sat-

* The Theory of Exchange Value.   Fortnightly Review. new series, xvii, 243.

isfaction by similar gestures, language, facial expression, and general conduct we speak of their satisfaction as very much the same. What however this may mean in the "noumenal" world is a mystery. If on the other hand differences of age, sex, temperament, etc. enter, comparison becomes relatively difficult and inappropriate. Very little could be meant by comparing the desire of a Fuegian for a shell-fish with that of a college conchologist for the same object and surely nothing is meant by comparing the desires of the shellfish itself with that of either of its tormentors.

§ 3.

When statistics becomes a developed science it may be that the wealth of one age or country will be compared with that of another as " gain " not money value. If the annual commercial product of the U. S. was in 1880 $9,000,000,000* and by increased facilities for production prices are lowered so much that the product in 1890 is only valued at (say) $8,000,000,000 it proves a gain not a loss. The country would be the richest possible when all things were as plentiful as water, bore no price, and had a total valuation of *zero*. Now money value simply measures utility by a marginal standard which is constantly changing. Statistical comparison must always be rough but it can be better than that. The statistician might begin with those utilities in which men are most alike—food utilities—and those disutilities in which they are most alike—as the disutilities of definite sorts of manual labor. By these standards he could measure and correct the money standard† and if the utility curves for various classes of articles were constructed he could make rough statistics of total utility, total disutility, gain, and utility-value which would have considerable meaning. Men are much alike in their digestion and fatigue. If a food or a labor standard is established it can be easily applied to the utilities in regard to which men are unlike as of clothes, houses, furniture, books, works of art, etc.

§ 4.

These inquiries however do not belong here. Let us instead of adding to the meaning of utility do the very opposite and strip it of all attributes unessential to our purpose of determining objective prices

---

* Edward Atkinson, Distribution of products, p. 141.

† Cf. Edgeworth, On the method of ascertaining and measuring variations in the value of the monetary standard, Report of the British Association for the Advancement of Science, 1887.

and distribution. Definition 3, Part I, Chap. I, § 4 yielded uniform results only on the assumption that the utility of each commodity was independent of the quantity of others. Similar assumptions are necessary in geometry. A unit of length is a yard. A yard is the length of a standard bar in London. To be used it must be assumed that its length is not a function of its position nor dependent on the changes in length of other bodies. If the earth shrinks we can measure the shrinkage by the yard stick provided it has not also shrunk as a necessary feature of the earth's change. Definition 3 was essential in Part I to give meaning to the cisterns used. Such a definition is essential to the analyses of Gossen, Jevons, Launhardt, Marshall, and all writers who employ coördinates. Yet it is not necessary in the analysis of Part II.

§ 5.

In fig. 28 the " lines of force " are drawn perpendicular to the in-

28 .

difference loci. The *directions* of these lines of force are alone used in the formulæ in Ch. II, § 9 which determine equilibrium. Therefore the *directions* alone are important. It makes absolutely no difference so far as the objective determination of prices and distribution is concerned what the length of the arrow is at one point compared with another. The ratios of the components at any point are important but these ratios are the same whatever the length of the arrow. Thus we may dispense with the total utility density and conceive the " economic world " to be filled merely with lines of force or " maximum directions."

§ 6.

Even if we should give exact meanings to the length of these arrows (so that the equation $\nabla U_1 = F(I)$ should signify not only that for each position in the economic world a definite "maximum direction " exists but also that the *rate* of increase of utility or the *length* of the vector along this line is given)—even then there would not be a complete primitive $U_1 = \varphi(I)$ unless certain conditions were fulfilled.* These conditions are (1) that the lines of force are so arranged that loci (*surfaces* in two dimensions, $m-1$ *spaces* in m dimensions) perpendicular to them can be constructed, and (2) that

---

* Osborne, Differential Equations, p. 12.

the rate of passing from one locus to the next along a line of force shall for all positions between the two loci be inversely proportional to the value of ∇U_1 already assigned to these positions. If ∇U_1 is not distributed in the above manner integration is impossible and *there is no such quantity as total utility or gain.*

§ 7.

Even if the integration were possible there would still be an arbitrary constant. We could even claim that total disutility exceeds total utility and all man can do is to minimize the disagreeable instead of maximize the agreeable. In other words, if we embrace hedonism, there is nothing in economic investigation to cause us to choose between optimism and pessimism.

§ 8.

Thus if we seek only the causation of the *objective facts of prices and commodity distribution* four attributes of utility as a quantity are entirely unessential, (1) that one man's utility can be compared to another's, (2) that for the same individual the marginal utilities at one consumption-combination can be compared with those at another, or at one time with another, (3) even if they could, total utility and gain might not be integratable, (4) even if they were, there would be no need of determining the constants of integration.

END OF PART II.

APPENDIX I.

MISCELLANEOUS REMARKS ON PART I.

I. FAILURE OF EQUATIONS.

Jevons (p. 118) discusses the failure of equations for simple exchange. It is clear that such failure must frequently occur in complex exchanges but no one has apparently commented on it. It would seem at first sight that this would introduce an indeterminate element into our results. Such however is not the case unless we take account of articles neither produced nor consumed ; then the highest price which any consumer will pay for the first infinitesimal is less than the lowest price at which any one will produce it; there is no production nor consumption and the term price has no determinate meaning. As soon as changes in industrial conditions, that is in the shape of the cisterns or their number makes this inequality into an equality, the article enters into our calculations.

Suppose A is produced by n_π people, consumed by n_κ, and exchanged or retailed by n_ϵ, where n_π, n_κ and n_ϵ are each less than n (the number of individuals.) Moreover from the nature of our former suppositions if any of the three are greater than zero all must be, for anything once in the system is supposed to be produced, exchanged and consumed within the given period of time.

The number of people who do not

produce A is $n - n_\pi$,

exchange A is $n - n_\epsilon$,

consume A is $n - n_\kappa$.

The number of unknowns dropped out of the equations in Ch. VI, § 2, is

$$3n - (n_\pi + n_\epsilon + n_\kappa) \text{ of the type } A_{1,\pi}, A_{1,\epsilon}, A_{1,\kappa}, \text{ etc.,}$$

and $3n - (n_\pi + n_\epsilon + n_\kappa)$ of the type $\dfrac{dU}{dA_1}$,

or $6n - 2(n_\pi + n_\epsilon + n_\kappa)$ altogether.

The failing equations in the first set are none,

"   "   "   " second " none,

"   "   "   " third " $3n - (n_\pi + n_\epsilon + n_\kappa)$,

"   "   "   " fourth " $3n - (n_\pi + n_\epsilon + n_\kappa)$,

"   "   "   " fifth " none,

or $6n - 2(n_p + n_e + n_c)$ altogether.

From the above agreement it appears that there can be no indeterminate case under the suppositions which were first made. Let us look at this somewhat more closely.

In the fourth set of equations there are really $n(3m-1)\left(\dfrac{3m}{2}\right)$ separate equations but only $n(3m-1)$ are *independent*. Which shall be selected is a matter of convenience. We may make every equation contain $p_{a,\pi}$ for instance and write

$$p_{a,\pi} : p_{b,\pi} = \frac{d\mathrm{U}}{d\mathrm{A}_{\pi,1}} : \frac{d\mathrm{U}}{d\mathrm{B}_{\pi,1}} = \frac{d\mathrm{U}}{d\mathrm{A}_{\pi,2}} : \frac{d\mathrm{U}}{d\mathrm{B}_{\pi,2}} = \text{etc.}$$

$$p_{a,\pi} : p_{c,\pi} = \text{etc.}$$

. . . .

$$p_{a,\pi} : p_{a,\kappa} = , \quad \cdots \cdots \cdots$$

. . . .

$$p_{a,\pi} : p_{a,\epsilon} = , \quad \cdots \cdots \cdots$$

. . . .

Now from the first two equations we may derive by division

$$p_{b,\pi} : p_{c,\pi} = \frac{d\mathrm{U}}{d\mathrm{B}_{\pi,1}} : \frac{d\mathrm{U}}{d\mathrm{C}_{\pi,1}},$$

but we might wish to use this last as one of the $n(3m-1)$ independent equations, if $\mathrm{A}_{1,\pi}$ should "fail." From the $n(3m-1)\dfrac{3m}{2}$ separate equations we are at liberty to select for use any $n(3m-1)$ independent ones; and if in this selection there occur any which by some change of quantities fail, we are compelled to change our selection so that the new $n(3m-1)$ equations shall avoid the "failing" magnitudes.

This is interpreted in the mechanism as follows : when a cistern is wholly above the surface of the tank (as IIIC fig. 8) and so contains nothing, the quantity of commodity and its utility "fail." The levers which keep the ordinates in proportion to the corresponding ordinates of other individuals may be far more numerous than the levers pictured in former diagrams. Thus for four cisterns there may be six levers (by joining each pair) but only three are necessary. The " failure " of any magnitudes will not invalidate any system of levers originally selected ; it will simply make their number greater than necessary.

II. THE CISTERNS AND DIAGRAMS OF PART I COMPARED WITH THE DIAGRAMS OF JEVONS AND OF AUSPITZ UND LIEBEN.

§ 1.

In order to represent geometrically the relations between quantity of commodity, marginal utility, total utility, and gain (any two of which four magnitudes are determined by a specified relation between the other two) it is only necessary to have a plane curve of appropriate form and to represent any two of the above economic magnitudes by any two geometrical magnitudes determined by the position of points in the curve.

Out of the numerous possible methods thus included, the one selected for the preceding discussion was to represent marginal utility by the Cartesian ordinate and commodity by the area included between the curve, the axes of coördinates, and the abscissa drawn from the point.

§ 2.

In order to show the connection between this system of coördinates and those of Jevons and of Auspitz und Lieben, the following scheme is presented :

	Jevons.	Auspitz & Lieben.	The new curves.
Commodity	$= x_j$	$= x_a$	$= \int x\,dy$
Marginal utility	$\dots = y_j$	$= \dfrac{dy_a}{dx_a} = \tan \theta$	$= y$
Total utility	$\dots = \int y_j dx_j$	$= y_a$	$= \int yx\,dy$
Gain	$= \int y_j dx_j - x_j y_j$	$= y_a - x_a \dfrac{dy_a}{dx_a}$	$= \int yx\,dy - y\int x\,dy$

29.

30.

31.

32.

33.　　　　　　　　　　　　34.

These curves are shown in figs. 29 and 30 (Jevons), 31, 32 (Auspitz und Lieben), and 33, 34 (new). The first in each case is for consumption the second for production.*

§ 3.

If Jevons' curve for consumption becomes a straight line, fig. 35, its equation is:†

$$x_j + qy_j = m.$$

Using the preceding table substituting for x_j and y_j we get in Auspitz und Lieben coördinates :

35.　　　　　　　　36.　　　　　　　　　37.

$$x_a - q\,\frac{dy_a}{dx_a} = m,$$

which integrated gives

$$2qy_a = 2mx_a - x_a^2 + C.$$

Since the curve must evidently pass through the origin, $C = 0$, and using new constants we may write :‡

$$y_a = \alpha x_a - \beta x_a^2,$$

which is a parabola (fig. 36).

---

* Jevons used no production curve. The one drawn is inserted to complete the comparison. Fleeming Jenkins' "Demand and Supply" curves are the same as Jevons save that price replaces marginal utility.

† Gossen, Launhardt, Whewell, and Tozer (the last two use no *geometric* analysis) employ such a linear supposition, though the meanings of their variables are not identical.　　　　　　　　　　　‡ Launhardt's equation.

For the new coördinates the substitutions from the table give :

$$\int x dy + qy = m,$$

which reduces to $\qquad\qquad x = -q,$

a straight line parallel to the axis of ordinates (fig. 37).

The Auspitz und Lieben curve does not reveal to the eye the special supposition (that commodity and marginal utility change proportionally). If we suppose that marginal utility decreases at a constant rate in relation to constant *second* differences of commodity, the new diagram reduces to a straight line :

$$x - qy - m = 0,$$

while the other curves would be :

$$(y_a + A x_a + B)^2 = C(D - x_a)^3$$

and $\qquad\qquad x_j = E - F y_j - G y_j^2.$

§ 4.

The value of Jevons' diagram consists in the use of a simple and familiar system of coördinates (the Cartesian) as representing the two chief economic quantities, and is probably the best for elementary purposes.

The value of Auspitz und Lieben's diagram together with a " derivative " curve* not shown above consists chiefly in the ease with which maxima are discovered and the clear association of maxima with equality of marginal utilities. It is believed that the third method will, by means of its applicability to the mechanisms of Part I, more clearly reveal the *interdependence* of the many commodities of many individuals and of their many utilities.

§ 5.

The properties which are essential to the curve we have adopted are :—

First. That the curve shall never admit of being intersected twice by a horizontal line (i. e. that it shall not cease to run in a general up and down manner), *to express the fact for consumption that marginal utility decreases as quantity of commodity increases and for production that marginal disutility increases as the quantity of commodity increases.*

---

* Whose Cartesian coördinates are x_a and $y_a \dfrac{dy_a}{dx_a}$.

Second. That the curve shall approach the axis of ordinates asymptotically and in such a manner that the whole area between it and the axis is finite, *to express the fact that marginal utility becomes infinitely minus for consumption of, and infinitely plus for production of finite limiting quantities of commodity.**

Third. The curves *begin* (have commodity equal to zero) at a finite vertical distance from the origin. (These assumptions are less generally true of production than of consumption, but they have been here employed throughout.)

§ 6.

It is evident that in comparing the forms of curves for different articles their differences and peculiarities are determined in a most delicate fashion by the form of the curve . . . far more delicately than, with our present statistical knowledge, is necessary.

Observe, then, what the *abscissa* of our curve stands for. An infinitely thin layer xdy is the amount *additional* demanded (or supplied) in response to an infinitesimal decrease (or increase) dy in marginal utility. The abscissa x is the ratio of the infinitesimal layer xdy to the infinitesimal change of price, dy. It is therefore *the rate of increase of quantity demanded*† (or supplied) in relation to change of marginal utility. AM (figs. 2 and 3) is the initial rate. Consulting II, § 2 of this appendix, we see that

$$x_j = \int xdy$$

Hence, $$dx_j = xdy$$
But $$y = y_j \text{ and } dy = dy_j$$
Hence $$\frac{dx_j}{dy_j} = x.$$

That is the abscissa of our curve is the *tangential direction* in Jevons' curve, considered with respect to the axis of ordinates.

Hence if Jevons' curve be subjected to the condition of being convex, the new curve must have the simple condition that successive abscissas diminish, etc., etc.

§ 7.

Hitherto nothing has been said as to the mode of representing total utility and gain.

If y_1 is the marginal utility (which may be figured in money) at which a consumer actually ceases to buy, y_k that at which he would

---

* Cf. Auspitz und Lieben. pp. 7 and 11.
† Cf. foot note Ch. IV, § 8, div. 3.

just begin to buy, then his consumer's rent or gain is (see Ch. I, § 8)

$$G = \int_{y_k}^{y_1} y\,x\,dy - y_1 \int_{y_k}^{y_1} x\,dy$$

or measuring this gain *in the given commodity* as valued at y_1 cents (say) per unit,

$$\frac{G}{y_1} = \int_{y_k}^{y_1} \frac{y}{y_1}\,x\,dy - \int_{y_k}^{y_1} x\,dy.$$

This may be interpreted by a simple geometrical construction. In fig. 38 OA $= y_k$ and OR $= y_1$.

38.　　　　　　　　　　　　　　39.

Selecting the point 3 make the evident dotted construction determining a point 5.

Evidently: $\dfrac{75}{73} = \dfrac{O5}{O4} = \dfrac{O7}{OR} = \dfrac{y}{y_1} \therefore 75 = \left(\dfrac{y}{y_1} \cdot x \right).$

Let 3 assume all positions from M to 6. Then 5 will trace a curve 26.

The area described by the moving line 73 is evidently $\displaystyle\int_{y_k}^{y_1} x\,dy$.

The area described by the moving line 75 is evidently $\displaystyle\int_{y_k}^{y_1}\left(\frac{y}{y_1}\,x\right)dy$.

Hence area described by the moving line 35 is the difference of these expressions or G/y_1.

That is the area M62 represents the gain measured in commodity.

Thus suppose a person buys corn measured by RAM6 and let corn at the valuation RO be the unit of utility. It is only the last layer R6 on which no gain is felt. For any preceding layer 75 the price really paid is OR while the price which it is worth to him is O7. The layer 73 may be considered as lengthened in his eyes by that ratio O7/OR so that by getting it at less than he was willing to pay, he has gained the element 35 measured in corn. His gain is *maximum* when he purchases such a quantity that its final utility equals its price.

Fig. 39 applies to " producer's rent " or " gain," substituting " sale " for " purchase "; " sell " for " buy."

To express the gain *in money* the area M26 must be multiplied by the price. On each cistern construct the curve 62 (fig. 38) and consider the area RA26 to move front and back one unit (say one inch) so as to trace a volume (fig. 40) adjacent to the front cistern and

40.

again to move *p* inches further back so as to trace a volume adjacent to the back cistern.

The front volume gives again the total utility measured in commodity. The back volume gives the total utility *measured in money*. That is the whole back cistern and its adjacent volume represent the money which if the individual paid he would neither gain nor lose, provided his marginal valuation of it is unchanged by the operation. The cistern portion is the money he actually pays and the outside volume 7, 10, 12, 9, 8, 11 is his "gain." Likewise for the producer.

III. GAIN A MAXIMUM.

§ 1.

In the case of a single individual distributing a fixed income over various commodities under fixed prices the distribution actually attained and specified in Part I yields the maximum total utility, for, since (Ch. IV, § 2):

$$\frac{dU}{dA_1} = \frac{dU}{dm_1} \cdot p_a \; ; \; \frac{dU}{dB_1} = \frac{dU}{dm_1} \cdot p_b \; ; \; \cdots$$

therefore:

$$\frac{\frac{dU}{dA_1}}{p_a} = \frac{\frac{dU}{dB_1}}{p_b} = \cdots = \frac{\frac{dU}{dM_1}}{p_m}. \tag{1}$$

The numerators are the marginal utilities per unit of commodity. To divide by the price is to make the unit of commodity the dollar's worth. Each fraction is thus the marginal utility per dollar's worth. The equation expresses the fact that the rate of increase of utility from spending more money on any one commodity equals the rate of increase for any other.   Hence by a familiar theorem of the calculus the total utility must be the maximum attainable by any distribution of a fixed income.   In like manner the individual distributes his production so that the marginal disutilities in all modes of producing dollar's worth of commodity are equal so that his total disutility is a minimum.   Hence the difference between his total utility and total disutility or his economic gain is a maximum .

§ 2.

In the distribution of a single commodity over many individuals since :

$$\frac{dU}{dA_1} = \frac{dU}{dm_1} \cdot p_a \; ; \; \frac{dU}{dA_2} = \frac{dU}{dm_2} \cdot p_a \; ; \; \cdots ; \; \frac{dU}{dA_n} = \frac{dU}{dm_n} p_a,$$

therefore,

$$\frac{\frac{dU}{dA_1}}{\frac{dU}{dm_1}} = \frac{\frac{dU}{dA_2}}{\frac{dU}{dm_2}} = \cdots = \frac{\frac{dU}{dA_n}}{\frac{dU}{dm_n}}, \tag{2}$$

that is, the marginal utilities (when the unit of utility is the marginal utility of money for each individual) are equal and the total utility is maximum.   In like manner the total disutility is a minimum and gain therefore a maximum.

§ 3.

The first continuous equation may be divided by $\dfrac{dU}{dm_1}$ and the second by p_a and since the first members will become identical we have a common continuous equation:

$$\frac{\dfrac{dU}{dA_1}}{\dfrac{dU}{dm_1} \cdot p_a} = \frac{\dfrac{dU}{dB_1}}{\dfrac{dU}{dm_1} \cdot p_b} = \cdots = \frac{\dfrac{dU}{dA_2}}{\dfrac{dU}{dm_2} \cdot p_a} = \text{etc.} \qquad (3)$$

that is, the marginal utilities of all commodities to all consumers are equal when the unit of utility is the marginal utility of money and the unit of commodity the dollar's worth. Hence the total utility in whole market thus measured is a maximum.*

§ 4.

However it may justly be objected that the marginal utility of money to one person is not equatable to that of another, that is that it is unfair to use the unit of utility for the poor man the high marginal utility of his small income and add the small number of such large units in a poor man's gain to the corresponding rich man's gain in which the unit of measure is small and the number of units large.

If we suppose by some mysterious knowledge an exact equivalence of utilities were possible between different individuals (see Part II, Ch. IV, § 2) and by some equally mysterious device of socialism we could *without changing the aggregate commodities* alter their distribution so as to make the whole market utility a maximum our condition would be

$$\frac{dU}{dA_1} = \frac{dU}{dA_2} = \text{etc.} \qquad (4)$$

This could be brought about by a change in the relative incomes, taking from the rich and giving to the poor until

$$\frac{dU}{dm_1} = \frac{dU}{dm_2} = \text{etc.}$$

which applied to equation (3) will evidently afford the required (4), or by breaking down the condition of uniformity of price and making each man's price inversely as his marginal utility of money, which applied to (3) will evidently yield (4).

To interpret equation 4 in the mechanism we may alter the position of the stoppers in fig. 8 until the ordinates in each front and back row are equal. (This will not be when " incomes are equally divided " nor when " gains " are equal, for persons differ in their power of enjoyment, and it would still be true that those whose

---

* Cf. Auspitz und Lieben, p. 23 and 435.

capacities for pleasure were great would consume the most in order to make the aggregate gain in the whole market a maximum). Or we may destroy all the levers and re-arrange the rear thicknesses until the front and back ordinates are made equal.

In like manner the minimum disutility would be attained if all marginal disutilities were equal. The maximum gain would then result. This is the maximum gain obtainable *when the amounts of each commodity consumed and produced are fixed and given.* If we are permitted to rearrange these amounts also, we shall secure the maximum gain when the marginal utilities equal the marginal disutilities ; i. e.

$$\frac{d\mathrm{U}}{d\mathrm{A}_{1,\,\pi}} = \frac{d\mathrm{U}}{d\mathrm{A}_{1,\,\kappa}} = \frac{d\mathrm{U}}{d\mathrm{A}_{2,\,\pi}} = \text{etc.}$$

Under such a socialistic regime more "necessaries" and less "luxuries" would be consumed and produced than previously. The "rich" or powerful would produce more and consume less than previously ; the poor or weak would consume more and produce less. Yet for each the marginal utilities and disutilities would be equal.

It is needless to say that these considerations are no plea for socialism, but they serve to clear up a subject sometimes discussed by mathematical economists and reconcile Launhardt's contention[*] that utility is not a maximum with Auspitz und Lieben's that it is. The former unconsciously has reference to equation (4) which is not true, the latter to equation (3) which is.[†]

IV. ELIMINATION OF VARIABLES.

The four sets of equations, Part I, Ch. IV, § 10, can be reduced. We may substitute for $\frac{d\,\mathrm{U}}{d\mathrm{A}_1}$ its value $\mathrm{F}(\mathrm{A}_1)$ and thus eliminate all marginal utilities. Moreover we can get an expression for p_a, p_b, etc., in terms of commodities. First, if $m = n$ the second set of equations are easily solved by determinants[‡] giving :[§]

---

[*] Volkswirthschaftslehre under "Widerholte Tausch."

[†] Auspitz und Lieben appear to overlook this difference of standpoint. Preface, p. xxv.

[‡] Burnside and Panton. Theory of Equations, p. 251.

[§] This equation does not mean that any *arbitrary* values can be assigned to A_1, B_1, etc., and the resulting price of A be so simply expressed ; only when A_1, B_1, etc. satisfy *all* the conditions of Ch. IV, § 10 will the price be expressible as the quotient of the two determinants.

$$p_a = \left\{ \begin{array}{cccc} K_1 & B_1 & \ldots & M_1 \\ K_2 & B_2 & \ldots & M_2 \\ \hline & & & \\ K_n & B_n & \ldots & M_n \end{array} \right\} \div \left\{ \begin{array}{cccc} A_1 & B_1 & \ldots & M_1 \\ A_2 & B_2 & \ldots & M_2 \\ \hline & & & \\ A_n & B_n & \ldots & M_n \end{array} \right\}$$

in which obviously in general a change in A will produce a greater influence on p_a then an equal change in B, etc. But it shows clearly that p_a is not a function of A alone.

Usually $n > m$. Hence we may use the first m equations of the second set, or in fact any m equations. The resulting determinant-quotients must be equal and must equal also the several like determinates for production.

The corresponding values of p_b, p_c, etc., may be found and may be substituted in the fourth set.

If wherever A_1 now occurs in the fourth set, we substitute $K_a - A_2 - A_3 - \ldots - A_n$ from the first set, and likewise for B_1, etc., the resulting fourth set is self-sufficient. We have thus eliminated the variables $\dfrac{dU}{dA}$, etc., p_a, etc., A_1, B_1, etc., and have gotten rid of the first, second and third set of equations. We can proceed no further, however, until the explicit forms of the functions $F(A_1)$, etc., are given.

APPENDIX II.

LIMITATIONS OF THE PRECEDING ANALYSIS.

§ 1.

No pretense is made that the preceding analysis is perfect or exhaustive. There is no such analysis of any phenomena whatever even in physics. The suppositions in Ch. II, § 2 of Part I, are of course ideal. They only imperfectly apply to New York City or Chicago. Ideal suppositions are unavoidable in any science. In fact it is an evidence of progress when the distinction between the ideal and the actual arises.* Even in hydrostatics the assumption of perfect fluidity is never fully realized. The physicist has never *fully* explained a single fact in the universe. He approximates only. The economist cannot hope to do better. Some writers, especially those of the historical school are disposed to carp at the introduction of *a refined mathematical analysis.* It is the old story of the

---

* See Prof. Simon Newcomb. The Method and Province of Pol. Econ., N. Am. Rev., CCXI, IX.

"practical" man versus the scientist. A sea-captain can sail his vessel and laugh at the college professor in his elaborate explanation of the process. What to him is all this resolution of forces and velocities which takes no account of the varying gusts of wind, the drifting of the keel, the pitching and tossing, the suppositions which makes of the sail an ideal plane and overlook the effect of the wind on the hull? There is no need to point the moral. Until the economist is reconciled to a refined ideal analysis he cannot profess to be scientific. After an ideal statical analysis the scientist may go further and reintroduce one by one the considerations at first omitted. This is not the object at present in view. But it may be well to merely enumerate the chief of these limitations.

§ 2.

In Part I the utility of A was assumed to be a sole function of the quantity of A, and in Part II a function of all commodities consumed by a given individual. We could go on and treat it as a function of all commodities produced and consumed, treating not *net* production for each article, but the actual amounts separately produced and consumed by the given individual.

Again we could treat it as a function of the quantities of each commodity produced or consumed by *all persons* in the market. This becomes important when we consider a man in relation to the members of his family or consider articles of fashion as diamonds,* also when we account for that (never thoroughly studied) interdependence, the division of labor.

This limitation has many analogies in physics. The attraction of gravity is a function of the distance from the center of the earth. A more exact analysis makes it a function of the revolution of the earth, of the position and mass of the moon (theory of tides) and finally of the position, and mass of every heavenly body.

§ 3.

Articles are not always homogeneous or infinitely divisible. To introduce this limitation is to replace each equation involving marginal utilities by two inequalities and to admit an equilibrium *indeterminate* between limits.† As an extreme case we may imagine an article of which no one desires more than a single copy as of a book. The utility of (say) Mill's Pol. Econ. is considerably greater than

---

* See David Wells, Recent Economic Changes, on Diamonds.
† Auspitz und Lieben, 117–136 and 467.

its cost, but the utility of a second copy is considerably less than its cost. In the aggregate market, however, there will be a *marginal person* whose utility is very close to the price. A change in price will not alter the amount purchased by everyone, but will alter the *number* of purchasers.*

§ 4.

Producing, consuming and exchanging are discontinuous in time. The theory of utility when applied to a *single act* of production or consumption or of sale or purchase, is independent of time, or rather the time element is all accounted for in the form of the utility function.† But an analysis of a number of such acts must take account of their frequency. The manner in which the time element enters has puzzled not a few economists.

An example from physics may not be amiss. In the kinetic theory of gases the pressure on the walls of the containing vessel is explained by its continual bombardment by molecules. But an apparent difficulty must be observed. A rebound of a molecule involves the idea of *momentum* only while that which we wish to explain is *pressure* or *force* which is not by any means momentum, but momentum divided by *time*. How does this time enter? By regarding not one but many molecules and taking account of the *frequency* of their collision. The average momentum of each blow divided by the average interval between the blows is the pressure sought.

So a produce exchange is a channel connecting production and consumption. Instead of an even flow of one bushel per second, the machinery of the exchange is such that by an instantaneous blow of a bat, so to speak, a thousand bushes are knocked along. Time is inappropriate to explain the single blow but necessary to explain the many.

§ 5.

The ideal statical condition assumed in our analysis is never satisfied in fact.

No commodity has a constant yearly rate of production or consumption. Industrial methods do not remain stationary. Tastes and fashions change. Panics show a lack of equilibrium. Their explanation belongs to the dynamics of economics. But we have

---

* The analysis of H. Cunynghame in the Ec. Jour., March '92, applies to this case.   † Cf. Jevons, 63–68.

again a physical analogue. Water seeks its level, but this law does not fully explain Niagara. A great deal of special data are here necessary and the physicist is as unfit to advise the captain of the Maid of the Mist as an economist to direct a Wall street speculator. The failure to separate statics from dynamics appears historically* to explain the great confusion in early physical ideas. To make this separation required the reluctant transition from the actual world to the ideal. The actual world both physical and economic has no equilibrium. " Normal "† price, production and consumption are sufficiently intricate without the complication of changes in social structure. Some economists object to the notion of "normal " as an ideal but unattainable state. They might with equal reason object to the ideal and unattainable equilibrium of the sea.

The dynamical side of economics has never yet received systematic treatment. When it has, it will reconcile much of the present apparent contradiction, e. g. if a market is out of equilibrium, things may sell for "more than they are worth," as every practical man knows, that is the proper ratios of marginal utilities and prices are not preserved.

§ 6.

We have assumed a constant population. But population does change and with it all utility functions change. An analysis whose independent variable is population‡ leads to another department of economics. In the foregoing investigation the influence of population was included in the *form* of the utility function. So also with all causes physical, mental and social not dependent on the quantities of commodities or services.

§ 7.

Individuals are not free to stop consuming or producing at any point. Factory operatives must have uniform working hours. The marginal undesirability of the last hour may for some workmen equal, for others exceed or fall short of the utility of its wages.

§ 8.

No one is fully acquainted with all prices nor can he adjust his actions to them with the nicety supposed ; both these considerations are starting points for separate discussion.

---

* Whewell, Hist. Induct. Sci., I, 72–3 and 186.   † Marshall, p. 84.
‡ See article of Prof. J. B. Clark. Distribution as determined by a law of rent. Quart. Jour. Econ., Apr. '91, p. 289.

§ 9.

The "fundamental symmetry of supply and demand worked out by Auspitz und Lieben should not bind us to the fundamental *asymmetry*. The symmetry enables us to investigate the general dependence of consumption and production but special investigation of production, e. g. of railroad rates should be independently pursued.

(1.) Production of a commodity always precedes its consumption.

(2.) The maximum advantage in *production* involves few commodities for each individual, in *consumption* many.

(3.) Increasing social organization intensifies the former fact not the latter.

(4.) There are more successive steps in production than consumption.

(5) Social organization intensifies this distinction.

(6) Owing to (4) and (5) *service* rather than *commodity* becomes increasingly the unit in production.

(7.) Freedom to leave off consuming at any point is greater than for producing.

(8.) Social organization intensifies this.

(9.) Combination and monopoly are more feasible and frequent in production than in consumption.

(10.) In production the distinction of fixed charges and running expenses often plays an important rôle. This deserves a separate treatment. The transportation charges on a steamship are not what it costs to transport an extra ton but it is this quantity plus the proportionate share of that ton in the fixed charges (interest, insurance, etc). That is, the marginal cost of service involves the margin of capital invested as well as the marginal cost of running the ship) (which is purely nominal). This is so in theory of railroad rates but the railroad investor cannot foresee the results of his enterprise as well nor can he change his road when built from one route to another as a steamship can do. To apply the theory to railroads assumes that railroad projectors know what the traffic will be. Consequently the proper discussion of railroad rates, *assuming that the railroads are already built,* takes no account of fixed charges but becomes formulated as "what the traffic will bear."*

A complete theory of the relation of cost of production to price in its varying and peculiar ramifications is too vast a subject to be treated here.

---

* See Hadley, Railroad Transportation.

§ 10.

It has been assumed throughout this investigation that marginal utility decreases as quantity of commodity increases. This is not always true, e. g. it is obviously not true of intoxicating liquors. A study of the liquor traffic would require a somewhat different treatment from that of most other commodities. Still less is it always true that marginal cost of production always increases as the quantity produced increases. It is clearly not true that it costs more in a shoe factory to produce the second shoe than it costs to produce the first. Yet it is probably quite generally true that at the actual margin reached in business the disutility of extending the business grows greater. When this is not true and when it is not true that marginal utility decreases as quantity of commodity increasess an instability is the result. The matter of instability is one element at the bottom of the present industrial tendency toward trusts and pools.

§ 11.

There is no isolated market. Not only this but a "market" itself is an ideal thing. The stalls in the same city meat market may be far enough apart to prevent a purchaser from behaving precisely as if he stood before two counters at once. The relation of the counters ten feet apart differs in degree rather than in kind from the relation of London to New York.

APPENDIX III.

THE UTILITY AND HISTORY OF MATHEMATICAL METHOD IN ECONOMICS.

§ 1.

Mathematics possesses the same *kind* though not the same degree of value in every inquiry. Prof. B. Peirce,* in his memorable *Linear Associative Algebra*, says : "Mathematics is the science which draws necessary conclusions. * * * * * Mathematics is not the discoverer of laws, for it is not induction, neither is it the framer of theories for it is not hypothesis, but it is the judge over both. * * * * * It deduces from a law all its consequences.

Mathematics under this definition belongs to every inquiry, moral as well as physical. Even the rules of logic by which it is rigidly bound could not be deduced without its aid. The laws of argu-

---

* Amer. Jour. Math., IV., p. 97.

ments admit of simple statement, but they must be curiously transposed before they can be applied to the living speech and verified by observation.

In its pure and simple form the syllogism cannot be directly compared with all experience, or it would not have required an Aristotle to discover it. It must be transmuted into all the possible shapes in which reasoning loves to clothe itself. The transmutation is the mathematical process in the establishment of the law."*

I make this quotation for I believe many persons, especially economists, do not understand the character of mathematics in general. They imagine that a physicist can sit in his study and with the calculus as a talisman spin out some law of physics. Some economists have hoped for a similar mysterious use of mathematics in their own science.

§ 2.

We must distinguish carefully between what may be designated as *mathematics* and *mathematical method*. The former belongs, as Prof. Peirce says, to every science. In this sense economics has always been mathematical. The latter has reference to the use of *symbols and their operations*. It is this which is to be discussed here. A symbol may be a letter, a diagram, or a model. All three are used in geometry and physics.†

By an *operation* on symbols is meant a rule the formulation of which depends on the mention of those symbols (as the operation of differentiation). To employ mathematical method is to pass from what is given to what is required by the aid of such a rule. To avoid mathematical method is to do it without the rule. Symbols and their operations are aids to the human memory and imagination.

§ 3.

The utility of mathematical method is purely relative, as is all utility. It helps greatly some persons, slightly others, is even a hindrance to some.

Before a schoolboy studies "mechanics" he is usually given in his arithmetic problems of uniform motion. It would sorely puzzle him if he were compelled to use the formula $s = ut$. The employment of symbols has for him only *disutility*. But when in

---

* Cf. Grassmann, Ausdehnungslehre, Introduction.

† Few are aware how important models sometimes are in the treatment of these sciences. Maxwell's model to represent the relations of volume, entropy and energy in thermodynamics is an excellent example.

"mechanics" proper a few years later the same boy studies "falling bodies" he finds it helpful to use the formula $v = gt$ which contrasts with the preceding formula only in that space (s) is replaced by space per unit of time (v) and velocity (u) by velocity acquired per unit of time (g). The increased complexity of the magnitudes makes a formula relatively desirable. Yet for some minds the latter formula is of no use. Experience in teaching this very subject has convinced me that there are a few who understand it better without the aid of the formula, but they are just those individuals whose comprehension of the relations involved is the vaguest and the weakest.

The formulæ, diagrams and models are the instruments of higher study. The trained mathematician uses them to clarify and extend his previous unsymbolic knowledge. When he reviews the mathematics of his childhood, the elementary mechanics is to him illumined by the conceptions and notation of the calculus and quaternions. To think of velocity, acceleration, force, as fluxions is not to abandon but to supplement the old notions and to think of momentum, work, energy, as integrals is greatly to extend them. Yet he is well aware or ought to be that to load all this on the beginner is to impede his progress and produce disgust. So also the beginner in economics might be mystified, while the advanced student is enlightened by the mathematical method.

§ 4.

The utility of a mathematical treatment varies then according to the characteristics of the user, according to the degree of his mathematical development and according to the intricacy of the subject handled. There is a higher economics just as there is a higher physics, to both of which a mathematical treatment is appropriate. It is said that mathematics has given no new theorems to economics. This is true and untrue according to the elasticity of our terms· The challenge of Cairnes might be answered by a counter challenge to show the contents of Cournot, Walras, or Auspitz und Lieben in any non-mathematical writer.

If I may venture a speculation, those who frown on the mathematical economist because he "wraps up his mysterious conclusions in symbols" seem to me in some cases to point their finger at those "conclusions" which when "unwrapt" of symbols they recognize as old friends and lustily complain that they are not new; at the same time they seem to ignore completely those "mysterious" conclusions which *are* new because they think the former and admitted theorems exhaust all that is important on the subject. Why should the mathematician be obliged to vindicate the exercise of his science by overturning economics or by deducing some "laws" more fundamental than those already admitted?

Elementary physics is the fundamental physics and it can be taught with little or no mathematical symbols. Advanced physics is relatively less popular while more mathematical. By actual count Ganot's elementary physics of 986 pages contains a formula for every three and one-third pages. The chapter on electricity and magnetism of 320 pages, a formula for every $4\frac{1}{2}$ pages, while the profound treatise of Mascart and Joubert on Electricity and Magnetism, vol. I, of 640 pages, contains $3\frac{3}{4}$ formulæ for each page or 15 times as many per page as the same subject in Ganot.

Similarly in economics, mathematical treatment is relatively useful as the relations become relatively complicated. The introduction of mathematical method marks a stage of growth—perhaps it is not too extravagant to say, the entrance of political economy on a scientific era.

§ 5.

Has the mathematical method attained a firm footing? Before Jevons all the many attempts at mathematical treatment fell flat. Every writer suffered complete oblivion until Jevons unearthed their volumes in his bibliography. One chief reason for this is that these writers misconceived the application of mathematics. I think this was true even of the distinguished Whewell. Jevons thinks it is so of Canard though his work was crowned by the French institute. The second reason for this oblivion is that the world was not prepared for it. The movement was too advanced and premature. Cournot certainly, Gossen possibly, now exert considerable influence on economic thought. Marshall, whose recent book is acknowledged to be to modern economics what Mill's was to the economics of a generation ago repeatedly expresses his admiration for and obligation to Cournot.

Thus the mathematical method really began with Jevons in 1871. Up to this time pol. econ. had been the favorite field for those persons whose tastes were semi-scientific and semi-literary or historical. But the scientific and literary temper are seldom equally balanced and as might have been expected after once beginning to divide they have steadily differentiated. On the one extreme is the historical school of Roscher and Leslie, on the other the mathematical, deductive, or so-called Austrian school of Jevons, Menger and Walras, while the "orthodox" economists the legitimate successors of Adam Smith, Ricardo and Mill constitute the central body from which both have split. This cleavage is, however, largely a division of the field of research rather than opposed theories or methods on the same field.

The mathematical economics apparently has its warmest adherents in Austria, Italy and Denmark. France occupies the next position, while England, America and Germany have their individual enthusiasts but are still restrained largely by classic traditions. Prof. Pantaleoni thinks "the most active movement in Italian pol. econ. is that of the new school styled rather inexactly the "Austrian,"[*] while Graziani says that the utility theory of value "seems to close the evolutionary cycle of Italian thought."[*]

In England, Prof. Edgeworth, noted for his enthusiasm on mathematical economics, has recently been elected to the chair of pol. econ. at Oxford, while Prof. Marshall is carrying forward the same movement at Cambridge.

There has been a great increase in mathematico-economic literature since 1871. Just two decades have passed by since Jevons' epoch-making books appeared. Of the mathematico-economic writings[†] appearing in this period which here come to my notice, the number in the first decade was 30, representing 12 writers, while in the second decade it was 66, representing 23 writers. From all apparent evidence the mathematical method has come to stay.

§ 6.

We can see why this is so if we glance at the work which the mathematical method has already accomplished. It is perhaps fair to credit the idea of marginal utility to mathematical method. This idea had five independent origins with Dupuit, Gossen, Jevons, Menger, and Walras. All except Menger presented this idea and presumably attained it by mathematical methods. No idea has been more fruitful in the history of the science. This one achievement is a sufficient vindication of the mathematical method.

---

[*] Article on Economics in Italy, by Prof. Ugo Rabberio, Pol. Sci. Quart., Sept., 1891, pp. 439–473.

[†] I have not even included here Menger, Böhm-Bawerk and other writers of the Austrian school, who in spite of a mathematical tone have omitted to use mathematical symbols.

To pass in review all that has been done in expanding and applying the idea of marginal utility (and most of this expansion has been purely mathematical) would not be possible here, nor would it be possible to state all the other notions which have grown out of a mathematical treatment. It has corrected numerous errors and confusion of thought. This correcting function has really been the chief mission of mathematics in the field of physics though few not themselves physicists are aware of the fact.

In fact the ideas of marginal utility and disutility may be regarded as corrections of two old and apparently inconsistent theories of value—the utility theory and the cost of production theory. Utility was first thought of as proportional to commodity. (That this was never *explicitly* assumed is a splendid illustration of how without a careful mathematical analysis in which every magnitude has definite meaning, tacit assumptions creep in and confuse the mind). It was next pointed out that utility could not explain price since water was useful. So "utility" and "scarcity" were jointly privileged to determine price. It was Jevons' clear and mathematical exposition of utility which showed the shallowness of the former discussion and brought to light the preposterous tacit assumption, unchallenged because unseen, that each glass of water has an inherent utility independent of the number of glasses already drunk.

Jevons laid emphasis on *demand*. Many who accepted his work were still applying the analogous errors to supply. Ricardo* had indicated the idea of marginal cost. But even Mill did not perceive its extension beyond agricultural produce. Considerable credit belongs to Auspitz und Lieben for working out the legitimate consequences and showing by a beautiful mathematical presentation that the marginal utility theory and the marginal cost theory are not opposed but supplementary. In fact the "margin" itself is determined by the condition that the utility and the cost of final increments shall be equal (when measured in money).

Mathematical method is to be credited with the development of the ideas of consumers' and producers' rent or gain so ingeniously applied by Auspitz und Lieben and so conspicuous in the original article of Prof. J. B. Clark on the law of the three rents.† The intimate and mathematically necessary relation between the equality of marginal utilities and disutilities and the maximum sum of consumers' and producers' rent, a theorem emphasized by Auspitz und Lieben, and Edgeworth, is of course due to the mathematical instrument.

---

* Pol. Econ., Ch. 2.   † Quart. Jour. Econ., April, 1891.

Mathematical method is making a new set of classifications based on mathematical properties. Thus the classification by Auspitz und Lieben of all commodities into three groups* is, I believe, a new one, and one suggested by, and readily discussed by the use of their diagrams. The classification of capital into free and sunk is one which is emphasized by the mathematical writers, as Marshall, and is bearing fruit.†

I believe therefore that mathematical method has made several real contributions to economics, and that it is destined to make more. To verify this statement I would refer the reader to the books mentioned in the bibliography among recent writers, especially Walras, Auspitz & Lieben, Marshall, Edgeworth, Wicksteed and Cunynghame ; also, if it is proper to include those writers, who while avoiding mathematical language are interpreting and extending the same ideas, Menger, Wieser, Böhm-Bawerk, Clark and Hobson.

§ 7.

It may not be amiss to present a list of quotations from those who have pursued or admired the mathematical path :

Whewell‡ says : [Mathematical method in mechanics saves scientists three errors, viz :] "They might have assumed their principles wrongly, they might have reasoned falsely from them in consequence of the complexity of the problem, or they might have neglected the disturbing causes which interfered with the effect of the principal forces. * * * It appears, I think, that the sciences of mechanics and political economy are so far analogous that something of the same advantage may be looked for from the application of mathematics in the case of political economy." Again :§ "This mode of treatment might be expected to show more clearly than any other within what limits and under what conditions propositions in political economy are true."

Cournot :‖ L'emploi des signes mathématiques, est chose naturelle toutes les fois qu'il s'agit de discuter des relations entre des grandeurs ; et lors même qu'ils ne seraient pas rigoureusement nécessaires, s'ils peuvent faciliter l'exposition, la rendre plus concise, mettre sur la voie de développements plus étendus, prévenir les écarts

---

* Page 46.

† See Cunynghame, Geom. Meth. of treating exchange value, monopoly, and rent. Econ. Jour., March, '92, p. 35.

‡ Cambridge Philosophical Transactions, 1830, p. 194.

§ Cambridge Philosophical Transactions, 1856, p. 1.

‖ Principes math. de la théorie des richesses, 1838. Preface, p. viii.

d'une vague argumentation, il serait peu philosophique de les rebuter, paree qu'ils ne sont pas également familiers à tous les lecteurs et qu'on s'en est quelquefois servi à faux."

Gossen: Was einem Kopernikus zur Erklärung des Zusammenseins der Welten im Raum zu leisten gelang, das glaube ich für die Erklärung des Zusammenseins der Menschen auf der Erdoberfläche zu leisten. * * * Darum ist es denn eben so unmöglich, die wahre Nationalökonomie ohne Hülfe der Mathematik vorzutragen, wie dieses bei der wahren Astronomie, der wahren Physik, Mechanik u. s. w."

Jevons:† "I have long thought that as it deals throughout with quantities, it must be a mathematical science in matter if not in language. I have endeavored to arrive at accurate quantitative notions concerning utility, value, labor, capital, etc., and I have often been surprised to find how clearly some of the most difficult notions, especially that most puzzling of notions *value*, admits of mathematical analysis and expression."

Walras:‡ "Je crois bien que les notations qui y sont employées paraitrout tout d'abord un peu compliquées; mais je prie le lecteur de ne ponit se rebuter de cette complication qui est inhérents au sejet et qui en constitue d'ailleurs le seule difficulté mathématique. Le système de ces notations une fois compris le systeme des phénomènes économiques est en quelque sorte compris par cela même."

Newcomb:§ "To ultimately expect from pol. econ. results of such certainty and exactness, that it can present the legislator with numerical predictions like those we have described is by no means hopeless." * * * * "Mathematical analysis is simply the application to logical deduction of a language more unambiguous, more precise, and for this particular purpose, more powerful than ordinary language."

Launhardt:‖ "Es ist ja die Mathematik nichts anderes als eine Sprache, welche in strenger Folgerichtigkeit die Beziehungen messbare Dinge zu einander darstellt, was durch die gewohnliche Sprache entweder gar nicht oder doch nur in weitschweifiger ungenauer Weise erreicht werden kann."

---

* Menschlicher Verkehr. Preface, p. v.

† Preface to first edition, p. vii.

‡ Econ. pol. pure, 1874, Preface, p. vi.

§ The method and province of pol. econ. [Review of Cairne's logical method in pol. econ.], N. Amer. Rev., No. CCXLIX, 1875, p. 259.

‖ Volkswirthschaftslehre : Preface, p. v.

*Wicksteed :** "The diagrammatic method of studying economics may be regarded from three points of view : (I) many teachers find in it a stimulating and helpful appeal to the eye and use it as a short and telling way of making statements and registering results. (II) a few students treat it as a potent instrument for giving precision to hypotheses in the first instance and then for rigorously analysing and investigating the results that flow from them. (III) a very few investigators (among whom I think we must rank Jevons), have hoped ultimately to pass beyond the field of pure hypotheses and analysis and to build up constructive results upon empirical curves of economic phenomena established by observation."

Foxwell† [speaking of the mathematics of Jevons and Marshall] : "It has made it impossible for the educated economist to mistake the limits of theory and practice or to repeat the confusion which brought the study into discredit and almost arrested its growth."

Auspitz und Lieben :‡ "Wir haben uns bei unseren Untersuchungen der analytischen Methode und namentlich der graphischen Darstellung bediehnt, nicht nur weil sich diese Behandlungsweise überall, wo sie überhaupt anwendbar ist, und namentlich in den naturwissenschaftlichen Fächern glänzend bewährt hat, sondern hauptsächlich auch darum weil sie eine Prazision mit sich bringt, welche alle aus vieldeutigen Wort-definitionen entspringender Missverständnisse ausschliest."

Edgeworth :§ * * * "the various effects of a tax or other impediment, which most students find it so difficult to trace in Mill's laborious chapters, are visible almost at a glance by the aid of the mathematical instrument.   It takes Prof. Sidgwick a good many words to convey by way of a particular instance that it is possible for a nation by a judiciously regulated tariff, to benefit itself at the expense of the foreigner.   The truth in its generality is more clearly contemplated by the aid of diagrams. * * * * There seems to be a natural affinity between the phenomena of supply and demand, and some of the fundamental conceptions of mathematics, such as the relation between function and variable * * * and the first principle

* On certain passages in Jevons' "Theory of pol. econ."   Quart. Jour. Econ., April, '89, p. 293.

† The Economic Movement in England, Quart. Jour. Econ., Oct., '88.

‡ Untersuchungen.   Preface, p. xiii.

§ Address before Brit. Assoc. as president of the section on economic science and statistics.   Published in *Nature*, Sept. 19, '89, p. 497.

of the differential calculus ; especially in its application to the determination of *maxima* and *minima*." [It seems to] "supply to political economy what Whewell would have called 'appropriate and clear' conceptions. * * * Algebra and geometry are to ordinary language in political economy somewhat as quaternions are to ordinary algebraic geometry in mathematical physics" (Quotes Maxwell on quaternions : "I am convinced that the introduction of the ideas as distinguished from the operations and methods * * * will be of great use.")

Again :* "I do not mean that the mathematical method should form part of the curriculum as we make Greek obligatory for the students of philosophy. But may we not hope that the higher path will sometimes be pursued by those candidates who offer *special subjects* for examination."

Marshall :† "It is not easy to get a clear full view of continuity in this aspect without the aid either of mathematical symbols or diagrams. * * * * experience seems to show that they give a firmer grasp of many important principles than can be got without their aid ; and there are many problems of pure theory, which no one who has once learnt to use diagrams will willingly handle in any other way.

The chief use of pure mathematics in economic questions seems to be in helping a person to write down quickly, shortly and exactly, some of his thoughts for his own use : and to make sure that he has enough, and only enough, premises for his conclusions (i. e. that his equations are neither more nor less in number than his unknowns). But when a great many symbols have to be used, they become very laborious to any one but the writer himself. And though Cournot's genius must give a new mental activity to every one who passes through his hands, and mathematicians of calibre similar to his may use their favorite weapons in clearing a way for themselves to the center of some of those difficult problems of economic theory, of which only the outer fringe has yet been touched ; yet it is doubtful whether any one spends his time well in reading lengthy translations of economic doctrines into mathematics, that have not been made by himself. A few specimens of those applications of mathematical language which have proved most useful for my own purpose have, however, been added in an Appendix."

---

* An introductory lecture on pol. econ. delivered before the University of Oxford, Oct. 23d, 1891, published in Economic Journal, Vol. i, No. 4, p. 629.

† Prin. of Econ. Preface to first Ed., p. xiv ; in 2d ed.

*Cunynghame:** "But curves play in the study of pol. econ. much the same part as the moods and figures play in logic. They do not perhaps assist in original thought, but they afford a system by means of which error can be promptly and certainly detected and demonstrated. And as in logic so in graphic pol. econ. the chief difficulty is not to solve the problem, but to state it in geometrical language."

§ 8.

Contrast with the preceding the following statements from a few who can see nothing good in mathematical method :

A writer in the "Saturday Review" (Nov. 11, 1871), quoted by Prof. Edgeworth† says of Jevons : "The equations, * * * assuming them to be legitimate, seem to us to be simply useless so long as the functions are obviously indeterminable." [Mathematics studies *relations* as well as *calculations*. Numerical indeterminability is common even in mathematical physics.]

Cairnes :‡ "Having weighed Prof. Jevons's argument to the best of my ability, and so far as this is possible for one unversed in mathematics, I still adhere to my original view. So far as I can see, economic truths are not discoverable through the instrumentality of mathematics. If this view be unsound, there is at hand an easy means of refutation—the production of an economic truth, not before known, which has been thus arrived at ; but I am not aware that up to the present any such evidence has been furnished of the efficiency of the mathematical method. In taking this ground, I have no desire to deny that it may be possible to employ geometrical diagrams or mathematical formulæ for the purpose of exhibiting economic doctrines *reached by other paths*, and it may be that there are minds for which this mode of. presenting the subject has advantages. What I venture to deny is the doctrine which Prof. Jevons and others have advanced—that economic knowledge can be extended by such means ; that mathematics can be applied to the development of economic truth, as it has been applied to the development of mechanical and physical truth ; and, unless it can be

---

* Geometrical methods of treating exchange value, monopoly and rent. H. Cunynghame. Econ. Jour., March, '92, p. 35.

† Math.-Psychics, p. 119.

‡ The Character and Logical Method of pol. econ. *New York*, 1875. Preface. See also, p. 122 ; also: Some leading principles of pol. econ. newly expounded. Preface.

shown either that mental feelings admit of being expressed in precise quantitative forms, or, on the other hand, that economic phenomena do not depend upon mental feelings, I am unable to see how this conclusion can be avoided." [There are examples in Cournot, Walras, Auspitz und Lieben, Marshall, etc., which I think are fair instances of the "production of an economic truth, not before known." It is admitted, however, that each of these truths could have been discovered without "mathematical method" by some remarkably clear headed reasoner. *But the same is true in physics.* The deduction used in every physical truth could be reasoned out without diagrams or formulæ. A railway will best convey a man from New York to San Francisco though it is perfectly possible to walk. Cairnes certainly has an erroneous idea of the use of mathematical method in physical investigations. Mathematics afford the physicist a complete and precise view of his subject, and this condition of mind permits and facilitates his discovery. The discovery is only indirectly due to mathematics though it might never have been made without it. Cairnes apparently thinks that physical truth has been discovered by the manipulation of equations. The history of physics will not bear him out. So far as I know only one physical discovery was made in that way—a discovery in light. See the quotation from Peirce at the beginning of this appendix.]

*Wagner** [in reviewing Marshall's Prin. of Econ.]: "I do not believe that this mode of treating the subject has an independent value of its own for solving our problems. Indeed Marshall himself admits as much [does he? Cf. preceding statement of Marshall.] * * * He has used diagrams and formulæ only for purposes of illustration and for greater precision of statement." [Diagrams and formulæ are never used for any other purpose yet they surely have an independent value in (say) physics. Cf. § 1.]

Ingram :† "There is not much encouragement to pursue such researches, which will in fact never be anything more than academic playthings, and which involve the very real evil of restoring the metaphysical entities previously discarded." Also,‡ "Units of animal or moral satisfaction, of utility and the like are as foreign to positive science as a unit of dormative faculty would be." [See Part I, Ch. I]. Also:§ "Mathematics can indeed formulate ratios of exchange when

---

* Quart. Jour. Ec., April, '91, p. 327.
† Ency. Brit., 9th ed. Vol. xix, p. 399.
‡ Ency. Brit., 9th ed. Vol. xix, p. 386.
§ Hist. Pol. Econ., *New York*, 1888, p. 182.

they have once been observed; but it cannot by any process of its own determine those ratios; for quantitative conclusions imply quantitative premises and these are wanting. There is then no future for this kind of study, and it is only waste of intellectual power to pursue it." [What a "therefore"! Why require mathematics to predict prices in order to be admitted into good society with the historical school? No mathematical economist has ever tried to do this. Dr. Ingram does not discuss what mathematics has done or attempted, but complains loudly that it cannot do everything and therefore has no future.]

*Rabberio** in speaking of Prof. Pantaleoni's Principi di Economia Pura says: "As a monument of abstract logic, it bears fresh witness to the unusual qualities of the author's genius; but it is based on a method which, frankly speaking, I consider dangerous. In the face of pressing practical problems of every kind, both in production and in distribution, economic thought is drawn off into the field of barren abstractions. Under an attractive semblance of mathematical accuracy these abstractions conceal much that is really false; for they do not correspond in the least to the complexity of concrete facts. While they distract the student with an imaginary logical construction, they lessen his interest in that positive study which tells us what is, whereas logic by itself gives us only what is thought. Thus in last result they deprive economic science of that great practical importance which it should have in society." [I am not acquainted with Prof. Pantaleoni's book nor with any Italian writer. As to the criticism on mathematical method, however, I may say that experience in other sciences shows that "in face of many practical problems" it is wisest to "draw off thought" for a time to pure theory. Before solving the problems of cannon projectiles it is best to solve the problem of projectiles in general. Before an engineer is fit to build the Brooklyn bridge or to pronounce on it after it is built it is necessary to study mathematics, mechanics, the *theory* of stress and of the natural curve of a hanging rope, etc., etc. So also before applying political economy to railway rates, to the problems of trusts, to the explanation of some current crisis, it is best to develop the *theory* of pol. econ. in general. When these special "practical problems" are examined the mathematical instrument will, I believe, often be the one to get the best results.

I am far from denying, however, that some mathematical economists have exhibited a "false accuracy." It has been due to

---

* Economics in Italy, Prof. Ugo Rabberio, Pol. Sci. Quart., Sept. 1891, p. 462.

making special assumptions not with the purpose of facilitating economic investigation but for permitting algebraic transformation. A writer who intentionally parades his mathematics really does the cause of mathematical economics much harm. I venture to think that Launhardt's Volkswirtschaftslehre which contains some excellent things would have exhibited these excellencies better if the author had contented himself with solving problems in all their generality].

§ 9.

I cannot refrain from venturing an opinion the application of which may not apply to all of those writers just quoted but which certainly applies to many: Mathematics is looked upon as an intruder by those students of economics who have not had the mathematical education to understand and make use of them, and who are unwilling to believe that others enjoy a point of view unattainable by themselves. A friend of mine much interested in economics asked me what was the service of mathematics in the subject. On hearing my reply he said: " Well, I don't like to admit that I can't understand economics as well as those who have studied higher mathematics."

Thus part at least of the opposition to mathematical method is a mere incident to its novelty. It must be remembered that the character of economists is itself a variable and from generation to generation those choose or reject the pursuit of economics according to what it is at the time of choice. It may not be rash to expect that the next generation of the theoretical (as distinct from historical) economists will have fitted themselves by mathematical training for this mode of treating their theme, and that they will be such men as by natural aptitude can so fit themselves.

§ 10.

The effort of the economist is to *see*, to picture the interplay of economic elements. The more clearly cut these elements appear in his vision, the better; the more elements he can grasp and hold in mind at once, the better. The economic world is a misty region. The first explorers used unaided vision. Mathematics is the lantern by which what before was dimly visible now looms up in firm, bold outlines. The old phantasmagoria disappear. We see better. We also see further.

APPENDIX IV.

BIBLIOGRAPHY OF MATHEMATICO-ECONOMIC WRITINGS.

§ 1.

A bibliography of mathematico-economic writings was constructed by Jevons and extended* by his wife up to 1888. This list contains a number of works mathematical in tone only. I have selected out of the whole number (196), those 50 which are either undoubtedly mathematical or are closely associated logically or historically with the mathematical method. Thus Menger, though his writings are not explicitly mathematical, is included for he founded the "Austrian School" which has ever since been allied with the mathematical method. In this selected list the references are much abbreviated and only the first edition of each work is cited.

The second list is intended to be an extension of that of Jevons up to the present date. I shall be indebted for information as to inaccuracies and omissions. A star has been placed opposite those writings in which mathematical method is employed only occasionally or whose mathematical character is not explicitly expressed in symbols or diagrams. In the case of Italian and Danish writings, with which I am wholly unacquainted and in the case of a large number of others which I have not been able to see and examine, I have been guided by book notices or the wording of the title.

The list in Jevons' appendix and the second list here given may be taken as a reasonably complete bibliography of mathematico-economic writings in the broadest sense, while the unstarred writings in the abridged list of Jevons here quoted together with the unstarred writings in the second list represent the economic literature which is strictly and avowedly mathematical. The distinction between these two classes is tolerably well marked.

§ 2.

SELECTED FROM JEVONS.

1711   CEVA—De re nummaria quoad fieri potuit geometrice Nactata.
1765   BECCARIA—Tentativo analitico sui contrabandi. Etc.
1801   CANARD—Principes d'economie politique.
1824   THOMPSON—Instrument of Exchange.
1826   von THÜNEN—Der isolirte Staat, etc.

* Pol. Econ., Appendix I to third edition, 1888.

1829 WHEWELL—Mathematical Exposition of some Doctrines of Pol. Econ.
1838 COURNOT—Recherches sur les principes math. de la théorie des richesses.
1838 TOZER—Math. Investigation of the Effect of Machinery, etc.
1840 ANONYMOUS—On Currency.
1840 TOZER—On the Effect of the Non-Residence of Landlords, etc.
1844 DUPUIT—De la mesure de l'utilité des travaux publics.
1844 HAGEN—Die Nothwendigkeit der Handelsfreiheit, etc.
1847 BORDAS—De la mesure de l'utilité des travaux publics.
1849 DUPUIT—De l'influence des péages sur l'utilité des voies de communication.
1850 LARDNER—Railway Economy (chapter xiii).
1850 WHEWELL—Mathematical Exposition of Certain Doctrines of Pol. Econ.
1854 GOSSEN—Entwickelung der Gesetze des menschlichen Verkehrs, etc.
1856 BENNER—Théorie mathématique de l'economie politique.
1863 MANGOLDT—Grundriss der Volkswirthschaftslehre.
1864 FAUVEAU—Considérations math. sur la théorie de l' impôt.
1867 FAUVEAU—Considérations math. sur la théorie de la valeur.
1870 JENKIN—The Graphic Representation of the laws of Sup. and Demand, etc.
1871 JEVONS—The Theory of Political Economy.
1871* MENGER—Grundsätze der Volkswirthschaftslehre.
1872 LAUNHARDT—Kommerzielle Trassirung der Verkehrswege.
1873 POCHET—Géométrie des jeux de Bourse.
1874 WALRAS—Principe d'une théorie math. de l'échange.
1874 WALRAS—Éléments d'économie politique pure.
1874* LETORT—De l'application des math. à l'étude de l'econ. pol.
1875* DARWIN—The Theory of Exchange Value.
1875* BOCCARDO—Dell' applicazione dei metodi quantitativi, etc.
1876 WALRAS—Equations de l'échange, etc.
1876 WALRAS—Équations de la capitalisation.
1876 WESTERGAARD—Den moralske Formue og det moralske Haab.
1878* WEISZ—Die mathematische Methode in der Nationalökonomie.
1879 WALRAS—Théorie math. du billet de banque.
1881 EDGEWORTH—Mathematical Psychics.
1881 WALRAS—Théorie math. du bimétallisme.
1883 LAUNHARDT—Wirthschaftliche Fragen des Eisenbahnwesens.
1884* WIESER—Hauptgesetze des wirthschaftlichen Werthes.
1885 LAUNHARDT—Math. Begründung der Volkswirthshaftslehre.
1886 GROSSMAN—Die Math. im Dienste der Nationalökonomie. I Lieferung.
1886* NEWCOMB—Principles of Political Economy.
1886* BÖHM-BAWERK—Theorie des wirtschaftlichen Güterwerts.
1886 ANTONELLI—Teoria math. della economica politica.
1886 GROSSMAN—Die Math. im Dienste der Nationalökonomie. II Lieferung.
1887 VAN DORSTEN—Math. onderzoekingen op het gebied Staathuishoudkunde.
1887 WESTERGAARD—Math. i Nationalökonomiens Tjeneste.
1887 PANTALEONI—Teoria della pressione tributaria, etc.
1888 WICKSTEED—The Alphabet of Economic Science.

§ 3.

EXTENSION OF JEVONS' BIBLIOGRAPHY.

1867 WITTSTEIN—Mathem. Statistik. *Hanover.*

1882 PANTALEONI (M.)—La Traslazione dei Tributi. *Rome. Paolini.*

1884 SCHROEDER (E. A.)—Das Unternehmen und der Unternehmergewinn vom
historischen, theoretischen und praktischen Standpunkte. *Wien.* 92 pp.

1884* SAX (E.)—Das Wesen und die Aufgabe der Nationalökonomie.

1887* SAX (E.)—Grundlegung der theoretischen Staatswithschaft.

1887 PICARD (A.)—Traité des Chemins de fer. 4 vols. *Paris: Rothschild.*

1888 EDGEWORTH (F. Y.)—New method of measuring variations in general
prices. *Jour. Stat. Soc. London,* p. 347.

1888* SAX (E.)—Die neusten Fortschritte der nationalökonomischen Theorie.
Vortrag gehalten in Dresden märz. *Leipzig: Duncker & Humblot.* 8vo.
38 pp.

1888* MENGER (C.)—Contribution à la théorie du Capital. [Trans. from Jahrb.
für Nat. Oek., by C. Secrétan.] *Rev. d'Écon. Pol.,* Dec. '88.

1888* SALERNO (Ricca)—Manuale di Scienza delle Finanze. *Florence. Barbera.*

1888 HADLEY (A. T.)—Railroad Transportation, its History and its Laws. *New
York and London.* 269 pp. [Appendix II.]

1888 GOSSEN (H. F.)—Entwickelung der Gesetze des menschichen Verkehrs.
[New edition.] *Berlin: Prager.* 8vo. 286 pp.

1888* MENGER (C.)—Zur Thoorie des Kapitals. *Jahrb. Nat. Oek., 17 Heft 1.*

1889 PANTALEONI (M.)—Principi di Economia Pura. *Florence. Barbera.*

1889 AUSPITZ UND LIEBEN—Untersuchungen über die Theorie des Preises.
Leipzig: Duncker & Humblot. 555 pp.

1889* ZUCKERKANDL (R.)—Zur Theorie des Preises mit besonderer Berücksichtigung der geschichtlichen entwicklung der Lehre. *Leipzig.* 348 pp.

1889* WIESER (F. von)—Der natürliche Werth. *Wien.* 237 pp.

1889* BÖHM-BAWERK (E.)—Kapital und Kapitalzins. Translated into English
by Wm. Smart. 1890. *London and New York: Macmillan.*

1889* LEHR (J.)—Wert, Grenzwert, und Preise. *Jahrb. Nat. Oek., 19 Heft 1.*

1889 SUPINO (C.)—La Teoria del Valore e la Legge del minimo mezzo. *Giorn.
degli Econ. Aug. '89.*

1889 WALRAS (L.)—Théorème de l'Utilité maxima des Capitaux Neufs. *Rev.
d'Econ. Polit., June '89.*

1889* MACLEOD (H. D.)—The Theory of Credit. Vol. I. *London: Longmans &
Co.* 8vo. 342 pp.

1889 ST. MARC (H.)—Les Procédés d'Analyse Graphique à l'Exposition Uni-
verselle. *Rev. d'Écon. Polit., Aug. '89.*

1889 VIRGILII (F.)—La Statistica Storica e Mathematica. *Giorn. degli Econ.,
Aug. '89, concluded Oct. '89.*

1889* HEARN (W. E.)—Plutology; or, The Theory of the Efforts to satisfy Human Wants. [New edition.] *Melbourne: Robertson.* 8vo. 486 pp.

1889* KOMARZYNSKI (J.)—Der Werth in der isolirten Wirthschaft. *Wien.
Manz.* 8vo. 105 pp.

1889 ROSSI (G.)—La Mathematica applicata alla Teoria della Ricchezza Sociale:
*Studî Bibliografici. Storici, e Critici. Vol. I, fasc. 1. Reggio Emilia
Artegianelli.* 8vo. 103 pp., 4 charts.

1889* BÖHM-BAWERK (E. von)—Une Nouvelle Théorie sur le Capital. *Rev. d'Écon. Pol., April, 1889.*

1889* BÖHM-BAWERK (E. von)—Kapital und Kapitalzins. Zweite Abteilung: Positive Theorie des Kapitals. *Innsbrück.* 8vo.

1889* CLARK (J. B.)—Possibility of a Scientific law of Wages. [Publ. of Am. Econ. Assoc.] *Baltimore.* 8vo. 32 pp.

1889 WICKSTEED (P. H.)—On certain Passages in Jevons' "Theory of Political Economy." *Quart. Jour. Econ., April, '89,* p. 293.

1889 EDGEWORTH (F. Y.)—On the application of Mathematics to Pol. Econ. *Journ. Stat. Soc. London, Dec. '89.*

1890* DIETZEL—Die Klassische Werttheorie und die Theorie vom Grenznutzen. *Conrad's Jahrbuch N. F. Band 20.* pp. 561–606.

1890* MACLEOD (H. D.)—The Theory of Credit. Vol. II, Part I. *London: Longmans.* 8vo.

1890 MARSHALL (A.)—Principles of Economics. Vol. 1, 1st ed. *London: Macmillan.* 770 pp. [Mathematical Footnotes and Appendix.]

1890 PANTALEONI (M.)—Principi di Economia Pura. *Florence: Barbèra.* 16mo. 376 pp.

1890 JURISCH (K. W.)—Mathematische Diskussion des Eutwickelungsgesetzes der Werterzengung durch industrielle Produktionsgruppen. *Viertelj. f. Volksw. 27 Band 3, 1.* Second paper, same title, *27 Band 3, 2.*

1890 VAUTHIER (L. L.)—Quelques Considérations Élémentaires sur les Constructions Graphiques et leur Emploi en Statistique. *Journ. de la Soc. Statist., June, '90.*

1890* AUSPITZ (R.)—Die klassische Werttheorie und die Lehre vom Grenznutzen. *Jahrb. Nat. Oek. 21 Heft 3;* reply to Dietzel, same journal, 20 Heft 6.

1890* ZUCKERKANDLE (R.)—Die klassische Werttheorie und die Theorie vom Grenznutzen. *Jahrb. Nat. Oek. 21 Heft 5.* Reply to Dietzel.

1890 COLSON (G.)—Transports et Tarifs. Précis du Régime, Lois Économiques de la Détermination des Prix de Transport, Tarifs de Chemins de Fer, etc. *Paris: Rothschild.* 8vo. 479 pp.

1890 LAUNHARDT (W.)—Theorie der Tarifbildung der Eisenbahnen. *Berlin: Springer.* 8vo. 84 pp.

1890 WESTERGAARD (H.)—Die Grundzüge der Theorie der Statistik. *Jena: Fischer.* 8vo. 286 pp.

1890 COSSA (E.)—Le Forme Naturali della Economia Sociale. *Milan: Hoepli.*

1890 MARSHALL (A.)—Principles of Economics. Vol. I, 2nd ed. *London: Macmillan.* 770 pp. [Mathematical Footnotes and Appendix.]

1891* HOBSON (J. A.)—The law of the three rents. *Quart. Jour. Econ., April, 1891,* p. 263.

1891* CLARK (J. B.)—Distribution determined by a law of rent. *Quart. Jour. Econ., April, 1891,* p. 289.

1891 EDGEWORTH (F. Y.)—Osservarioni sulla Teoria matematica dell' Economia Politica con riguardo speciale ai Principi di Economia di Alfredo Marshall. *Giorn. degli Econ., March, '91.*

1891* SMART (W.)—An Introduction to the Theory of Value on the lines of Menger, Wieser and Böhm-Bawerk. *London and New York: Macmillan.* 16mo. 88 pp.

1891* CLARK (J. B.)—The statics and the dynamics of Distribution. *Quart. Jour. Econ., Oct. '91,* p. 111.

1891* WIESER (F.)—The Austrian School and the Theory of Value. *Economic Journal, March,* '91.

1891* BÖHM-BAWERK (E. von)—The Austrian Economist. *Annals of Am. Acad. of Polit. Sci., Jan.* '91.

1891 EDGEWORTH (F. Y.)—La Théorie Mathematique de l'Offre et de la Demande et le Coût de Production. *Rev. d'Écon. Polit., Jan.* '91.

1892* BÖHM-BAWERK (E. von)—Wert, Kosten und Grenznutzen. *Jahrbücher für Nationalökonomie und Statistik, Dritte Folge, Dritter Band, Drittes Heft,* pp. 321–378.

1892 BILGRAM (H.)—Comments on the "Positive Theory of Capital" [of Böhm-Bawerk]. *Quart. Jour. Econ., Jan. '92,* pp. 190–206.

1892 GROSSMAN (L.)—Die Mathematik in Dienste der Nationalökonomie unter Berücksichtigung auf die praktische Handhabung der Finanzwissenschaft und der Versicherungstechnik [schluss Lieferung]. *Vienna.*

1892* WIESER (F. von)—The Theory of Value. A reply to Prof. Macvane. *Annals of Am. Acad. of Pol. and Soc. Sci., March,* '92.

1892* SELIGMAN (E. R. A.)—On the Shifting and Incidence of Taxation. *Publ. of Amer. Econ. Asso., Vol. VII, Nos. 2 and 3.*

1892* PATTEN (S. N.)—The Theory of Dynamic Economics. *Publ. of Univ. of Penn., Pol. Econ. and Public Law Series, Vol. III, No. 2.* *Phila.* 8vo. 153 pp.

1892* BÖHM-BAWERK (E.)—Wert, Kosten, und Grenznutzen. *Jahrb. Nat. Oek., 3, Heft 3.*

1892 CUNYNGHAME (H.)—Geometrical methods of treating Exchange-value, Monopoly, and Rent. *Econ. Journ., March,* '92.

1892 PARETO (V.)—Considerazione sui Concipi Fondamentali dell' Economia Politica Pura. *Giorn. degli Econ., May,* '92.

1892 PARETO (V.)—La Teoria dei Prezzi dei Signori Auspitz e Lieben e la Osservazioni del Professore Walras. *Giorn. degli Econ., March,* '92.

1892* VOIGT (A.)—Der Oekonomische Wert der Güter. *Zeitschr. f. Ges. Staatsw., 48, Heft 2.*

1892 WALRAS (L.)—Geometrical Theory of the Determination of Prices. *Annals Amer. Acad. Polit. and Social Sci., Phila., July,* '92. Translated under the supervision of Irving Fisher. Part I was published in French in the *Bulletin of Soc. of Civil Eng. of Paris, Jan. 1891,* and Parts II and III in the *Recueil inaugural of Univ. of Lausanne,* July (?) '92.

1892 FISHER (I.)—Mathematical Investigations in the Theory of Value and Prices. *Transactions of the Connecticut Academy of Arts and Sciences.* Vol. IX, pp. 1–124.

REVIEWS OF "MATHEMATICAL INVESTIGATIONS IN THE THEORY OF VALUE AND PRICES."

From review by F. Y. Edgeworth. *The Economic Journal*, March, 1893, pp. 108-109, 112. Also reprinted in *Papers Relating to Political Economy*, Macmillan, 1925, Vol. III, pp. 36-41.

Dr. Fisher is distinguished above most writers on Economics in that he does not attempt to carry the reader over the whole ground, however familiar, but confines himself to those parts where he is himself a path-breaker. Or, if it is necessary to start by beaten ways, yet even these he makes straighter, and improves them by depositing new materials.

The last remark applies especially to the first part of the *Investigations*, in which the author restates many of the conclusions of his predecessors. He imparts new clearness to the idea of marginal utility by introducing a 'unit of utility.' . . .

The theory of exchange which is based upon marginal utility has received from Dr. Fisher some very happy illustrations. Observing that most economists employ largely the vocabulary of mechanics—equilibrium, stability, elasticity, level, friction and so forth—and profoundly impressed with the analogy between mechanical and economic equilibrium, Dr. Fisher has employed the principle that water seeks its level to illustrate some of the leading propositions of pure economics. . . .

. . . we may at least predict to Dr. Fisher the degree of immortality which belongs to one who has deepened the foundations of the pure theory of Economics.

From *The Application of Mathematics to the Theory of Economics*. Review by Thomas S. Fiske in *Bulletin of the New York Mathematical Society*, Vol. II, No. 9, June, 1893, pp. 205, 211.

The most careful scientific analysis of these conceptions [utility and marginal utility] that has come to the writer's notice is contained in the first few pages of Dr. Fisher's paper. . . .

The preceding ideas are developed with much skill in Dr. Fisher's paper. Its most conspicuous feature, however, consists in the systematic representation of different questions in the equilibrium of supply and demand through the agency of an elaborate mechanism in the construction of which the greatest ingenuity is displayed. The equilibrium is brought about by means of a liquid in which float a number of cisterns representing the individual consumers and producers. These are made to fulfil the requisite conditions and relations through a series of connecting levers. This dynamical solution of economic problems is both novel and instructive.

From review by Enrico Barone. *Giornale Degli Economisti*, May, 1894, pp. 413, 428.

Il Prof. Irving Fisher, dell'università di Yale, ha nel '92 pubblicato uno studio, piccolo di mole, ma ricco di idee originali, sulla teoria del valore e dei prezzi (1). L'originalità di questo notevole contributo alla scienza consiste in ciò essenzialmente, che per alcuni problemi di economia pura, l'autore ha immaginato—ed ha realmente fatto costrurre—un apparecchio che ne dà meccanicamente la soluzione. . . .

L'apparecchio del Fisher, come dicemmo, è tutt'altro che una mera curiosità scientifica.

From *L'Emploi des Mathématiques en Économie Politique* by Jacques Moret. M. Giard & É. Brière, Paris, 1915, p. 136.

Dans sa remarquable étude intitulée *Mathematical investigations in the theory of value and prices* (2), il a, en effet, tout en faisant état des travaux de ses prédécesseurs, notamment de ceux de Jevons et de MM. Auspitz et Lieben, posé les principes ou du moins fourni les germes des théories les plus récentes.

From review of French translation. *The Economic Journal*, September, 1917, p. 451.

A translation of Professor Irving Fisher's celebrated work. The author in a preface to the French edition arranges the leading ideas of the book under four heads: (1) the use of mathematics in economic science, and (2) of physical, especially hydrostatic analogies; (3) utility as a measurable quantity; (4) interdependent utilities—"competive" and complementary goods. Among the hydrostatic analogies akin to those of the author the illustration in *The Economic Journal*, September, 1895, p. 434, is mentioned by him too modestly. It was fathered by him.

PUBLICATIONS

OF THE

AMERICAN ECONOMIC ASSOCIATION

THIRD SERIES.	ISSUED QUARTERLY.
VOL. XI. NO. 4.	PRICE, $4.00 PER YEAR.

APPRECIATION AND INTEREST

BY

IRVING FISHER, PH.D.

AUGUST, 1896.

PUBLISHED FOR THE

AMERICAN ECONOMIC ASSOCIATION

BY THE MACMILLAN COMPANY

NEW YORK

LONDON : SWAN SONNENSCHEIN & CO.

PRICE IN PAPER, 75 CENTS

APPRECIATION
AND
INTEREST

CONTENTS.

Part I. Theory.

Part II. Facts.

Part III. Applications.

STATISTICAL TABLES.

PREFACE.

The connection between monetary appreciation and the rate of interest has received very scant attention from economists. The writer has been led to believe that this neglect has somewhat retarded the progress of economic science and the successful interpretation of economic history — in particular the monetary history of the last twenty years. The views here put forward were first stated in brief before the American Economic Association at Indianapolis, December, 1895. They differ radically from those expressed by Mr. Giffen and many other eminent economists. For this reason it has been necessary to make a statistical examination of all available facts bearing on the subject. Such a study could not be properly conducted without a definite economic theory as a starting point. The idea on which this theory is founded appears to have occurred independently to several writers. of whom Mr. Jacob de Haas, Jr., of Amsterdam, seems most fully to have realized its importance. To develop the theory in a quantitative form, some simple mathe‧ matics have been employed. With numerical illustrations at each step, it is hoped that those to whom mathematics are distasteful will find few, if any, impediments to easy reading. The mathematical reader, on the other hand, may feel that the discussions are too much encumbered by numerical illustration and detail; but these presentations are usually in such a form that they can easily be passed over by those who find them superfluous. The gist of the theory is contained in Chapter II, but its statement would not be complete, nor the apparent objections to it fully answered, without the discussions of Chapters III-VI.

The writer is greatly indebted to the many persons whose names are mentioned in the text, who have supplied him with important facts and references; also to Professor Sumner for the privilege of consulting his collection of works on banking; to Professor Hadley, for valuable suggestions and criticisms; to Mr. Horace White for pointing out the important pamphlet of the eighteenth century mentioned in Chapter I; and to Mr. Sakata for translating several statistical tables from Japanese.

New Haven, August, 1896.

PART I. THEORY.

CHAPTER I.

INTRODUCTION.

§ 1.

The chief issues in the bimetallic controversy center about the question of justice between debtor and creditor. The bimetallic propaganda succeeds just so far as it spreads a belief that an injustice has been done by the adoption of the gold standard, which the re-adoption of bimetallism would correct.

The question therefore arises, does the appreciation of gold necessarily aggravate debts? Are contracting parties powerless to forestall the gains or losses of an upward or downward moving currency? It is clear that if the unit of length were changed and its change were foreknown, contracts would be modified accordingly. Suppose a yard were defined (as once it probably was) to be the length of the king's girdle, and suppose the king to be a child. Everybody would then know that the "yard" would increase with age and a merchant who should agree to deliver 1,000 "yards" ten years hence, would make his terms correspond to his expectations. To alter the mode of measurement does not alter the actual quantities involved but merely the numbers by which they are represented.

§ 2.

Hitherto monometallists have usually replied to the argument "gold has appreciated, therefore the debtor has been robbed" by challenging, not the inference, but the premise. Thus the discussion has been shunted off from economic theory and turned into a controversy over the fact of "appreciation". This controversy has been, to a large extent, a mere war of words, because, by "appreciation" the monometallists mean one thing and the bimetallists, another. No one has yet provided a meaning for that much abused word acceptable to both parties. The bimetallists prove the appreciation of gold by the fall in prices. The monometallists reply that wages have risen, and hold that the fall in prices is due to progress in the arts. Some bimetallists, *e. g.,* Leonard Courtney,[1] accept the distinction between a fall in prices through causes connected with gold and a fall through causes connected with commodities, but most of them assert that a "fall of prices" and "appreciation of gold" are synonymous expressions, and that, if progress cheapens other commodities, it ought justly to cheapen gold also. Generally speaking, bimetallists set up the "commodity standard" and monometallists, the "labor standard".

Others attempt to find the "just" standard in "marginal utility", "total utility", and so forth. On all sides it is tacitly assumed that a "just" standard must in some sense be an "invariable" standard; that is, a standard such that the principal of the debt when due should be equivalent in some way to the original loan. "All writers on the subject of money have agreed that uniformity in the value of the circulating medium is an object greatly to be desired—a currency to be perfect, should be absolutely invariable in value."[2] Proposals to define and secure such invariability have been made by many writers.

---

[1] Report of the Indian Currency Committee, 1893, p. 39; also, *Nineteenth Century,* April, 1893.

[2] Ricardo, "Proposals for an Economic and Secure Currency", Secs. I, II.

Within the last few years, the problem has become a
favorite one, and scarcely an issue of the economic journals appears without discussions on "The ultimate standard of value", "The just standard of deferred payments",
"Has gold appreciated?" "The measurement of the value
of money", and kindred subjects.[3]

§ 3.

It is not proposed to deny that the terms of appreciation
and depreciation may have an "absolute" as distinct from
a "relative" meaning.[4] But such definitions and distinc-
tions can throw no light whatever on the question of
justice in contracts. We shall see that a standard to be
perfect need not be invariable. What is required is
simply that it shall be *dependable,* so that contracting
parties may be able to forecast all required elements of
their economic future in terms of that standard as accurately as in terms of any other. If a standard is thus
dependable, the terms of the contract will be as "just"
as they could possibly be under any system.

§ 4.

At a later stage the general question of "justice" will
be discussed. Here the effort will be to show that losses
due to "appreciation", however defined, will tend to be
forestalled. For this, it is not necessary to scale the
principal of a debt. The principal is not the only or
even the chief element in a loan contract. The other
element is the *rate of interest.* It is an astonishing fact

---

[3] See, *e. g.,* the connected discussions in the *Annals of the American Academy of Political and Social Science, 1892-95,* and the *Journal of Political Economy, 1893-95,* by Ross, Merriam, Fetter, Com-
mons, Newcomb, Cummings, Orton and Taylor.

[4] See Chapter XII.

that the connection between the rate of interest and appreciation has been almost completely overlooked, both in economic theory and in its bearing upon the bimetallic controversy.

Of the few writers who have conceived this connection, apparently the earliest was the anonymous author of the remarkable pamphlet entitled: "A Discourse Concerning the Currencies of the British Plantations in America." Boston, 1740 (Reprinted in the "Overstone Tracts" 1857). He writes:

The Arguments current amongst the Populace in favour of Paper Money, are,

I.   In most of the Paper Money Colonies one of the principal Reasons alledged for their first Emissions; was, *to prevent Usurers imposing high Interest upon Borrowers, from the Scarcity of Silver Money.* It is true, that in all Countries the increased Quantity of Silver, falls the Interest or Use of Money; but large Emissions of Paper Money does naturally rise the Interest to make good the sinking Principal: for Instance, in the Autumn, *A.* 1737, Silver was at 26 s. to 27 s. per Ounce, but by a large *Rhode Island* Emission, it became in Autumn 1739, 29 s. per Oz. this is 7 per Cent. Loss of Principal, therefore the Lender, to save his Principal from sinking, requires 13 per Cent. natural Interest (our legal Interest being 6 per Cent.) for that Year. In Autumn A. 1733, Silver was 22 s. per Oz. by large Emissions it became 27 s. in the Autumn, *A.* 1734; is 22 per Cent. loss of Principal; and the Lender to save his Principal; requires 28 per Cent. *natural Interest* for that Year. Thus *the larger the Emissions, natural Interest becomes the higher;* therefore the Advocates for Paper Money (who are generally indigent Men, and Borrowers) ought not to complain, when they hire Money at a dear nominal Rate.

If Bills were to depreciate after a certain Rate, Justice might be done to both contracting Parties, by imposing the Loss which the Principal may sustain in any certain Space of Time (the Period of Payment, upon the Interest of a Bond or Price of Goods: but as Depreciations are uncertain, great Confusions in Dealings happen.

John Stuart Mill expresses the same view,[5] as do also Jacob de Haas[6] and Professor John B. Clark.[7] A principle which apparently has been independently discovered by each of these economists and quite possibly by others, is likely to be of some importance. It is the object of the present essay to develop the theory in a quantitative form, to bring it to a statistical test, and to apply it to current problems, and to the theory of interest.

[5] "Principles of Political Economy", Book 3, Chapter 23, § 4. [A single paragraph.]

[6] "A Third Element in the Rate of Interest." *Journal of the Royal Statistical Society*, March, 1889. [A more extended discussion, with statistics.]

[7] "The Gold Standard in the Light of Recent Theory." *Political Science Quarterly*, September, 1895. [Applied to the current bimetallic controversy.]

CHAPTER II.

ONE YEAR CONTRACTS.[1]

§ 1.

We must begin by noting the distinction between a foreseen and an unforeseen change in the value of money. Only the losses or gains of the former can be forestalled. A sudden and unexpected inflation, as in the United States in 1862, works enormous losses to creditors, while an unforeseen contraction is equally harmful to debtors.

How far foresight in such matters actually exists will be discussed in Part II. At present we wish to discover. what will happen, *assuming* this foresight to exist.

If a debt is contracted optionally in either of two standards and one of them is expected to change with reference to the other, will the rate of interest be the same in both? Most certainly not. Only a few months ago the Belmont-Morgan syndicate offered the United States government the alternative of taking some 65 millions at 3% in gold or at 3¾% in "coin". Everyone knew that this additional ¾% was due to the mere *possibility* of free silver coinage. If the alternatives had been between repayment in gold and—not possible, but actual—repayment in silver, the additional interest would certainly have been much more than ¾%.

§ 2.

To fix our ideas, let the two standards be gold and wheat. and. while to-day a bushel of wheat is worth a

---

[1] More properly speaking, in place of "one year" should be put "one interest interval".

dollar, let it be known that one year hence it will be worth but 96 cents. One hundred dollars (gold standard) or its equivalent one hundred bushels (wheat standard) are borrowed to-day and are to be repaid with interest in one year. If the rate of interest in the gold standard is 8%, what will be the rate in wheat?

We note that the repayment, if in gold, will be, not $100, but $108, and our problem is solved by finding what will be the equivalent of this sum in wheat at the end of the year. This is easily obtained from the expected price of wheat, thus:[2]

$$
\begin{array}{lll}
\text{96 cents gold} \backsim & \text{1} & \text{bushel wheat.} \\
\text{Hence 1 dollar "} \backsim & \tfrac{100}{96} \text{ bushels "} & i.\,e.,\ 1.04\tfrac{1}{6} \text{ bu.} \\
\text{108 dollars "} \backsim 108 \times 1.04\tfrac{1}{6} \text{ bushels "} & i.\,e.,\ 112\tfrac{1}{2} \text{ bu.}
\end{array}
$$

Thus the repayment of 112½ bushels will be equivalent to $108. The alternative contracts would therefore be:

For 100 dollars borrowed to-day, 108 dollars are due one year hence.
For 100 bushels   "   "   112½ bushels " "   "   "   "

Hence 8% interest in the gold standard is equivalent to 12½% in the wheat standard.

Now the relative change in the two standards may be spoken of either as an appreciation of gold relatively to wheat or as a depreciation of wheat relatively to gold. We are not compelled to inquire which is the "absolute" change. If we speak in terms of appreciation, we say $1 changes in value from 1 bushel of wheat to 1.04⅙ bushels, and hence has appreciated 4⅙%; while we may also say, wheat has depreciated from $1 to $.96 or 4%. Our results can be stated in either of two ways:

1. If the rate of interest in one standard is 8%, then in another, which depreciates 4% relatively to the first, it will be 12½%; that is, a depreciation of 4% is offset by an increase of interest of 4½%.

---

[2] The symbol "$\backsim$" is used for "are equivalent to".

2.　If the rate of interest in one standard is $12\frac{1}{2}\%$, in another, which appreciates $4\frac{1}{6}\%$ relatively to the first, it will be 8%; that is, an appreciation of $4\frac{1}{6}\%$ is offset by a decrease of interest of $4\frac{1}{2}\%$.

§ 3.

Leaving this numerical case, we may state the problem more generally.　Suppose gold is to appreciate relatively to wheat a certain known amount in one year.　What will be the relation between the rates of interest in the two standards?　Let wheat fall in gold price (or gold rise in wheat price) so that the quantity of gold which would buy one bushel of wheat at the beginning of the year will buy $1 + a$ bushels at the end, a being therefore the rate of appreciation of gold in terms of wheat.

Let the rate of interest in gold be i, and in wheat be j, and let the principal of the loan be D dollars or its equivalent B bushels.

Our alternative contracts are then:

For D dollars borrowed $D+Di$ or $D(1+i)$ dollars are due in one year.
For B bushels　　"　　$B+Bj$ or $B(1+j)$ bushels　"　"　　"　"

and our problem is to find the relation between i and j, which will make the $D(1 + i)$ dollars $\backsim$ the $B(1 + j)$ bushels.

At first,	D	dollars $\backsim B$		bu.
At the end of the year	D	"　$\backsim B(1+a)$		"
Hence　"　"　"	$D(1+i)$	"　$\backsim B(1+a)(1+i)$		"

Since $D(1 + i)$ is the number of dollars necessary to liquidate the debt, its equivalent $B(1 + a)(1 + i)$ is the number of bushels necessary to liquidate it.　But we have already designated this number of bushels by $B(1 + j)$.

Our result, therefore, is:

At the end of 1 year $D\,(1+i) \backsim B\,(1+j) = B\,(1+a)\,(1+i)$ (1)

(Dollars.) (Bushels.) (Bushels.)

which, after B is canceled, discloses the formula:

$$1 + j = (1 + a)\,(1 + i)$$ (2)

or $\quad j = i + a + i\,a$ (3)

or in words: *The rate of interest in the (relatively) de-preciating standard is equal to the sum of three terms, viz., the rate of interest in the appreciating standard, the rate of appreciation itself, and the product of these two elements.*

Thus, to offset appreciation, the rate of interest must be lowered by slightly more than the rate of appreciation.[3]

We may introduce depreciation in a similar manner. Instead of saying, gold appreciates at the rate a, rela-tively to wheat, we may say, wheat depreciates at the rate d, relatively to gold.[4] This means that wheat has sunk in terms of gold in the ratio 1 to $1 - d$, and reason-ing similar to the foregoing shows that

$$1 + i = (1 - d)\,(1 + j).$$ (4)

Equations (2) and (4) may be conveniently combined, thus:

$$\frac{1+j}{1+i} = \frac{1+a}{1} = \frac{1}{1-d}.$$ (5)

---

[3] Professor Clark (*Political Science Quarterly*, September, 1895) implies that 1% appreciation is offset by *less* than 1% reduction of interest. But in making his calculation he has failed to "compound". The numerical illustrations of the eighteenth century pamphleteer (*supra*) are also erroneous. E. g., instead of 28%, should be 29.32%. Professor Marshall ("Principles of Economics", Vol. I, 3rd ed., p. 674) gives a correct example. His example is designed to show the losses from a fluctuating currency and not the effort to offset these losses. He appears, however, to have in mind this effort when he postpones to the next volume the discussion of "the influences which changes in the purchasing power of money do actually exert on the terms on which loans are arranged" (p. 673).

[4] The relation between d and a is $(1 + a)\,(1 - d) = 1$, which is evident from equation (5) or can be easily shown independently.

Since $\dfrac{1+a}{1}$ is the ratio of the value of gold at the end of the year to its value at the beginning (all in terms of wheat), that is, the ratio of divergence of the two standards expressed in wheat, while $\dfrac{1}{1-d}$ is the same ratio of divergence expressed in gold, and since $1+i$ is the "amount" of $1 put at interest for one year while $1+j$ is the "amount" of one bushel; we may state equation (5) as follows:

The ratio of divergence between the standards equals the ratio between their "amounts".

This is, perhaps, the simplest mode of conceiving the relation, and stress is laid upon it because it brings into prominence the "amount", or ratio of future payment to present loan, a magnitude which in most questions of interest plays a more important rôle than the rate of interest itself.[5]

Equation (5) gives the relation between i and j in terms of a or d. From it, follows the value of j in terms either of i and a or of i and d, and also the value of i in terms either of j and a or of j and d, thus:

$$\frac{1+j}{1+i} = \frac{1+a}{1} \qquad = \frac{1}{1-d} \tag{5}$$

whence
$$j = i + a + ia = \frac{i+d}{1-d} \tag{6}$$

or
$$i = j - d - jd = \frac{j-a}{1+a} \tag{7}$$

---

[5] In fact, except for convenience in computation, the conception of the rate of interest might well be dispensed with, giving place to the conception of a year's "amount" or "ratio of accumulation." In his "Positive Theory of Capital", Professor Böhm-Bawerk expresses the same view. (English Translation, p. 296.) We should then speak, not of a 6% rate of interest, but of 1.06 as the "ratio of accumulation". In like manner "rate of appreciation" would give place to "ratio of appreciation". Denoting the ratio of accumulation, $1+j$, by r' and $1+i$ by r, and the "ratio of appreciation", $1+a$, by p, our theorem becomes simply $\dfrac{r'}{r} = p$.

It follows that j exceeds i by more than the rate of appreciation, which in turn is more than the rate of depreciation (*i. e.; $j—i > a > d$*).

§ 4.

It is to be noted that we have been regarding money as a standard of value and not as a medium of exchange. In either contract the actual liquidation need not be made either in gold or wheat, but in some other medium, as bank notes. The speculator who sells wheat "short" really uses wheat as a standard and not necessarily as a medium. In consideration of value received to-day (which, though reckoned by the speculator in money, may readily be thought of as measured in wheat) he promises to deliver, at a later date, so many bushels oi wheat, it being perhaps understood that he need not actually deliver the wheat so long as he delivers its equivalent in money. This operation, as actually practiced, involves great uncertainties, and therefore occurs as a gambling transaction. Moreover, the wheat is not usually paid for in advance. But if wheat were a more reliable standard, selling it "short" in consideration of present advances might be a true method of business borrowing, and would then exactly exemplify the case we have supposed. In fact, such contracts are identical in form with those which would be made under the oft-proposed "multiple standard".

CHAPTER III.

§ 1.

A prominent bimetallist, in conversing with the writer on the subject of interest and appreciation, raised the following objection: "Interest and principal are separate; the one is paid regularly in installments; the other remains to the end; hence appreciation must affect them in totally different ways. I do not see how it is possible by a uniform reduction in interest applied to contracts of different periods to offset the appreciation of both interest and principal." This view, as we shall soon see. is quite erroneous and arises from the habit of separating in thought interest and principal.

§ 2.

First consider the case in which no interest is paid until the end of the term of years. Let us suppose, for instance, a savings bank which receives $100, gold standard, and repays the depositor in five years at 5% compound interest. If there were an alternative standard, say wheat, in terms of which gold is known to appreciate[1] constantly by 1% per annum, what would be the rate of interest in this standard? We shall suppose for convenience that at first the price of wheat is $1 per bushel.

---

[1] Or what is equivalent, wheat depreciates $\frac{100}{101}$% relatively to gold. As it will be understood that there are always these two modes of expressing the relative change of two standards, we shall hereafter adhere to "appreciation".

If the repayment were to come in one year, we know from Chapter I, § 3, that the rate of interest in wheat is given by the formula

$$j = i + a + i\,a$$
$$= .05 + .01 + .0005$$
$$= .0605$$
$$= 6\tfrac{1}{20}\%$$

This result is as truly the answer to our problem for a series of years as for one year. The proof consists simply in separating the contract into several contracts of one year each. Thus, by Chapter II, we know if we deposit to-day $100 or its equivalent, 100 bushels, it will amount in 1 year to $105 at 5% or its equivalent, 106.05 bushels, at 6 1-20%. We may now regard these equivalent amounts as withdrawn but immediately redeposited for one year. Then, with the same rate of interest in gold and the same rate of relative appreciation, we shall obtain the same rate of interest in wheat, so that $105.00 or its equivalent, 106.05 bushels, will amount in 1 year to $110.25 at 5%, or its equivalent, 112.47 bushels at 6 1-20%. In this way each successive pair of "amounts", including the last, will be equivalent.

§ 3.

The principle employed in § 2 is to resolve the contract into a series of one year contracts. The general case is precisely similar. For the first year we have, by formula (1), Chapter II,

Dollars due.   Bushels due.   Bushels due.
$$D\,(1 + i) \frown B\,(1 + j) = B\,(1 + a)\,(1 + i)$$

In the second year the same formula applies, except that in place of D, the principal is now $D\,(1 + i)$, and in place of B, $B\,(1 + j)$ or $B\,(1 + a)\,(1 + i)$. Making these substitutions in the formula, we obtain

$$D (1 + i)^2 \backsim B (1 + j)^2 = B (1 + a)^2 (1 + i)^2$$

and similarly in the third year,

$$D (1 + i)^3 \backsim B (1 + j)^3 = B (1 + a)^3 (1 + i)^3$$

and so on. Each of the results discloses the principle

$$1 + j = (1 + a) (1 + i).$$

§ 4.

In §§ 2 and 3, we began for simplicity with the case in which the debt is allowed to accumulate to the end. The most general case, however, is one in which the repayments are in installments.

Suppose, as in § 2, that the interest in gold is 5% and that gold is known to appreciate 1% per annum relatively to wheat. A farmer mortgages his land for $1,000 or its then equivalent, 1,000 bushels of wheat, and agrees to pay annually the interest and such parts of the principal as he can save, making the repayment complete in 7 years. Our problem is to find that rate of interest in wheat which will make the contracts in gold and wheat equivalent in every respect.

The solution of this problem is precisely the same as that of § 2, viz., 6 1-20%. For, at the end of one year, the farmer's debt amounts to $1050 or its then equivalent, 1060.50 bushels. Let us suppose that he finds himself able to pay, not only the "interest", $50, but also $50 of the "principal", that is, $100 altogether. The equivalent of this in wheat is 101.00 bu.

Hence he can either

pay $100.00   on $1,050.00,   leaving $950.00
or   101.00 bu. on   1,060.50 bu., leaving 959.50 bu.

and, since the "amounts" $1,050 and 1,060.50 bu. are equivalent and the deductions $100 and 101.00 bu. are equivalent, the remainders $950 and 959.50 bu. must also be equivalent; and, in fact, this may be seen directly since, with gold appreciating 1%, $950, originally worth 950 bu., becomes worth 1% more, or 959.50 bu.

Thus the farmer's remaining debt at the end of the first year is the same whether measured in wheat or gold, and since the same reasoning applies to the second year, third year, etc., the equivalence remains to the end of the contract.

It is worth noting here that the $100 payment in gold will be regarded as consisting of half interest and half principal, whereas the equivalent payment in wheat, 101.00 bu., consists of 60.50 bu., interest and 40.50 bu., principal.

The liquidation of the contract during the 7 years may be supposed to take place in either of the following equivalent ways:

GOLD STANDARD.

	Interest	Amount	Payment	Principal
At beginning	. . . . .	. . . . .	. . . . .	$1,000.00
In 1 year	$ 50.00	$1,050.00	$100.00	950.00
" 2 years	47.50	997.50	97.50	900.00
" 3 "	45.00	945.00	145.00	800.00
" 4 "	40.00	840.00	150.00	690.00
" 5 "	34.50	724.50	174.50	550.00
" 6 "	27.50	577.50	277.50	300.00
" 7 "	15.00	315.00	315.00	0.00

WHEAT STANDARD.

	Interest	Amount	Payment	Principal
At beginning	. . . . .	. . . . .	. . . . .	1,000.00 bu.
In 1 year	60.50	1,060.50	101.00	959.50 "
" 2 "	58.05	1,017.55	99.46	918.09 "
" 3 "	55.54	973.63	149.39	824.24 "
" 4 "	49.87	874.11	156.09	718.02 "
" 5 "	43.44	761.46	183.40	578.06 "
" 6 "	34.97	613.03	294.57	318.46 "
" 7 "	19.27	337.73	337.73	0.00 "

In these two tables every entry in one is equivalent to

the corresponding entry in the other, except those in the interest columns.

We thus see that the farmer who contracts a mortgage in gold is, *if the interest is properly adjusted,* no worse and no better off than if his contract were in a "wheat" standard or a "multiple" standard.

§ 5.

The principle involved in § 4 is that equivalent payments subtracted from equivalent "amounts" will leave equivalent remainders. The payment in any year forms the same fractional part of the "amount" in the two standards. We may designate this fraction at the end of the first year by f, the second year by f', etc., and we have the following results:

END OF FIRST YEAR.

	Dollars.	Bushels.	Bushels.
Amount	$D(1+i) \backsim$	$B(1+j) =$	$B(1+a)(1+i)$
Payment	$fD(1+i) \backsim$	$fB(1+j) =$	$fB(1+a)(1+i)$
Remainder	$(1-f)D(1+i) \backsim (1-f)B(1+j) = (1-f)B(1+a)(1+i)$

In like manner the unpaid remainder at the end of the second year can be shown to be

Dollars	Bushels.	Bushels
$(1-f')(1-f)D(1+i)^2 \backsim (1-f')(1-f)B(1+j)^2 = (1-f')(1-f)B(1+a)^2(1+i)^2$

and so on for any number of years. Each result again yields the formula $(1+j) = (1+a)(1+i)$.

This includes, of course, the case of § 1, in which no partial payments are made, f, f', etc., being then zero.

§ 6.

One special case may seem to require separate consideration. Suppose the interest alone is annually paid and the principal redeemed at the end, as in the case of a bond not subject to a sinking fund. What correspondence between the two standards is then possible? The following tables answer this question, the first, for the case where the wheat interest, the second, where the gold interest is annually paid:

TABLE I.

	Interest	Amount	Payment	Principal
At beginning (Bushels)	. . . .	. . . . .	. . . . .	1,000.00
In 1 year . . . "	60.50	1,060.50	60.50	1,000.00
" 2 years . . . "	"	"	"	"
" 3 " . . . "	"	"	"	"
" 4 " . . . "	"	"	"	"
" 5 " . . . "	"	"	"	"
" 6 " . . . "	"	"	"	"
" 7 " . . . "	"	"	"	"
" 8 " . . . "	"	"	"	"
" 9 " . . . "	"	"	"	"
" 10 " . . . "	"	"	1,060.50	0.00
At beginning (Dollars)	. . . .	. . . . .	. . . . .	1,000.00
In 1 year . . . "	50.00	1,050.00	59.90	990.10
" 2 years . . . "	49.50	1,039.60	59.31	980.29
" 3 " . . . "	49.01	1,029.30	58.72	970.58
" 4 " . . . "	48.53	1,019.11	58.14	960.97
" 5 " . . . "	48.05	1,009.02	57.56	951.46
" 6 " . . . "	47.57	999.03	56.99	942.04
" 7 " . . . "	47.15	989.19	56.43	932.76
" 8 " . . . "	46.63	979.39	55.87	923.52
" 9 " . . . "	46.17	969.69	55.32	914.37
" 10 " . . . "	45.71	960.08	960.08	0.00

TABLE II.

	Interest	Amount	Payment	Principal
At beginning (Bushels)	. . .	. . . . .	. . . . .	1,000.00
In 1 year . . . "	60.50	1,060.50	50.50	1,010.00
" 2 years . . . "	61.10	1,071.10	51.00	1,020.10
" 3 " . . . "	61.72	1,081.82	51.52	1,030.30
" 4 " . . . "	62.32	1,092.62	52.03	1,040.59
" 5 " . . . "	62.96	1,103.55	52.55	1,051.00
" 6 " . . . "	63.59	1,114.59	53.08	1,061.51
" 7 " . . . "	64.22	1,125.73	53.61	1,072.12
" 8 " . . . "	64.86	1,136.98	54.14	1,082.84
" 9 " . . . "	65.51	1,148.35	54.68	1,093.67
" 10 " . . . "	66.17	1,159.84	1,159.84	0.00
At beginning (Dollars)	. . . .	. . . . .	. . . . .	1,000.00
In 1 year . . . "	50.00	1,050.00	50.00	1,000.00
" 2 years . . . "	"	"	"	"
" 3 " . . . "	"	"	"	"
" 4 " . . . "	"	"	"	"
" 5 " . . . "	"	"	"	"
" 6 " . . . "	"	"	"	"
" 7 " . . . "	"	"	"	"
" 8 " . . . "	"	"	"	"
" 9 " . . . "	"	"	"	"
" 10 " . . . "	"	"	1,050.00	0.00

From Table I, it will be seen that the case in the wheat standard, in which only the interest is annually paid and the principal redeemed in ten years is equivalent, step by step, in the gold standard to a series of small partial payments. Thus, instead of paying merely the annual interest of $50, the sum paid the first year is $59.90, reducing the principal by $9.90. At the end there is due $914.37 of principal and $45.71 of interest, making $960.08 in all, which at that date is, of course, precisely equivalent to the 1,060.50 bushels, the final payment in wheat.

On the other hand, the case in which the gold interest payments are kept up, corresponds to a series of wheat payments *less* than the annual interest, so that the unpaid interest accumulated to the end makes the sum then due, 1,159.84 bu., of which 1,093.67 bu. are principal.

It is thus clear that the case in which in one standard the interest is paid annually and the principal at the end, can be exactly matched in the other standard either by minute partial payments or minute arrears of interest. Without such partial payments or arrears in one of the standards, the two would not be equivalent step for step. We shall see, however, that they would still be equivalent as a whole.

CHAPTER IV.

§ 1.

In practice, of course, no such minute partial payments of principal or minute remissions of interest would be made. Any advantages to be derived from such calculations of trifles would not be worth the trouble. But even if we destroy the precise step-for-step equivalence between the wheat and gold tables, we do not destroy their equivalence as a whole. The *"present values"* remain exactly equal.

The ordinary definition of the "present value" of a given sum due at a future date is "that sum which put at interest to-day will 'amount' to the given sum at that future date". "Present value" and "amount" are thus correlative terms. In fact, we may extend the preceding definition to include the present value of *past* sums as the accumulated "amount" to-day of the past sum put at interest then.

The literal meaning of "present value" implies that it is the actual market price to-day of a future sum due. This is, in fact, the case. We need not stop to prove it in theory, for we are all familiar with it in practice. Elaborate tables are constructed on this principle for the practical use of insurance companies in calculating their premiums, and for brokers in determining the comparative merits of various bond investments. What we are here concerned with is applying the principle to our problem.

§ 2.

If a debt of $1,000 is contracted to-day, interest being 5%, the "present value" of all payments, principal and interest, by which that debt is to be liquidated is exactly $1,000.[1]   Again, the debt's present value, reckoned at a later date than the time of contract, is the "amount" of $1.000 at interest from the time of contract to that date, and this is true, whether or not any of the debt has already been paid.   Thus if the present values at the date of contract are computed for the gold and the wheat debts of the last chapter, they will be $1,000 and 1,000 bushels, which are then equivalent.   If the present values one year later are taken, they are $1,050 and 1,060.50 bushels, which at that date are also equivalent, gold having appreciated 1%.

From these familiar principles, it follows that the present values of the two debts, reckoned at any date whatever, are identical whether the individual payments correspond or not.   Thus, to take the case first referred to, suppose the wheat debt to be discharged as in Table I and the gold debt as in Table II.   The present value, at the date of contract, of the interest and principal, separately computed, will be:[2]

		Dollars.	Bushels.
Present value of all interest payments		386.09 $<$	444.24
" " principal due in 10 years . . .		613.91 $>$	555.76
" " total		1000.00 $\rightleftharpoons$	1000.00

If the present values (including "amounts" of past

---

[1] This and the other general theorems on present value are not proved here because their proof is accessible in most treatises on interest, annuities, insurance, etc.   See, *e. g.,* the "Encyclopædia Britannica", "Annuities".

[2] The symbol $<$ is here used for "is less than the equivalent of" and $>$ for "is more than the equivalent of".

interest) were computed 5 years after the date of the contract, the items would be:

	Dollars.	Bushels.
Interest	492.75 <	595.88
Principal	783.53 >	745.50
Total	1276.28 $\backsim$	1341.38

We thus see that it would be just as much a hardship to pay the high interest in wheat as to pay the more onerous principal in gold.

§ 3.

The case of a perpetual annuity may be given special consideration. As is well known, the present value of a perpetual annuity is its "capitalized" value. Thus, if the rate of interest is taken at 5%, the present value of a perpetual annuity of $50 per annum is $1,000. Applying the same principle to the wheat annuity of 60.50 bushels and extending the previous reasoning, we find that the two annuities are equivalent.

At first sight this seems impossible, since 6 1-20% is a higher rate of interest than 5%. This is true in the numerical sense, and it is also true that the early payments of 60.50 bushels are actually more valuable than $50. But after a certain time (in this case 19 years) the reverse is true. The 19th payment of $50 in gold is worth 60.40 bushels, while the 20th is worth 61.01 bushels. That is, the recipient of the wheat annuity has at first a slight advantage over the recipient of the gold annuity, which ceases and becomes a slight disadvantage after 19 years.

§ 4.

To derive the formula for the time at which the relative values of the two annuities become reversed, let the rate of interest in gold be i, in wheat, j; let the two annuities be $D\,i$ and $B\,j$, their capitalized values being D and B $(D \backsim B$ at the beginning$)$ and let x be the number of years in which $B\,j$ is as valuable as or more valuable than $D\,i$. Then

Bushels.   Dollars.

At the end of x years, ... $B\,j \gtreqless D\,i$

At the end of $x + 1$ years, . . . $B\,j < D\,i$

and since we know that in x years, $D \backsim B\,(1 + a)^x$ and hence $D\,i \backsim B\,i\,(1 + a)^x$; and likewise in $x + 1$ years, $D\,i \backsim B\,i\,(1 + a)^{x+1}$, we see that the previous inequalities become:

Bushels.   Bushels.

At the end of x years, $B\,j \gtreqless B\,i\,(1 + a)^x$

At the end of $x + 1$ years, $B\,j < B\,i\,(1 + a)^{x+1}$

which may be combined in the formula:

$$i\,(1 + a)^x \leq j < i\,(1 + a)^{x+1}$$

or $x \leq \dfrac{\log j - \log i}{\log\,(1 + a)} < x + 1.$ (8)

That is, x is the integral part of the number

$$\frac{\log j - \log i}{\log\,(1 + a)}$$

Thus, if $i = .05$, $a = .01$, and hence also $j = .065$, then

$$\frac{\log j - \log i}{\log\,(1 + a)} = \frac{\bar{2}.7818 - \bar{2}.6990}{.0043} = \frac{.0828}{.0043} = 19.3$$

Hence $x = 19$.

CHAPTER V.

VARYING RATES OF INTEREST AND APPRECIATION.

§ 1.

Hitherto we have assumed that the appreciation proceeded (during the period of the contract) at a constant percentage rate per annum, and that the rate of interest (in one standard, and consequently in the other) remained constant also. The more general case is one in which these elements are changing.

Beginning with a numerical case, let us suppose that the United States government is offered an alternative loan, not in gold or "coin", but in gold or silver. Let it be known that 100 gold dollars will remain at par the first year, but in two years will be worth 150 silver dollars, that is, gold will "appreciate", in the second year, 50% relatively to silver; also that in the third and fourth years it will appreciate 10% and 5% respectively. We shall suppose that the rate of interest, if the contract be in gold, is 3% for each year of the contract.

Our problem is to discover what will be the interest in silver. It is perhaps already evident that it will be a different rate for each year. If the contract were made for one year only, the rate of interest in silver would also be 3%, since silver remains so far at par with gold. If the contract (or any unpaid part of it) were then renewed for a second year, the rate of interest would be, by formula (3):

$$
\begin{aligned}
j &= i + a + a\,i \\
&= .03 + .50 + .015 \\
&= \quad .545 \\
&= \quad 54\tfrac{1}{2}\,\%
\end{aligned}
$$

In like manner, we may deduce the rate of interest in each year, with the following results:

	Gold Standard	Silver Standard	Appre-ciation
1st year	3%	3 %	0%
2d year	3	54½	50
3d year	3	$13\frac{3}{10}$	10
4th year	3	$8\frac{15}{100}$	5
Etc.			

§ 2.

The question arises, can a single "average" rate of interest be substituted for the above irregular series?

We answer that such an average is not possible if the debtor has the option of arbitrary partial payments. If, for instance, the average were 20%, and the government could pay off at any time, it would evidently be tempted to refund the debt at the end of the second year, to which the lending syndicate would not agree. If, however, the conditions as to repayment are stipulated for in advance, an average can easily be computed on the principle of present values.

Suppose the government agrees to extinguish the debt in four years by paying at the end of successive years 20, 40, 30, and 10 millions (these to include "interest"). The present value of these sums is 66.321 millions, which is therefore the amount of the loan received from the syndicate. This sum is obtained by adding the present values of several payments. The present value of 20 millions, due one year hence, is

$$\frac{20}{1.03} = 19.418 \text{ millions.}$$

and of 40 millions, due two years hence, is

$$\frac{40}{(1.03)(1.545)} = 25.136 \text{ millions,}$$

for evidently if this be put at interest for one year at

3%, and the next at 54½%, it will amount to 40 millions. Likewise the third and fourth payments have present values of

$$\frac{30}{(1.03)\,(1.545)\,(1.133)} = 16.639 \text{ millions}$$

$$\frac{10}{(1.03)\,(1.545)\,(1.133)\,(1.0815)} = 5.128 \text{ millions.}$$

The sum of these four present values is 66.321 millions. Now if we compute the present values of the four payments on the basis of a uniform rate of 20.26% interest, we obtain the same sum, thus

$$\frac{20}{(1.2026)} = 16.631 \text{ millions}$$

$$\frac{40}{(1.2026)^2} = 27.659 \quad ``$$

$$\frac{30}{(1.2026)^3} = 17.250 \quad ``$$

$$\frac{10}{(1.2026)^4} = 4.781 \quad ``$$

$$\overline{\text{Total,} \quad = 66.321 \quad ``}$$

The separate present values are here fictitious, that is, no one of them is the actual present selling price of the future payment to which it refers, but the deviations so offset each other that their sum is the actual present selling price of the whole set of future payments. It follows from principles already stated that the debt, 66.321 millions, can be liquidated by precisely the same payments (20, 40, 30, and 10 millions), whether the interest is reckoned separately at 3, 54½, 13 3-10, and 8 15-100%, or uniformly at 20.26%. In fact, the details of the bookkeeping in the two cases are:

	At 3, 54½, 13$\frac{3}{10}$, 8$\frac{15}{100}$%				At 20.26% uniformly.			
	(In Millions)				(In Millions)			
	Interest	Amount	Payment	Principal	Interest	Amount	Payment	Principal
Date	. . .	. . .	.	66.32	. . .	. . .	. .	66.32
In 1 year . .	1.99	68.31	20.00	48.31	13.44	79.76	20.00	59.76
In 2 years . .	26.33	74.64	40.00	34.64	12.11	71.87	40.00	31.87
In 3 years . .	4.61	39.25	30.00	9.25	6.45	38.32	30.00	8.32
In 4 years . .	.75	10.00	10.00	0.00	1.68	10.00	10.00	0.00

We thus see that 20.26% is the "average" of 3, 54½, 13 3-10, and 8 15-100 %s in the sense that, by it, the same payments will cancel the same debt. It is not identical with the arithmetical average, which is 19.74%.

§ 3.

Let us suppose that the rate of appreciation of one standard in terms of the other is foreknown to be a_1 the first year, a_2 the second year, a_3 the third year, and so on; also, to be as general as possible, that the rates of interest in both standards are variable, being in the appreciating standard i_1 the first year, i_2 the second, etc., and in the depreciating standard, j_1, j_2, etc. Let the final settlement occur in n years. Then, as in § 2, we may regard the contract as equivalent to a series of one-year contracts successively renewed in whole or in part. the difference being only that the terms are all made in advance. As equation (2) applies to each of these contracts, we have

$$1 + j_1 = (1 + a_1)(1 + i_1)$$
$$1 + j_2 = (1 + a_2)(1 + i_2) \qquad (9)$$
$$1 + j_n = (1 + a_n)(1 + i_n)$$

§ 4.

To obtain an expression for the average rate of interest in either standard, *i. e.*, i_a (or j_a), we require a given series of payments D_1, D_2, . . . D_n in the gold standard (or their equivalent B_1, B_2, . . . B_n in the silver standard). The aggregate present value of these payments, reckoned by the separate rates of interest, i_1, i_2, . . i_n (or j_1, j_2 . . j_n) is

$$\frac{D_1}{1+i_1} + \frac{D_2}{(1+i_1)(1+i_2)} + . . + \frac{D_n}{(1+i_1)(1+i_2)...(1+i_n)}$$

(or the corresponding expression in terms of B's and j's). Now the "average" rate i_a must be such that if applied to the same set of payments it will make the same sum of present values; that is, i_a is determined by

$$\frac{D_1}{1+i_a} + \frac{D_2}{(1+i_a)^2} + . . + \frac{D_n}{(1+i_a)^n} =$$

$$\frac{D_1}{+i_1} + \frac{D_2}{(1+i_1)(1+i_2)} + . . + \frac{D_n}{(1+i_1)(1+i_2) . . (1+i_n)}$$

(10)

and j_a is determined by the corresponding formula in B's and j's.

This equation has only one real and positive root or value of i . It can readily be obtained by Horner's Method.[1] We shall call i_a and j_a the "actuarial average" of i_1, i_2, . . i_n and of j_1, j_2, . . j_n respectively.[2]

---

[1] For, by substituting for $\frac{1}{1+i_a}$, the single letter x and for $\frac{1}{1+i_1}$, $\frac{1}{1+i_2}$, etc ., the letters x_1, x_2, etc., the equation becomes:

$$D_1x + D_2x^2 + . . + D_nx^n = D_1x_1 + D_2x_1x_2 + . . + D_nx_1x_2 . . x_n$$

In the exampel of § 2, the equation becomes:

$$20\,x + 40\,x^2 + 30\,x^3 + 10\,x^4 = 66.321,$$

the required root of which is $x = .83155,$

which, applied to $x = \frac{1}{1+j_a}$, gives $j_a = .2026.$

[2] $1 + i_a$ reduces to the " geometrical average " of $1 + i_1$, $1 + i_2$, etc., when $D_1 = D_2 = . . = D_{n-1} = 0$.

§ 5.

We may define the average rate of appreciation of one of the two standards in terms of the other as that rate which would connect the two average interest rates if the latter were actual (instead of averages of actual) rates.[3] That is, the average appreciation, a_a is given by the equation

$$1 + j_a = (1 + i_a)(1 + a_a)$$

or

$$a_a = \frac{j_a - i_a}{1 + i_a} \tag{11}$$

Thus in the example of § 1, the average silver interest is 20.26% and gold interest 3%, so that

$$a_a = \frac{.2026 - .03}{1 + .03} = .1676,$$

or 16.76%. This average is not identical with the arithmetical average of 0, 50, 10, and 5%s, which would be 16.25%, nor is it identical with that rate which if uniform would result in four years in the same divergence between silver and gold as was produced by the four successive rates 0, 50, 10 and 5%s; this would be 14.70%. For the statistical purposes of Part II, however, the latter method is adopted for simplicity and is doubtless correct within the limit of error.

§ 6.

It may seem that the subject of this chapter can have no practical application. In Part II we shall see that this is not the case. A government bond, for instance, is a promise to pay a specific series of future sums, the price of the bond is the present value of this series and

---

[3] It may be proved that this definition of a_a, satisfies the general condition of an average, viz., that a_a reduces to a_1, a_2, etc., when the latter are all equal, whether i_1, i_2, etc. (and j_1, j_2, etc.) be all equal or not.

the "interest realized by the investor" as computed by actuaries is nothing more nor less than the "average" rate of interest in the sense above defined. Of course, the investor puts no specific values on the individual yearly rates of interest of which the "interest realized" is the average, but that this interest is truly an average is attested both by the comparative stability of the rate of interest realized on long time bonds as compared with the fluctuations of the rate of interest in the short time money market (a stability which the rate realized on the bonds does not possess when near maturity[4]) and by the fact that interest realized on a very long bond, say 50 years, is often lower than on a 25 years' bond. This is explainable by the prevailing opinion that interest tends to fall, so that if the 50 years' investment were in two successive bonds of 25 years each, the interest realized in the second would be lower than in the first. The "actuarial average" of the two is equal to the interest realized on the 50 years' bond.

---

[4] This is abundantly verified by market quotations, as is also the fact that the interest realized to him who buys a bond and sells it again in a short time is even more variable than rates on money. Thus, if in a fortnight (in which no interest falls due) the bond advances ⅛, the speculator realizes at the rate of about 3% per annum; if the rise is ½, he realizes over 12%. The investor who holds a bond a long time realizes an interest which is an "average" of the oscillating rates of those who speculate during the interim.

CHAPTER VI.

ZERO AND NEGATIVE INTEREST.

§ 1.

Having established the truth and generality of the principle $1 + j = (1 + a)(1 + i)$, we next inquire what limits, if any, are imposed on the three magnitudes j, a, i. The foregoing equation seems to require that, when the appreciation is sufficiently rapid, the rate of interest in the upward moving standard should be zero or negative. Thus if $a = j$, the equation gives us $i = 0$. Again, if $a > j$ then $i < 0$. For instance, if j, the rate of interest in wheat, is 8%, and if gold appreciates relatively to wheat 20% per annum, we have $1 + .08 = (1 + .20)(1 + i)$ whence $i = -.10$; that is, the rate of interest in gold would be *minus* 10%!

Now it is clear that negative interest is impossible. Any possessor of $100 of gold (or its equivalent in goods which can be sold for gold) would hoard the gold rather than lend it at a loss. That is, the relation $i < 0$ is impossible and therefore also $a > j$ is impossible. Thus our magnitudes are restricted within certain limits, viz.,

$$i \geq 0$$
$$a \leq j$$
(12)

or, in words, the rate of interest in a money which can be hoarded (without trouble, risk or expense) can never sink below zero and the money itself can never undergo an *expected* appreciation (relatively to another standard) greater than the rate of interest in that standard.

.§ 2.

This last result will not seem mysterious when we reflect that the same cause, viz., hoarding, which prevents the interest from being negative, also checks the expected rate of appreciation. An example will make this clear. It is a familiar fact that the expected rate of appreciation of real estate (relatively to money) can never be more rapid than the rate of interest (in money). If the latter is 5%, the (money) value of land can never advance faster than 5% per annum, except when that advance is unforeseen.

The explanation is simple. If it were foreknown that certain land values would rise 10%, owners would be able to make twice as much by holding as by selling and investing the proceeds at 5%. The land would be hoarded. This decreases the supply and sends up the price until it is within at least 5% of the expected selling price one year hence. It thus happens that holding city lots for speculation comes to be regarded as a regular investment from which the same return is to be expected as from investing in a productive enterprise. The same could be said of wheat, cotton, or other speculation. Hoarding money is but a particular form of "holding for a rise". In all cases the process tends to lessen the rise—not to obliterate it, but to make it equal to the rate of interest (in the standard in which the rise itself is measured).

In the case of appreciating money we saw that, of the two conditions $i \geq 0$ and $a \leq j$, the first was the more obvious, while in the case of appreciating real estate the second was the more obvious. The reason is that in both cases we are accustomed to think in terms of money. We say, "the rate of interest cannot be negative", "the expected rise of real estate cannot exceed the rate of interest", but, as we have seen, each of these statements implies another. It may strike the reader as a new idea that land speculation presents an actually existing case of zero interest. And yet this is undoubtedly so, if we take as our standard an acre of speculative land. The land speculator is "making money", but not "making land". His 100 acres remains 100 acres. We could even imagine all loan contracts translated from "dollars" into "acres" (though still keeping money as the *medium*). A debt of 100 "acres" would be liquidated one year hence by 100 "acres" and interest would be *nil*. There is no intrinsic reason why this same zero interest (for absolutely safe loans) might not sometime be true of money, and this without implying any change in the abundance of capital.

§ 3.

It is important to emphasize the fact that these limits imposed on the magnitudes i and a come from the possibility of hoarding money without loss. If the money were a perishable commodity, such as fruit, the limit would be pushed into the region of negative quantities. One can imagine a loan based on strawberries or peaches contracted in summer and payable in winter with *negative* interest.[1] Or, again, we may define a "dollar" as consisting of a constantly increasing number of grains of gold.[2] If the weight doubles yearly, such "dollars" cannot be hoarded without growing fewer with time. and if interest was previously 5% it will now be minus 47½%, for he who borrows $100 (2580 grains) to-day

---

[1] Cf. Böhm-Bawerk, "Positive Theory of Capital", pp. 252, 297.

[2] Such a definition for either the gold or silver "pound" is implied in Professor Foxwell's proposal for a "climbing" ratio.

375] *Appreciation and Interest* 33

will pay back $52.50 (2709 grains) one year hence. Again we find a real example by recurring to land specu- lation. Since to hold land usually involves paying taxes upon it, the rate of interest in terms of such "acres" is often, in actual fact, negative.

§ 4.

In this connection, an apparent difficulty needs to be explained. If gold should appreciate up to the maxi- mum limit so that the interest rate were zero for safe loans, would not all investment cease? What object would a capitalist have in investing when he could gain as much by hoarding? Nothing could be more natural than the fallacy here involved, and we ought not to be surprised on finding it among the arguments of certain bimetallists. For example, the Free Coinage Conven- tion at Memphis, Tenn., a year ago, adopted the follow- ing resolution: "The demonetization of either silver or gold means a fall in the prices of commodities, a dimin- ution of the profits of legitimate business, a continuing increase in the burden of debts, with consequent hard times, idle labor and *idle capital, the increasing value of money promising a surer return to a hoarded dollar than to an invested one."*

The error here contained is the ancient confusion of capital and money. It is true that a *limited*[3] amount of gold would be withdrawn and hoarded, but this would not check the investment of capital any more than the similar withdrawal of so much copper. If a hoarded dollar yields a "sure return", a hoarded *dollar's worth of*

---

[3] As in the case of land, the hoarding would reach its limit when it had raised the value (marginal utility) of present money up to the present value of future money. Hoarding beyond this point would bring loss.

goods as surely brings loss. The possessors of stocks of cotton or grain, machinery or ships, the prices of which are falling, have no disposition to keep them unemployed. A retail dealer fills his store with carpets and gives the wholesale dealer his note for three months. He is said to borrow "money", but he really borrows carpets. He may pay no (money) interest, and yet the wholesaler gains by the loan. He is saved a loss in the (money) value of the carpets which he would have incurred had he failed to get rid of them. In terms of carpets he may be making 5%. Similar considerations apply when the loan is negotiated through a third party, as a bank, and apply in fact to all forms of loans and investments. But the case supposed is so highly hypothetical and the error involved has been so often explained[4] that no further treatment of it seems necessary here. However turned or twisted and from whatever point of view examined, lending "money" at no per cent. may under certain circumstances be a very profitable transaction. It goes without saying that the foregoing conclusions apply only to "pure" or "net" interest. That part of market interest representing risk, and that part representing commissions for transacting the business of lending and borrowing would not disappear.

[4] *E. g.,* F. A. Walker, "Money" (New York, 1878), p. 94.

PART II. FACTS.

CHAPTER VII.

INTRODUCTION.

§ 1.

No study of the relation between appreciation and interest would be complete without verification by facts. In imaginary illustrations, such as those used in Part I, it is easy to make calculations agree to the last decimal place; but the figures in which we are really interested must come from actual market quotations. Through these alone can we test our assumption that foresight in regard to the appreciation or depreciation of money actually exists.

At the outset the question arises, how can a merchant be said to foresee the appreciation of money? Appreciation is a subtle conception. Few business men have any clear ideas about it. Economists disagree as to its definition, and statisticians as to its measurement. If you ask a merchant whether he takes account of appreciation, he will say he never thinks of it, that he always regards a dollar as a dollar. Other things may change in terms of money, but money itself he is accustomed to think of- as the one fixed thing. But though we do ordinarily regard the value of a dollar as a fixed magnitude, this does not really prevent our taking account of its changes. In our daily life we think of the earth as fixed, but we virtually take account of its rotation whenever we speak of sunrise or sunset. During a period of inflation the ordinary man conceives the premium on gold as a rise of

gold, not a fall of money. But if he takes account of
rising wages and rising prices he arrives at the same results as if he had thought of falling money. We need
not ascribe to the practical man any knowledge of "absolute" appreciation, but whatever absolute appreciation
is, it is included, though unseparated, in the practical
man's forecast in terms of money of all the economic
elements which concern him—prices of his product, cost
of living, wages of his workmen, and so forth. If he
expects falling prices and rising wages, as is often the
case, he may be said to foresee an appreciation of gold
as defined by the ordinary bimetallist and at the same
time a depreciation as measured by difficulty of attain-
ment. What is more, he takes account of the relative
importance, as affecting himself, of the various changes
which he expects, and not of their relative importance
in the elaborate averages of the statistician, averages
which may emphasize some commodity or some labor
whose fluctuations have absolutely no concern for him.
His effort is not to predict the index numbers of Sauerbeck or Conrad, but so to foresee his own economic future
as to make reasonably correct decisions, and in particular
to know what he is about when contracting a loan. If
gold appreciates in such a way or in such a sense that
he expects a shrinking margin of profit, he will be cau-
tious about borrowing unless interest falls; and this very
unwillingness to borrow, lessening the demand in the
"money market", will bring interest down. Further
explanation of this process is postponed to Chapter X.

§ 2.

Before proceeding to specific statistics, it is important
to emphasize the broad fact that, in general, business
foresight exists and that the accuracy and power of this
foresight is greater to-day than ever before. It is one of

the distinguishing marks of modern business. Multitudes of trade journals and investors' reviews have their sole reason for existence in supplying data on which to base prediction. Every chance for gain is eagerly watched. An active and intelligent speculation is constantly going on, which, so far as it does not consist of fictitious and gambling transactions, performs a well-known and provident function for society. Is it reasonable to believe that foresight, which is the general rule, has an exception as applied to falling or rising prices? Or, if so, can the academic bimetallist assume himself possessed of a foresight of which he says the practical man is incapable? It is the practical man's business to foresee. It is he who first gathers the facts and statistics on which forecasts must be based. It is he who watches the trend of past price movements and notes the slightest signs of a change. And it is in his trade journals that we find the first discussions of the probable effect of gold discoveries or silver legislation on prices and trade. The theorist can aid in these predictions only by supplying the principle on which they are constructed.

CHAPTER VIII.

GOLD AND PAPER.

§ 1.

General evidence that an expected change in the value of money has an effect on the rate of interest can be obtained from several sources. Municipalities often find they can sell gold bonds at better terms than currency or coin bonds. The very desire of lenders to insert a gold clause in their contracts is strong proof that they are willing to yield something for it. This was strikingly shown in California[1] during the war inflation period, where, for a time, gold contracts could not be enforced, and in consequence interest rates were very high.

During a period of progressive paper inflation it is also true that interest is high, even when the contract is drawn on a paper basis. As we shall see at a later stage, this was partially true during the civil war, though its effect was not very pronounced, owing to the over-sanguine hopes of an early termination of the war and a return to a specie basis. It was also true during the currency troubles in the thirties. Raguet wrote:[2] "In the six months before the suspension of '37, although the amount of the currency was greater than it had ever been before in the United States, yet the scarcity of money was so great that it commanded from 1% to 3% per month." It would be unsafe to found much inference on these facts. Their significance may be partly or wholly differ-

---

[1] Bernard Moses, "Legal Tender Notes in California", *Quarterly Journal of Economics*, October, 1892, p. 15.

[2] "Currency and Banking" (1839), p. 139; also Sumner, "History of Banking" (1896), p. 264.

ent. But they raise a presumption in favor of the theory
here advanced and against the theory that the rate of
interest is lowered by inflation of the currency.

§ 2.

A definite test must be sought where two standards
are simultaneously used. An excellent case of this kind
is supplied by two kinds of United States bonds, one
payable in coin and the other in currency. From the
prices which these bonds fetch in the market it is possible
to calculate the interest realized to the investor. The
currency bonds are known as currency sixes and mature
in 1898 and 1899. The coin bonds selected for comparison are the 4%s of 1907. The following table gives the
rates of interest realized in the two standards, together
with the premium on gold.

RATES OF INTEREST REALIZED FROM DATES MEN-
TIONED TO MATURITY [3]

	Coin	Currency	Price of Gold		Coin	Currency
Jan., 1870 .	6.4	5.4	119.9	Jan., 1879 .	3.7	4.5
July, 1870 .	5.8	5.1	112.2	Jan., 1880 .	3.8	4.0
Jan., 1871 .	6.0	5.3	110.8	Jan., 1881 .	3.3	3.4
July, 1871 .	5.8	5.0	113.2	Jan., 1882 .	3.0	3.5
Jan., 1872 .	5.3	4.9	109.5	Jan., 1883 .	2.9	3.3
July, 1872 .	5.6	5.0	113.9	Jan., 1884 .	2.6	2.9
Jan., 1873 .	5.7	5.1	111.9	May, 1885 .	2.7	2.7
July, 1873 .	5.4	5.0	115.3	Jan., 1886 .	2.6	2.6
Jan., 1874 .	5.0	5.0	110.3	Jan., 1887 .	2 3	2.6
July, 1874 .	5.0	4.9	110.7	Mar., 1888 .	2.3	2.9
Jan., 1875 .	5.1	4.7	112.6	Jan., 1889 .	2.2	2.6
July, 1875 .	5.1	4.4	117.0	May, 1890 .	2.1	2.6
Jan., 1876 .	4.7	4.4	112.9	July, 1891 .	2.4	3.0
July, 1876 .	4.5	4.2	112 3	Jan., 1892 .	2.6	3.1
Jan., 1877 .	4.5	4.4	107.0	Mar., 1893 .	2.8	3.1
July, 1877 .	4.4	4.3	105.4	Nov., 1894 .	2.7	3.5
Jan., 1878 .	5.0	4.6	102.8	Aug., 1895 .	2.8	3.6
July, 1878 .	3.9	4.4	100.7	Aug., 1896 .	3.2	4.3

[3] This table has been obtained by the aid of the usual brokers'
bond tables. In the case of currency bonds, it was only necessary to
deduct accrued interest (if any) from the quoted price and look in
the table for the interest which corresponds to the price so found

Several points in this table deserve notice. The quotations of 1894, '95, '96 show a considerably higher rate of interest in the currency standard than in the coin standard as well as a higher rate in both standards than in previous years. The difference is between 2.7% and 3.5% in 1894, and between 3.2% and 4.3% in 1896. Both the increase and the wedging apart of the two rates are explainable as effects of the free silver proposal and its incorporation (July, 1896) in the platform of the Democratic party. A free silver law would *certainly* reduce the value of returns from currency bonds and *possibly* also of those from coin bonds. If the mere dread of inflation has this effect, it might be supposed that, during the period of actual inflation, the discrimination in favor of coin bonds would be even greater. But we find the exact opposite to be true. In 1870 the investor made 6.4% in gold, but was willing to accept a return of only 5.4% in currency. This fact becomes intelligible in the light of the theory which has been explained. It meant the hope of resumption. Just because paper was so depreciated there was a prospect of a great rise in its value. It was not until 1878, when the prospect of a further rise disappeared, that the relative position of the two rates of interest was reversed. After resumption in 1879 the two remained very nearly equal for several years, until recent fears of inflation again produced a divergence.

---

and the number of years to maturity. In the case of gold bonds, since the quotations are given in currency, it is necessary to divide the quoted price by the price of gold in order to obtain their price in gold (*i. e.*, "coin") and then proceed as above indicated. The quotations of prices of bonds and gold are the "opening" prices for the months named and are taken from the *Financial Review*, 1895, the *Commercial and Financial Chronicle*, the (New York) *Bankers' Magazine*, and the *Bankers' Almanac*. After 1884, January quotations were not always available.

§ 3.

We have found so far that the facts agree with the
theory previously laid down.   But it is necessary further
to inquire *how close* is this agreement.   For this purpose,
the figures just given are of little value.   They represent
the rates of interest realized for the periods between the
dates named and the times at which the bonds mature.
These periods are not the same for the two bonds.   As
has been explained, such a rate of interest is a sort of
average of the rates of interest for the individual years
of the periods in question.   Thus, in the foregoing table,
the rate of interest in currency opposite January, 1870,
is 5.4%.   This is the rate realized between 1870 and 1899.
It is a sort of average of, say, the rate realized between
1870 and 1879 and between 1879 and 1899.   As we shall
see, the former was 6.3% and the latter, 4.5%.

It is clear that we must seek the rates of interest in
the two standards for the same periods.   In the following table the periods selected terminate on Jan. 1, 1879,
the date of resumption of specie payments.   We may
say, to fix our ideas, that the figures represent the rate of
interest realized to investors who buy the bonds at the
dates mentioned and sell them on January 1, 1879; but
it is obviously unnecessary to consider the bonds as actually either bought or sold, but only as owned.   This
is no new use of terms.   Business men reckon securities
in their assets at their market prices, and if these prices
rise or fall they count themselves as gainers or losers.
This gain (or loss) added to the annual interest receipts,
and properly distributed over the time considered, gives
the rate of interest realized.

RATES OF INTEREST REALIZED FROM DATES MENTIONED
TO JANUARY 1, 1879, (DATE OF RESUMPTION).[4]

	Coin j	Currency i	Appreciation of Currency in Gold	
			Expected a	Actual
January, 1870 . . .	7.1	6.3	.8	2.1
July, 1870	6.2	5.7	.5	1.4
January, 1871 . . .	6.7	6.3	.4	1.3
July, 1871	6.4	5.7	.7	1.8
January, 1872 . . .	5.9	5.7	.2	1.3
July, 1872	6.2	5.7	.5	2.1
January, 1873 . . .	6.5	6.2	.3	2.0
July, 1873	6.2	6.0	.2	2.8
January, 1874 . . .	5.6	6.1	—.5	2.1
July, 1874	5.7	5.8	—.1	2.4
January, 1875 . .	6.0	5.4	.6	3.1
July, 1875	6.1	4.2	1.8	4.9
January, 1876 . . .	5.4	4.1	1.2	4.3
July, 1876 . . .	5.2	2.4	2.7	4.9
January, 1877 . . .	5.5	4.0	1.4	3.5
July, 1877	5.7	3.1	2.5	3.6
January, 1878 . . .	8.2	6.0	2.1	2.8
July, 1878	4.8	2.6	2.1	1.4

[4] Since the figures in this table represent the rates of interest
which will render the "present value", at the date of purchase, of all
the future benefits to January, 1879, equal to the purchase price, they
can be calculated by Horner's method as indicated in Chapter V.
But the method which has been adopted is less laborious, as it
enables us to use the bond tables. It can best be explained by an
example. The opening price, January, 1870, of currency 6's was
109⅛, and January, 1879, 119½, which require no correction for
accrued interest. Our problem is, if a man spends $109⅛ in 1870
and receives $119½ in 1879 with $6 per annum (semi-annually) in
the meantime, what rate of interest does he realize? Now it is clear
that the answer is the same if all the benefits and sacrifices involved
are doubled or halved or increased or decreased in any common
ratio. Let us then divide them all by 1.19½. Then $91.3 would be
paid in 1870 for $100 due in 1879, and $5.02 per annum in the meantime. That is, the interest realized is exactly as if the bond were a
5.02% bond maturing in 1879 and bought at 91.3 in 1870. This can
readily be obtained from the bond tables by interpolating between
the figures for a 5% and a 5½% bond purchased at 91.3 and having
9 years to run. For a 5% bond we obtain 6.28%, and for a 5½%
bond, 6.81%. Hence for a 5.02% bond the result is 6.30%, or
6.3%. The third column gives what may be called the expected rate

From this table we see that the interests realized for the period, January, 1870, to January, 1879, were, in coin, 7.1%, and in currency, 6.3%, which, according to the formula $1 + j = (1 + i)(1 + a)$, gives a rate of appreciation of .8%. This may be called the "expected appreciation". The actual rate of appreciation was 2.1%. That is, the estimated appreciation was about two-fifths of the appreciation as it really turned out. Thus those who held currency sixes had the better investment. In fact, it is well known that many speculators grew rich by exchanging gold bonds for currency bonds at this time. The table shows the same misjudgment in July, 1870, January, 1871, and July, 1871. From then to July, 1874, the outlook for resumption grew gloomy, due no doubt to the strong greenback sentiment. The inflation bill of 1874 actually produced a prospect of negative appreciation, *i. e.,* depreciation. This bill was vetoed by President Grant, and in December of that year the bill for resumption was passed by the Senate. Accordingly, January, 1875, opened with a more hopeful estimate. The bill became law on the 14th of January, and there was an immediate rise in the "expected" appreciation, which, from then on, averaged 2%. But during the same period the actual appreciation from the dates named to January,

---

of appreciation of currency in terms of gold, that is, that rate of appreciation which would have made the two interest rates equally profitable. It is obtained from the formula $1 + j = (1 + i)(1 + a)$. The last column gives the actual rate of appreciation between the dates mentioned and January 1, 1879. This is calculated from the quoted prices of gold. Thus the opening price of gold January, 1870, was 119.9, and January, 1879, 100. Hence currency appreciated in nine years in the ratio 100 to 119.9, which is at the rate of 2.1% per annum. If the appreciation proceeded uniformly this method would be strictly correct. As it is, a more elaborate method would be required, in accordance with the principles explained in Chapter V, to take account fully of the fluctuations of the annual appreciation. But for our present purposes, and for results worked out to but one decimal place, the simpler method here adopted is sufficiently correct.

1879, averaged 3.6%, so that even after the government promised resumption, investors and speculators did not put implicit confidence in that promise, the "expected" appreciation being only a little more than half the actual appreciation.   This corresponds to the well-known fact that the resumption act was then looked upon as a political manœuvre, likely to be repealed.

§ 4.

It should be observed that the method employed to determine the rate of interest realized is open to one danger.   It correctly represents the rate of interest actually realized between two dates, but, unless the later of the two dates is maturity, it does not necessarily represent the rate of interest *expected* at the first date.   The investor could not know in January, 1870, what the price of bonds would be in January, 1879, unless the bonds matured at that time.   To compare, in 1870, the relative advantages of coin and currency bonds for the period 1870-79, a forecast was necessary, not only of the relation of currency to gold, but also of the prices of the two bonds in 1879.   These prices in turn depend on a new forecast made in 1879.   It follows that a mistake in this forecast of 1879 and embodied in the prices of that year will affect the rate of interest realized between 1870 and 1879 in the same manner as a mistake of the opposite kind in the forecast of 1870.

But in most cases the method given is sufficiently exact. For, although in 1870 it would have been impossible to predict exactly the prices of the two bonds in 1879, yet it can usually be depended upon that any great change in price is apt to affect both alike (provided they have approximately the same time to run), and thus eliminates itself for the most part in the comparison.   For this reason it is clearly better to take bonds whose dates of maturity approximately correspond, in order that any abnormal influence in 1879 may affect both alike, than to take, for instance, currency sixes of 1899 and coin bonds of 1881.

CHAPTER IX.

GOLD AND SILVER.

§ 1.

We turn next to the problem of the monetary disturbance since 1873. The question whether the relations between debtor and creditor have been disturbed during this period resolves itself simply into the question whether the rate of interest has been properly adjusted. If it be discovered that this adjustment was inadequate, it is still of great importance to find out *how much* the debtor has lost or gained. The comparison must be between gold and silver contracts in the same market and with the same security. Such contracts are fortunately available in the London market of government securities. The loans of India have been raised partly in gold and partly in silver, and both forms of securities are bought and sold in London.[1] The interest on the silver bonds is paid by draft on India. The sums actually received in English money depend on the state of the exchanges. The rate of interest in the silver standard is calculated in the same way as for gold bonds in the last chapter.[2]

The results are contained in the following table:

---

[1] The silver bonds or "rupee paper" were issued to raise loans in India, but they have also been enfaced for payment in England and in 1893-4 some Rx 25,000,000 were on the London books.—Burdett's "Official Intelligencer" (1894), p. 75.

[2] Thus in 1880 the average price paid in London for "rupee paper" of face value 1,000 Rs yielding 4% or 40 Rs per annum was £79. In order to find the rate of interest realized by the investor, we must translate £79 into silver. The average of exchange in 1880 was 20d. per rupee. Hence £79 were equivalent to 948 rupees. That is, speaking in terms of silver (or, more exactly, in terms of exchange on India), the price of a 4% bond was 94.8, which, treated as a perpetual annuity, yields the investor 4.3%. In the same year, an India bold bond yielded 3.6%.

RATES OF INTEREST REALIZED FROM DATES NAMED TO
MATURITY OR IN PERPETUITY.[3]

	Silver[4]	Gold[5]	Difference	Exchange on India Pence per rupee
1865	4.3	4.1	.2	23.2
1868	4.3	4.0	.3	23.0
1870	4.3	4.0	.3	23.6
1871	4.1	3.8	.3	23.2
1872	3.9	3.7	.2	22.6
1873	3.9	3.7	.2	22.4
1874	3.9	3.8	.1	22.2
1875	4.0	3.6	.4	21.9
1876	4.1	3.7	.4	20.5
1877	4.1	3.7	.4	20.9
1878	4.2	3.9	.3	20.2
1879	4.4	3.7	.7	19.7
1880	4.3	3.6	.7	20.0
1881	4.0	3.4	.6	19.9
1882	3.9	3.5	.4	19.5
1883	4.1	3.4	.7	19.5
1884	4.1	3.3	.8	19.5
1885	4.1	3.5	.6	18.5
1886	4.1	3.5	.6	17.5
1887	4.1	3.4	.7	17.2
1888	4.1	3.1	1.0	16.5
1889	4.1	3.0	1.1	16.5
1890, 1st half . .	4.0	3.0	1.0	17.6
1890, 2nd half, . .	3.9	3.1	.8	19.3
1891	3.8	3.1	.7	17.1
1892	3.9	3.1	.8	15.3
1893	3.9	3.0	.9	15.0
1894	3.9	3.0	.9	13.5
1895	3.4[4]	2.8	.6	13.4

[3] This table is formed from averages of (usually ten) quotations distributed through each year, taken from the *Economist,* the *Investor's Monthly Manual,* and the (London) *Banker's Magazine.* The fourth column is founded on the table in the Report of the Indian Currency Committee (1893), p. 27, but is corrected to apply to calendar instead of official years.

[4] The quotation from which the interest was computed for 1895 is for 3½% rupee paper. All other quotations are for 4%'s. The 4%'s were repayable on three months' notice; this notice was given in 1894, and the bonds redeemed or converted into 3½%'s before the close of the year. To obtain the rate of interest realized, the London quotations in pounds sterling are first converted into rupees at the current rates of exchange, and then the bonds are treated as perpetual annuities. The results differ from those given in the *Investor's Monthly Manual,* because the rupee is there converted at a conventional value, not the market value.

[5] To 1880 inclusive the figures refer to 4%'s, repayable October, 1888, or later; those of 1881-84 are for 3½%'s maturing in 1931, and those for 1885-95 are for 3%'s maturing in 1948.

From this table it will be seen that the rates realized
to investors in bonds of the two standards differed but
slightly until 1875, when the fall of Indian exchange
began. The average difference before 1875 was .2%,
while the average difference since 1875 has been .7%, or
more than three times as much.

From 1884 exchange fell much more rapidly than before, and the difference in the two rates of interest rose
accordingly, amounting in one year to 1.1%. Since the
two bonds were issued by the same government, possess
the same degree of security, are quoted side by side in the
same market and are in fact similar in all important respects except in the standard in which they are expressed,
the results afford substantial proof that the fall of exchange (after it once began) was discounted in advance.
Of course, investors did not form perfectly definite estimates of the future fall, but the fear of a fall predomi-
nated in varying degrees over the hope of a rise.

The year 1890 was one of great disturbance in exchanges, the average for the first six months being 17.6
and for the last six months 19.3. The gold price of
the silver bonds rose from an average for the first six
months of 73.8 to 83.5 for the last six months, but the
rise in their silver price was only from 100.6 to 103.7,
showing that the increase of confidence in the "future
of silver" was not great, and, in fact, only reduced the
disparity in the interest from 1.0 to .8%.

This great rise in exchange and the slight revival in
silver securities occurred simultaneously with the passage
of the Sherman act of July, 1890, by which the United
States was to purchase four and a half million ounces of
silver per month. There can be little doubt that the disturbance was due in some measure to the operation or
expected operation of that law.

This is not the only case in which the relative prices of
rupee paper and gold bonds were probably affected by

political action. The smallest difference (since 1874) in
the two rates of interest occurs in 1878, which was the
year of the Bland act and the first international monetary
conference.

After the closure of the Indian mints on June 26, 1893,
exchange rose from 14.7 to 15.9, the gold price of rupee
paper from 62 to 70, and consequently its rupee price
from 101.2 to 105.7.

§ 2.

The preceding comparisons serve to establish the influence of the divergence between the standards on the
rates of interest, but afford no measure of that influence.
The rates of interest which have been deduced for gold
bonds were the rates realized if the bonds were held to
maturity. The rupee bond had no fixed date of maturity
and had to be treated as a perpetual annuity, although it
differed from such an annuity in being terminable by the
government at par on three months' notice.

In order to measure the extent to which the fall of
silver was allowed for by investors, it is necessary to
examine the rates realized during specified periods. The
following table gives the rates realized between the first
five and the last five years of the period of falling exchange.

RATES OF INTEREST REALIZED ON INDIA BONDS FOR
PERIODS SPECIFIED.[6]

	Silver j	Gold i	Appreciation of Gold in Silver	
			Estimated a	Actual
1875–91	4.1	3.5	.6	1.6
1876–92	4.3	3.6	.7	1.8
1877–93	4.5	3.6	.9	2.1
1878–94	4.6	3.8	.8	2.6
1879–95	4.8	3.9	.9	2.4
Average	4.5	3.7	.8	2.1

The average estimated appreciation for the periods
taken is .8%, which is slightly more than one-third of
the average actual appreciation, 2.1%. Perhaps to obtain
the net estimate of investors as to the fall of exchange
we ought to deduct from the .8% another .1% due to the
trouble and expense of obtaining English money for
Indian exchange, for it will be remembered that even
before the fall of exchange began, the rates yielded to
investors differed by .2%.[7] We thus obtain .7% as
the extent to which, on the average, investors protected
themselves against the fall in silver during the period

---

[6] The methods by which the first column is computed are the same
as those explained in the preceding chapter, account being taken of
the fact that the price quotations for rupee paper are not "flat", so
that no corrections for accrued interest need be applied. For com-
puting the second column a more laborious method was necessary,
due to the fact that the quotations are not continuous for the same
bond. The earlier ones are for a 4% bond and the later for a 3%
bond. The buyer of a 4% bond is regarded as converting it into the
3% at the current price in 1888, the date of maturity of the earlier
bond. As no bond tables apply to such conversions, tables of present
values were used and that rate was found by trial (and interpola-
tion) which would make the present value of all benefits equal to the
purchase price.

[7] This probably included, besides the brokerage and trouble of
obtaining and selling "interest bills", the risks even at those early
dates of a falling or fluctuating exchange.

named. The remaining fall, 1.4%, implies a relative loss
to the holders of rupee paper and a gain to the holders of
gold bonds. Had the business world fully foreseen the
fall of Indian exchange, rupee paper would have been
cheaper or gold bonds dearer than they actually were, or
both. The rates of interest realized in the two standards
during the periods mentioned would have been spread
apart (at most) 1½% further.

§ 3.

The question arises at this point, how is this 1½% to
be distributed? Did investors overestimate silver or un-
derestimate gold most? There is nothing in the foregoing investigation to decide this vexed question. Our
quantitative result is purely a differential one. But other
sorts of evidence point strongly to the conclusion that the
major part of the miscalculation was on the silver side.
So far as "demonetization" is concerned, the effect on
silver must have been, according to any reasonable view,
greater than the effect on gold, and in consequence any
unforeseen part of these effects would be probably greater
in the case of silver than in the case of gold. So far as
production is concerned, the disturbance in silver was far
greater than that in gold, either when reckoned absolutely
or in proportion to the total masses whose values would
be affected. Finally, since the break-down of bimetallism
in 1873-4, the world-wide agitation to "rehabilitate silver"
has held out a delusive hope which must have acted to
give the silver bonds a higher price than they "were
worth". The strength of this agitation need scarcely be
dwelt on here. It found expression in many bills in Congress which were never passed and in two which were
passed, in numerous proposals in Germany, in silver commissions there and in England, and in three international
conferences. If any further evidence is needed that this

agitation contributed to mislead investors as to the future of silver, it can be found by examining the discussions and mistaken prophecies on silver, contributed to the *Economist* and other trade journals. It would seem extremely improbable that these hopes for the "rehabilitation of silver" have acted to depress the price of gold bonds rather than to raise the price of silver bonds.

For these reasons it seems likely that, of the $1\frac{1}{2}\%$ relative gain or loss, not more than half represents an unexpected gain on the gold bonds. That is, the interest realized on the gold bonds, if higher than it should be, was not higher by more than $\frac{3}{4}\%$. If this be true of one gold investment, it was undoubtedly true of all gold investments, and of the whole money market in London. This affords, therefore, a probable upper limit to the debtor's loss in England for contracts made since 1874. But even if the miscalculation was *twice* as great for gold as for silver, the upper limit becomes only 1%.

Our result, therefore, is that the average debtor's loss in London for contracts made since the fall of silver began, was probably less than $\frac{3}{4}\%$, and almost certainly less than 1% per annum. In Chapter X we shall attempt to find a lower limit.

§ 4.

A great deal has been written on the loss incurred by India in paying her annual interest to England in gold, but little is said of the interest paid at home in silver. Of India's national debt, about £100,000,000 are in gold and Rx 100,000,000 in rupees. This rupee debt was almost all in force twenty years ago and was then equivalent to £100,000,000, but to-day it is worth only £60,000,000. The difference may mean an added burden of gold debt, but it may also mean a lessened burden of silver debt, and it is by no means impossible that, so far as national indebtedness is concerned, India is better off than she would have been if a bimetallic tie between silver and gold had been maintained.

In this connection it may be worth while to point out a curious oversight in Mr. Elijah Helm's recent book.[8] In Chapter XVI he proposes the conversion of the 4% rupee debt into a 3% gold debt, and, assuming very plausibly that the gold bonds could be sold for 99, shows that so long as exchange remained at its present level, there would be an annual saving of interest of *Rs* 160,000. This is correct enough, but he next attempts to show that if exchange should gradually fall, there would continue to be a saving until it should sink to 10½d. This is entirely erroneous. It takes account only of the annual interest and not of the deferred principal, which, if in gold, grows progressively onerous in terms of silver. It is odd that a bimetallist who portrays so vividly the evils to the debtor from an appreciating gold principal should have found himself in the position of deliberately advising a debtor to adopt that standard to lessen his burden of interest. In the same year that Mr. Helm's book was written, the Indian Government converted its 4% rupee debt, not into gold, but into another rupee debt at 3½%.

---

[8] "The Joint Standard" (London and New York, 1894).

CHAPTER X.

§ 1.

In attempting to apply our theory to periods of rising and falling prices, we are met by the difficulty that comparison can only be made between *successive* periods. We can learn what the rate of interest has been since 1873, but we cannot know what it *would have been* if bimetallism had been extended or if the world's currency had been so expanded as to have prevented the fall of prices. Without this missing term of comparison, it is difficult to measure the influence of the progressive scarcity of gold, if such there has been, upon the rate of interest. It does not answer the purpose merely to compare the rates of interest before and after 1873. No two periods are so alike industrially that we can say they differ only in the state of the monetary standard. Other influences innumerable affect the "value of money" on the money market. Individual quotations at different times on the same market vary from one-half of one per cent. to fifty per cent., while yearly averages vary from one to seven per cent. We can never wholly eliminate all causes but one, and even partial elimination is possible only by taking averages for periods of several years each. In spite of these difficulties, however, certain general conclusions can be established.

§ 2.

Our main problem is not concerned with high and low prices, but with rising or falling prices. But we note in

passing an important generalization in regard to price
levels and the rate of interest. Shall we associate high
interest with high prices or with low prices? To answer
this question the following table is constructed. Two
rates of interest are given for each decade. The first,

MARKET RATES OF INTEREST IN RELATION TO HIGH
AND LOW PRICES.[1]

		1824 to 1831 incl.	1832 to 1841 incl.	1842 to 1851 incl.	1852 to 1861 incl.	1862 to 1871 incl.	1872 to 1881 incl.	1882 to 1891 incl.
London,	High prices	3.8	4.4	3.6	5.4	5.1	3.7	3.0
"	Low prices	3.2	3.2	2.6	3.0	2.6	2.5	2.5
New York,	High prices	. . .	. . .	. . .	9.1	7.4	7.0	5.3
"	Low prices	. . .	.	. . .	9.1	6.7	5.1	5.1
Berlin,	High prices	. . .	. . .	. . .	. . .	4.6	3.7	3.3
"	Low prices	. . .	. . .	. . .	. . .	3.4	3.2	2.7
Paris,	High prices	. . .	. . .	. . .	. . .	. . .	4.1	2 6
"	Low prices	. . .	. . .	. . .	. . .	. . .	2.4	2.6
[2]Calcutta,	High prices	. . .	. . .	. . .	. . .	. . .	6.2	5.4
"	Low prices	. .	. . .	. . .	. . .	.	5.6	6.2
[3]Tokyo,	High prices	. . .	. . .	. . .	. . .	. . .	12.3	10.1
"	Low prices	. . .	. . .	. . .	. . .	. .	12.0	10.1
[4]Shanghai,	High prices	.	. . .	. . .	. . .	. . .	. . .	6.0
"	Low prices	. . .		. . .	. .	. . .	. .	5.7

[1] This table is constructed from the data given in the Appendix.
For New York, the rates for the first decade are averaged from the
column in the Appendix headed "60 days", and are not to be compared with those for the remaining decades, which are averaged
from the column headed "Prime two name 60 days". The index
numbers of prices which have been employed are those of Jevons
(1824-51) and Sauerbeck (1852-91) for England, Soetbeer and
Heinz for Germany, the Aldrich Senate report for the United States
and France, and the Japanese report for India, Japan and China.
(See Appendix, § 3). The table ends in 1891 because there are no
index numbers for the United States since that year.

[2] For Calcutta the rate for the bank of Bengal is employed, no
"market" rate being available. The first column is for 1873-81 instead of 1872-81, for the reason that no index number for 1872 is
available.

[3] For Tokyo the first column is for 1873-81 for the same reason.

[4] For Shanghai the period is 1885-93 instead of 1882-91, for the
reason that the available rates begin in 1885 and the index numbers
end in 1893.

opposite "high prices", is the average rate for those years of the decade whose price levels, as shown by an index number, were above the average price level for the whole decade; the second is the average rate for the years whose prices were below the general average.

Of the 21 comparisons contained in this table, 17 show higher rates for high-price years than for low-price years, one shows the opposite condition, and three show equal rates in the two cases. As the table covers 68 years for London, 40 for New York, 30 for Berlin, 20 for Paris, 19 each for Calcutta and Tokyo, and 9 for Shanghai, or 205 years in the aggregate, the result may be accepted with great confidence that high and low prices are usually associated with high and low interest respectively.

There are two probable reasons for this connection. One is that high general prices usually mean scarcity of capital rather than abundance of money, while low prices generally mean abundance of capital, not scarcity of money. This corresponds to the observations of Jevons on the relation of the rate of discount to the price of wheat;[5] the other reason is connected with periods of speculation and depression and will be discussed in § 12.

§ 3.

The relation of high or low prices to the rate of interest must not be confused with the relation of *rising* or *falling* prices to the rate of interest,[6] to which we now turn.

---

[5] "Investigations in Currency and Finance" (1884), p. XIV.

[6] de Haas appears to have fallen into this confusion both in his criticism of Jevons and in his treatment of statistics. See "A third element in the rate of interest", *Journal of the Royal Statistical Society,* March, 1889.

It was predicted by Mr. Gibbs,[7] formerly a director of the Bank of England, and by other eminent bimetallists, that the progressive scarcity of gold would raise the rate of interest.   Such a scarcity makes a stringency in the money market, and the banks, each struggling to attract reserves from the others, will raise their rates.   This prophecy, however, has not been fulfilled.   Scarcely had Mr. Gibbs made his prediction when the rate fell enormously.   Some monometallists have argued from this fact that there has been no appreciation of gold.[8]   But the *theory* that appreciation raises interest has been confidently affirmed on both sides, and has even received the stamp of approval of Mr. Giffen.[9]   It is, however, utterly

---

[7] "The Bimetallic Controversy" (London, 1886), pp. 19, 231, 245-8-9, 373.

[8] Report of the Gold and Silver Commission (1888), p. 120; also Professor Laughlin in *Quarterly Journal of Economics,* Vol. I, p. 344.

[9] "Essays in Finance" (2d series, 1886), p. 70. "The years of *falling* prices and *rising* prices also correspond as a rule with those years in which high rates and low reserves, and low rates and high reserves, are combined." This (so far as prices and interest are concerned) is not only the exact opposite of the truth, but it is flatly contradicted by the few figures which Mr. Giffen himself brings forward. Of these he says: " . . . in years like 1865 and 1866 with which the Table begins, there is an obvious connection between the low reserve and high rate of discount of those years and the high Index No., leading in the following [!] years 1867-71 to a simultaneous fall in the Index No. and the rates of discount. . . . " He adds: " . . . the low prices rather succeed the high discount rates than exactly correspond. . . . " Coming to the recent period of gold contraction, he says: "Turning to the rate of discount, we find the facts once more in correspondence. What we find first is a striking disturbance of the money market at the maximum period of high prices, 1871-73 [a period of *rising* prices and high interest], when the contraction of gold begins." Of the period 1875-79 (falling prices and low interest), he writes: "With a minimum average monthly rate of 2 per cent. in each year, the following maximum monthly rates were nevertheless touched, viz.": [4½, 4⅝, 4⅜, 5⅝, 4½%s]. "In the present year (1885), when, with dull trade and low prices, the reserve should be full and discount rates low, we find that with a minimum of 2 per cent. there is again to be a compara-

at variance with facts. That an *abnormally* high or low
bank reserve is correlated with low and high interest is
abundantly justified in theory and verified in practice.[10]
But the *normal* bank reserve itself shrinks with a shrinkage of gold, and in consequence the inference that a contraction of the general gold supply will raise interest is
fallacious.[11]

When prices are rising or falling, money is depreciating or appreciating *relatively* to commodities. Our
theory would therefore require high or low interest according as prices are rising or falling, provided we assume
that the rate of interest in the commodity standard should
not vary. This assumption would be thoroughly justified
only in case the two periods were economically alike in all
respects except in the expansion or contraction of credit
and currency. In the following table for London the

---

tively high maximum (4%) within the year." "To sum up—what
I have to say of the recent discount rates is that, while there has
been an undoubted fall in recent years, corresponding to the abundance of capital, yet the market has been fevered by the demands on
the reserve. . . . " "The monetary history of recent years has
accordingly been very like what was to be expected on the theory
above set forth, assuming a contraction of gold to have occurred,
. . . finally the money market has been irritable and feverish in a
remarkable manner during the period of contraction." Thus, beginning with a statement that years of falling and rising prices correspond to years of high and low interest, Mr. Giffen cites facts which
show that the opposite is true, but proceeds complacently to compare
the rates of periods of rising (or falling) prices with the prices of
the *succeeding* period of falling (or rising) prices. As the period
of falling prices in which he writes is unfinished, he can only say of
it that the "money market has been irritable and feverish in a remarkable manner". Another monometallist, Clarmont Daniell, objects to bimetallism for India on the ground that it would deplete
India of silver and raise the rate of interest. ("The Bimetallic Controversy", p. 257). On this point see § 5.

[10] See, *e. g.*, Giffen's "Essays", *ibid.*, or the diagrams in Clare's
"Money-Market Primer", London, 1891; also F. M. Taylor, "Do we
want an Elastic Currency", *Political Science Quarterly*, March, 1896,
pp. 133-157.

[11] See, however, § 12, note.

periods are selected to correspond with the main movements of prices. Thus the period 1826-29 was a period
of falling prices, so that money appreciated in terms of
commodities at the average rate of 4.2% per annum.
This is indicated in the third column by the figure + 4.2.
In the period 1836-39 prices rose so that money fell at
the rate of 2.3% per annum, indicated by — 2.3.

LONDON RATES OF INTEREST IN RELATION TO RISING
AND FALLING PRICES.[12]

	Bank	Market i	Appreciation of Money in Commodities, a	Virtual Interest in Commodities (Market) j
1826—29	4.4	3.5	+4.2	7.8
1830—35	4.0	3.2	0.0	3.2
1836—39	4.7	4.2	—2.3	1.8
1840—44	4.2	3.5	+5.9	9.6
1845—47 . . .	3.7	4.2	—3.0	1.1
1848—52	2.9	2.5	+1.2	3.7
1853—57	4.1	5.3	—2.4	2.8
1858—64	4.4	4.2	—3.0	1.1
1865—70	3.8	3.6	+1.1	4.7
1871—73	3.9	3.7	—6.2	—2.7
1874—79	3.2	2.7	+4.3	7.1
1880—87	3.3	2.6	+3.8	6.5
1888—90 . . .	3.8	2.9	—1.4	1.5
1891—95	2.6	1.6	+3.8	5.5
Mean Variation,	.5	.7		2.6

[12] This table is constructed from the data in the Appendix. The
third column is based on index numbers (Jevons' for 1826-52, and
Sauerbeck's for the remaining years). The index numbers for two
dates, as 1826 and 1829, being given, their inverse ratio gives the
relative value of money (in commodities) at those two dates. From
these it is easy to calculate the average annual change in its value.
Theoretically, since the loans here included run usually, perhaps, 30
to 90 days, the quotations averaged should begin at the first of the
two dates, and cease, say, 60 days before the second. But the index
numbers are not always for definite points of time, nor can the
interest quotations be subjected to such minute corrections without
an immense expenditure of labor. Hence, the method adopted has
been to average the rates for all the years of a period, *e. g.*, for the
four years, 1826-29, while the "appreciation" is reckoned between
those dates, and thus is an average for only three years. If the

If this table be examined in successive periods, it will be found, in eleven out of thirteen sequences for bank rates and in ten out of thirteen for market rates, that interest is high or low according to the degree in which prices are rising or falling. Attention is called particularly to the period 1853-57, during which prices rose very fast simultaneously with and presumably because of the great gold production. The market rate of interest averaged 5.3%, which was far higher, not only than in any subsequent, but also than in any previous period, although it can scarcely be supposed that capital was less abundant. This fact has been commented upon by various writers,[13] and is usually attributed to trade activity and speculation. Such a reason, however, is not really explanatory unless the reason for the speculation is also given.

The theory here offered, that the high rate represented an effort to offset the depreciation of money, not only affords a complete explanation, but, in connection with another fact soon to be noted, explains the trade activity also.

§ 4.

The following table for Berlin displays the same connection between price movements and interest.

---

index numbers represent the price levels at the middle of 1826 and of 1829, then the average interest rates ought in theory to include only the last six months of 1826, and the first four months of 1829. But it seems better to include too much at both ends than to omit the averages for 1826 and 1829 altogether, for the reason that an average is the more valuable the greater the number of terms included. The method adopted also seems better than omitting either *one* of the extreme years, partly for the reason just given, and partly because both years usually belong to the same economic movement.

[13] *E. g.,* Sir Louis Mallet. Note to Report of Gold and Silver Commission (1888), p. 120; and Jevons' "Investigations in Currency and Finance" (1884), p. 95. The latter will be again referred to.

BERLIN RATES OF INTEREST IN RELATION TO RISING
AND FALLING PRICES.[14]

	Bank i_1	Mar- ket i_2	Apprecia- tion of Money in Commod- ities a	Virtual Interest in Commod- ities (Bank) j_1	Virtual Interest in Commod- ities (Market) j_2
1851–52	4.0	. . .	—1.5	2.4	. . . .
1853–57	4.7	. . .	—3.3	1.2	. . . .
1858–64	4.3	3.7[1]	—2.2	2.0	1.4
1865–70	4.7	4.0	0 0	. . . .	4.0
1871–73	4.5	4.1	—4.1	. . . .	—0.2
1874–79	4.3	3.2	+3.1	. . . .	6.4
1880–83	4.3	3.4	—0.1	. . . .	3.3
1884–88	3.6	2.5	+2.9	. . . .	5.5
1889–91	4 0	3.1	—1.4	. . . .	1.7
1892–95	3.4	2.2	+5.2	. . . .	7.5
Mean variation, 1858–91 .	.3	.4	. . . .	. . . .	2.1

In the foregoing table the relation is observed in six
out of nine sequences for bank rates (one being neutral)
and in six out of seven for market rates.

For France, index numbers covering a wide range of
articles are not available. Using those given in the
Aldrich report for sixteen articles, we have:

PARIS RATES OF INTEREST IN RELATION TO RISING
AND FALLING PRICES [15]

	Bank	Market	Appreciation in Commodities
1861–64	5.1		—8.1
1865–70	3.2		+3.6
1871–73	5.3	4.6[2]	—4.5
1874–79	3.1	2.6	+4.3
1880–86	3.2	2.8	+2.3
1887–90	3 1	2.6	—5.1
1891–95	2.6	2.0	

[14] This table is constructed from the data in the Appendix. The
average in the second column, marked (1), is for the years 1861-64,
not 1858-64. The "appreciation" is calculated from the figures of
Soetbeer and Heinz, as given in the Aldrich report.

[15] This table is constructed from the data in the Appendix. The
average in the second column marked (2) is for the years 1872-73,
not 1871-73.

Here the law is observed in five out of six sequences for bank rates and three out of four for market rates.[16]

It will be noted that the course of prices and interest has been very similar in England, Germany and France. For New York we have the following table:

NEW YORK RATES OF INTEREST IN RELATION TO
RISING AND FALLING PRICES AND WAGES.[17]

	Call	i, 60 days	Prime two name, 60 days	Appreciation of Money in Commodities	Appreciation of Money in labor	Virtual interest in Commodities (60 days)	Virtual interest in Commodities (Prime)	Virtual interest in Labor (60 days)	Virtual interest in Labor (Prime)
		i	i	a	a	j	j	j	j
1849–57	6.2	9.2	. . .	— 3.8	—1.1	5.1	. . .	8.0	. . .
1858–60	5.0	7.4	. . .	+ 6.4	—1.0	14.3	. . .	6.3	. . .
1861–65	5.9	8.4	6.8	—20.2	—9.3	—13.5	—14.8	—1.7	—3.1
1866–74	5.4	8.4	7.5	+ 4.7	—0.5	13.5	12.6	7.9	7.0
1875–79	.	. .	5.1	+ 7.9	+3.2	. . .	13.4	. . .	8.5
1880–84	.	. .	5 4	+ 0.6	—2.0	. . .	6.0	. . .	3.3
1885–91	. .	. .	5.1	— 0.2	—1.3	. . .	4.9	. . .	3.7
1892–95	.	. .	4.6	. . .	. . .	. . .	. . .	. . .	. . .
Mean variation, '66–91	. .	. .	.6	. . .	. . .	. . .	3.8	. . .	2.1

We find here the same association of appreciation and interest in all of the three sequences for call loans, in two of the three cases for 60 days paper (the third being neutral), and in three of the five cases for "prime" paper.[18] This is with reference to commodities. The same holds true in reference to wages. We find in the successive periods that interest is high or low according to the degree in which wages rise or fall. This is true in each of the three sequences for call loans, in two of the three for 60 days paper, and in three of the four for "prime" paper.

---

[16] Assuming that prices fell, 1891-95.

[17] This table is constructed from the data in the Appendix. The rates of appreciation are calculated from Falkner's figures for prices and wages in the Aldrich Report.

[18] Assuming that prices fell, 1892-95.

Perhaps the most remarkable fact in this table is the extremely low rate for 1875-79. The average is 5.1%, which is the next but lowest in the table, the lowest being 4.6% for 1892-95. The extraordinary change in interest rates beginning in 1875 has been observed before; but its connection with the resumption act (as it seems to the writer) has been misconstrued. Thus William Brough, referring to that act, says:[19] "The mere announcement of our intention to put our money on a sound metallic basis had brought capital to us in such abundance that the resumption was not only made easy, but the normal rate of interest was reduced. . . . This remarkable reduction . . . is explainable only on the ground of a large influx of foreign capital." But this explanation would naturally require a still lower rate of interest after resumption had been accomplished. As the facts are the opposite, there seems little room for doubt that the rate of interest was simply accommodating itself in some degree to the rapid appreciation involved in a return to specie payments.

§ 5.

The preceding statistics apply to gold standard countries. Index numbers for silver standard countries are not available prior to 1873. It is however, *a priori* probable that the relative price movements in gold and silver standard countries before and after the rupture of the bimetallic tie in 1874 presented a strong antithesis. This event marked a change in gold standard countries from rising to falling prices, while in silver standard countries prices began to rise. Unless, therefore, prices in silver countries had been rising previous to 1874, and rising very fast indeed, the antithesis referred to must have

---

[19] "Natural Law of Money" (New York, 1894), p. 124.

existed. It is, consequently, of much interest to inquire
whether the fall in the rate of interest which was so
marked for gold countries was shared in equal degree
by silver countries. The following table for periods of
five years before and after the silver and gold standards
began to diverge, throws some light on this problem:

AVERAGE BANK RATES IN GOLD AND SILVER STANDARD
COUNTRIES BEFORE AND AFTER THE BREAKDOWN
OF BIMETALLISM.[20]

	Calcutta	Tokyo	Shanghai	London	Berlin	Paris	New York	Average for Silver Countries	Average for Gold Countries
1870–74	5.1	16.4	10.6	3.7	4.5	4.9	7.5	10.7	5.2
1875–79	6.5	14.6	9.2	3.0	4.2	2.9	5.1	10.1	3.8

While the results are not conclusive, they go to con-
firm our theory. In all gold countries the rate fell after
the par of exchange with silver countries was broken,
while in India it rose, and this in spite of the flow of
capital to India from England and other gold countries.
It is true that in Japan and China the rates fell. But this
fall was much less than in the gold countries, whereas
we should expect it to be much greater if the only influence at work were the migration of capital. Such extra-

---

[20] This table is constructed from the data given in the Appendix.
Bank rates are selected rather than market rates, as the latter are not
available for Calcutta and Shanghai. For New York, however, the
rates for "prime two name 60 days paper" are employed. Although
the United States and Japan were on a paper basis at the periods
given, the premium on gold in the one case and silver in the other
moved in opposite directions, affording, therefore, as great or greater
antithesis than if the standards had been simply gold and silver. For
the American premium see Chapter VIII, § 2: for the Japanese, see
Appendix, § 3, note.

ordinary rates as ruled in China and Japan in the '70's must have been extremely sensitive to the influence of an influx of capital. Even though British investment in Japan and China may have been much less than in India, we should expect its tendency to reduce the native rate of interest to be more effective where that rate was 10% or 15% than where it was 5%. An added reason for a fall in rates in Shanghai and Tokyo is the narrowness of the areas affected by foreign capital, which, having little opportunity to penetrate inland, tends to glut the market in the open ports.

Turning to the period for which index numbers are available, we have the following table for India, Japan, and China:

RATES OF INTEREST IN RELATION TO RISING AND FALL-ING PRICES IN CALCUTTA, TOKYO AND SHANGHAI.[21]

		Bank	Market	Appreciation in Commodities
Calcutta . .	1873–75	5.3		+ 2.6
	1876–78	6.8		—11.0
	1879–85	5.9		+ 3.8
	1886–89	6.0		— 2.6
	1890–93	4.3		— 4.7
Tokyo. . . .	1873–77	14.0	12.0	— 0.2
	1878–81	16.3	12.2	—13.3
	1882–86	12.8	10.3	+10.4
	1887–93	9.3	9.4	— 2.8
Shanghai . .	1874–81	9.1		— 1.4
	1882–88	7.5	5.8[1]	+ 1.3
	1889–93	7.0	5.8	— 0.9

Here we find our theory confirmed in three out of four cases for India, two out of three for bank rates in Japan, and two out of three for market rates, one out of two for bank rates in China, while the one case for market rates is neutral.

[21] This table is constructed from the data given in the Appendix. The entry marked (1) is for 1885-88, not 1882-88.

Summarizing the cases for the seven countries examined, we find 57 favorable, and 16 unfavorable, to our theory, distributed as follows:

	England	Germany	France	United States	India	Japan	China	Total
Favorable . .	21	12	8	8	3	4	1	57
Unfavorable .	5	3	2	2	1	2	1	16

We therefore conclude with great confidence that, "other things being equal", the rate of interest is high when prices are rising and low when prices are falling.

§ 6.

We turn next to the question *how far* the rate of interest has been adjusted to price movements. The formula $(1 + j) = (1 + i) (1 + a)$, or its more convenient form for present purposes, $j = i + a + ia$, enables us to calculate the rate of interest in the *commodity standard* which was equivalent to the money interest paid in each period. Thus in London for 1826-29 the rate of interest (i) in money was 3.5%, but money was appreciating relatively to commodities 4.2% (a), so that the interest actually paid in terms of commodities (*i. e.*, the forty commodities averaged by Jevons) was $j = .035 + .042 + .035 \times .042 = 7.8\%$. It will be seen from the table in § 3 that the virtual rate of interest paid in commodities usually varies inversely with the rate paid in money. For 1853-57, money interest was 5.3%, and for 1891-95, 1.6%, but commodity interest for 1853-57 was 2.8%, and for 1891-95, 5.5%. Moreover, commodity interest fluctuated much more than money interest, the mean variation from the average being for money interest, .7%, and for commodity interest, 2.6%. All these facts suggest — indeed, practically demonstrate — that money interest was not adequately adjusted. It is, of

course, not to be assumed that commodity interest ought
to be invariable, but we can be practically certain that its
variations ought not to be three and a half times the
variations in money interest.   Such fluctuations must
mean that the price movements were inadequately predicted.   If any doubts were possible on this point, they
must disappear when we find that for 1871-73 commodity
interest was *minus* 2.7%.   Money lenders would have
been better off had they simply bought commodities in
1871 and held them till 1873.   Such losses are especially
apt to appear in short periods.   Thus, if we take the
period 1824-25, we find that the market rate was 3.7%,
the rate of appreciation was *minus* 14.5%, and the virtual
rate of interest in commodities *minus* 11.3%.

The same observations apply to the rates at Berlin.
Paris, New York, Calcutta, Tokyo, and Shanghai.   In
New York during the inflation period 1861-65, commodity interest sank to the fabulously low figure of
−14.8%, though the rate of interest in the labor standard
was only −3.1%.   This shows in a striking way how
thoroughly the greenback inflation upset all business calculations.   This fact has generally been recognized,
though probably underestimated.   It is amply confirmed
by examining the predictions as to the termination of
the war and the reduction of the gold premium which
were recorded from month to month in the "Notes on
the Money Market" in the (New York) *Banker's Magazine*.   In all probability this is always true of periods
of paper money inflation.   Our tables show it for the
Japanese inflation of 1878-81.

§ 7.

We can now understand why a high rate of interest
need not retard trade nor a low rate stimulate it.   These

facts have puzzled many writers. For instance,[22] "Public inquiry has been of late strongly directed to the reasons for the very low rate of interest upon loanable capital in the year 1875, the more especially as ten years ago the very high rates then prevailing created equal surprise". Again,[23] "The effect of such and many more changes effected during the last twenty years or so, is seen in a general increase in wealth and of mercantile industry and profits. Thus only can be explained the extraordinary high rate at which the interest of money has in the last ten years often stood. During 1854-57 the rate of interest was only for a few months below 5%, but for many months above it. For more than half a year it stood at 6 and 7%, and in the end of May, 1857, it remained for nearly two months at 10%. Again, in 1861, interest rose to 6 and 8%, and all this, *to the surprise of the elder generation, without the general stoppage of trade, the breach of credit, and the flood of bankruptcy, which has hitherto attended such rates of interest.* It is certainly not to increasing scarcity of capital we should attribute such rates, but rather to a greatly extended field for its profitable employment."[24] But were these rates high? If we turn to our table for London rates, we find that the average market rate for 1853-57 does appear to be the highest in the table, but, unmasking it of the money element, we find it is equivalent to a commodity interest of 2.8%. This is 1.0% *lower* than the average for the whole period, 1826-95. Should we be surprised that industry did not languish?

---

[22] Robert Baxter, *Journal of the Royal Statistical Society,* June, 1876.

[23] Jevons, "Investigations", p. 95. The italics are the present writer's.

[24] This view had also been expressed by Tooke and Newmarch, "History of Prices", Vol. V, p. 345.

Professor Bonamy Price,[25] writing at a time of very low interest rates, says: "Everyone remembers the agitations associated with 7%, the trepidation of merchants, the apprehension of losses in business. . . . If only a moderate rate could be reckoned on as steady, how happy would everyone have been! . . . Yet what are the facts and feelings to-day? Is every merchant, every manufacturer, rejoicing in the pleasant terms on which he obtains the accommodation so necessary for his business? . . . Alas! no such sounds meet our ears. . . . Commercial depression is the universal cry, depression probably unprecedented in the annals of trade, except under the disturbing action of a prolonged war. . . . In the export figures, the writer still fails to see any signs of the long-looked-for revival of trade. Both quantities and values continue to shrink in all save a few cases. . . . What then is the cause? *The explanation will certainly not be found in gold nor in any form of currency whatever. . . . nor has anyone said anything so ridiculous.* . . . That cause is one and one only: over-spending."

If we turn back to our London table we find, however, that for 1874-79 the commodity rate of interest was 7.1%! It would be astonishing if trade did *not* shrink under such a burden.

All these writers mistook high or low nominal interest for high or low real interest. Tooke apparently did the same. In his "History of Prices", vol. ii, p. 349, he names as the last of six reasons for the fall of prices for 1814-37, "a reduction in the general rate of interest". This is probably not only an inversion of cause and effect, but also, when the veil of money is thrown off, a misstate-

---

[25] "One per cent.", *Contemporary Review*, April, 1877. The italics are the present writer's.

ment of fact. The commodity interest for 1826-29 was
7.8%. It would seem that Tooke, Price, and Jevons all
overlooked the fact that interest, unlike prices, is not an
instantaneous but essentially a *time* phenomenon.

§ 8.

In order to make our results as certain as possible, the
following table is formed, in which the longer price
movements are selected. It consists of three periods, of
ten, twelve, and twenty-one years respectively.

LONDON MARKET RATES OF INTEREST IN RELATION TO
RISING AND FALLING PRICES, WAGES AND INCOMES.[26]

	Market Interest i	Appreciation of Money in Commodities. a	Virtual interest in Commodities j	Appreciation of Money in Labor a	Appreciation of Money in Income a	Virtual interest in Labor j	Virtual interest in Income j
1826–35	3.4	+1.2	4.6		. . .		. . .
1853–64	4.6	—0.9	3.7	. . .	. . .	. . .	. . .
1874–95	2.4	+2.4	4.9		. . .	. . .	
1860–74	4.0	. . .	. . .	—2.1	—2.5	1.8	1.4
1874–91	2.7	. . .	. . .	0.0	—0.2	2.7	2.5

In averages covering so many years, we may be sure
that accidental causes are almost wholly eliminated. We
find that during the period of rising prices, 1853-64, the
average rate of interest was 2.2% above the average for
the subsequent period of falling prices, 1874-95, and
1.2% higher than in the former period of falling prices,
1826-35. The rates in the commodity standard, however,
vary in the inverse order, the highest interest being for
1874-95 and the lowest for 1853-64. It is a noteworthy

[26] The rates of appreciations in labor and income are based on
"Changes in average wages in the United Kingdom between 1860
and 1891", by A. L. Bowley, in the *Journal of the Royal Statistical
Society,* June, 1895.

fact, in strong contrast with what we have found true of short periods, that the commodity interest in this table of long periods is less variable[27] than the money interest. Thus the adjustment of (money) interest to long price movements is more perfect than to short.

§ 9.

The foregoing table shows exactly how the English borrower has fared so far as commodities and labor are concerned. During 1853-64 he paid 3.7% in commodities, but during 1874-95 he had to pay 4.9%, an increase of 1.2%. In the labor standard, during 1860-74, he paid 1.8%, and during 1874-91, 2.7%, showing an increase of .9%, while in the income standard the rates were 1.4% and 2.5%, respectively, showing an increase of 1.1%. Now it is quite conceivable that *commodity* interest should normally be high during the latter period, if this period can be shown to be one of unusually rapid economic progress.[28]   That this was in fact the case has

---

[27] The mean variation for the three money rates is easily seen to be .8% and for the commodity rates only .5%. The two "labor" and "income" rates differ by .9 and 1.1%, while the money rates differ by 1.3%. In the New York table which follows, the money rates differ by 3.0% and the commodity rates by 3.2%, but the labor rates by only 2.2%.

[28] For when the future seems a time of relative plenty, future goods may be discounted at a high rate and profits measured in commodities may be large.   Contrariwise, during a period of progressive scarcity commodity interest may be normally low.   These theories may seem to conflict with current opinion; but only when the fundamental distinction is overlooked between a period of plenty and a period of progressive plenty, and between a period of scarcity and a period of progressive scarcity.   During stationary scarcity and stationary plenty, normal commodity interest may be high and low respectively.   But during the *transition* from scarcity to plenty instead of running through the intermediate rates, commodity interest may be normally higher than in either of the extreme states.   This is a case in which "dynamic" economics differ strikingly from "static" economics.

been pretty thoroughly established by the admirable researches of David A. Wells[29] and others, and by the statistics of wages compiled by Falkner[30] and Bowley.[30] But these considerations can scarcely apply to "labor interest" or "income interest". A man who borrowed the equivalent of a hundred days' income during 1860-74 could pay it back in a year with the equivalent of 101.4 days' income, while during 1874-91, for a similar loan he must return 102.5 days' income. This is the opposite of what we should expect as the influence of progress. It therefore seems safe to ascribe at least 1.1% as the borrower's loss since 1874, *compared* with his gain or loss before 1874. It may well be that part of this comparative loss for 1874-91 represents a gain for 1860-74. If we ascribe half to this gain, there remains the other half, .5% or .6%, as loss during 1874-91. Although this division is quite arbitrary, the conclusion that the borrower's loss was at least ½% seems reasonable when we consider that the total comparative loss, 1.1%, was itself a minimum. But even if we suppose the debtor's gain during the former period twice his loss during the latter (a supposition which, in view of all the facts, must be within the claims of all reasonable monometallists), we still have a minimum (English) debtor's loss since 1874 of ⅓%.

Combining the results just given with those of Chapter IX, we see that the average loss to English borrowers during the fall of prices since 1874-75 probably lies

---

[29] "Recent Economic Changes" (New York, 1890).

[30] *Loc. cit.* These statistics, taken in connection with price statistics, show that commodity wages, *i. e.,* money wages divided by the index number of prices (*wholesale* unfortunately), rose in England during 1860-74 at the rate of 1.8% per annum and during 1874-91 at the rate of 2.2%, while in America for 1849-57 they fell 2.7% per annum and for 1875-91 rose 2.4% per annum.

between ½% and ¾%, and almost certainly between ⅓% and 1%. The former result may be stated thus, ⅝ ± ⅛%, and the latter, ⅔ ± ⅓%. We may therefore say with considerable confidence that the average debtor's loss in England for contracts made since 1874-75 has been two-thirds of one per cent. per annum, with a possible error of one-third of one per cent. In other words, the average debtor's loss could have been corrected by a reduction in the rate of interest of from one-third of one per cent. to one per cent.

§ 10.

For contracts made before 1874, but continued to the present, the loss since 1874 must have been greater. We may therefore accept the former estimate of ⅔% as a lower limit, or, to be safe, ½%. To find an upper limit, we recur to the fact that India gold bonds purchased prior to 1875 yielded very nearly ½% more interest than the average subsequent to that date. Since we have estimated that the average from 1875 was at most 1% too high, the average for periods beginning before but ending after 1875 must have been at most 1½% too high for it can scarcely be claimed that the rate of interest for the part of the term of the bonds previous to 1875 ought to have been lower than that for the part subsequent to that date. We therefore conclude that, for English contracts made before 1874-75, the debtor's loss since 1874-75 has been between ½% and 1½%, *i. e.*, 1 ± ½%.

It follows that for contracts which were made prior to 1874-75, but subsequently converted or continued at a lower rate of interest, the loss since 1874-75 was 1 ± ½% per annum to the date of conversion and ⅔ ± ⅓% since that date.

It should be observed that the foregoing calculations are based on public prices of bonds and rates on money. Interest on private loans and farm mortgages, although influenced[31] by the same causes which affect the money market, is less flexible, and the debtor's losses or gains in these cases are doubtless somewhat greater.

§ 11.

The following table gives the long time averages for New York. The war period is omitted and a nine years' period of rising prices is compared with a seventeen years' period of falling prices.

NEW YORK RATES OF INTEREST IN RELATION TO RISING AND FALLING PRICES AND WAGES.

	Interest Prime Two name 60 days i	Appreciation of money in commodities a_1	Appreciation of money in labor a_2	Virtua interest in commodities j_1	Virtual interest in labor j_2
1849–57 . .	8.2[32]	—3.8	—1.1	4.1	7.0
1875–91 . .	5.2	+2.0	—0.4	7.3	4.8

We find for 1849-57 and 1875-91 that the money rates were 8.2 and 5.2%, the commodity rates 4.1 and 7.3%, but the labor rates 7.0 and 4.8%. We see, therefore, that in terms of labor, loans in America have actually been *easier* during 1875-91 than during 1849-57. This fact suggests the conclusion that the debtor's loss in America has not been as great as in England. This, if

---

[31] See Appendix, § 2, 4th title.

[32] The average of Elliott's figures (which are not for "prime" paper) is 9.2, but 1.0 has been deducted from this average in order that it may be properly compared with the average of Robbins' figures for 1875-91. The correction is based on the fact that 1.0 was the average excess of Elliott's figures over Robbins' during the fifteen years, 1860-74. See Appendix.

true, may be due to a more rapid rate of progress in the United States.[33]

§ 12.

Four general facts have now been established:

(1) High and low prices are directly correlated with high and low rates of interest; (2) Rising and falling prices and wages are directly correlated with high and low rates of interest; (3) The adjustment of interest to price (or wage) movements is inadequate; (4) This adjustment is more nearly adequate for long than for short periods.

These facts are capable of a common explanation expressing the manner in which the adjustment referred to takes place. Suppose an upward movement of prices begins. Business profits (measured in *money*) will rise, for profits are the difference between gross income and expense, and if both these rise, their difference will also rise. Borrowers can now afford to pay higher "money interest". If, however, only a few persons see this, the interest will not be fully adjusted[34] and borrowers will realize an extra margin of profit after deducting interest charges. This raises an expectation of a similar profit in the future, and this expectation, acting on the demand for loans, will raise the rate of interest. If the rise is still

---

[33] See page 72, note 2.

[34] It seems scarcely necessary to add as an independent cause of mal-adjustment the accumulation (or in the opposite case, depletion) of bank reserves, for this is but another symptom of mal-adjustment due to imperfect foresight. An increase of gold supply, as in 1852-53 (see Tooke and Newmarch, "History of Prices", vol. V, p. 345) may first find its way into the loan market instead of into circulation. But if foresight were perfect, this would not happen, or if it did happen, borrowers would immediately take it out (or increase the liabilities against it) to avail themselves of the double advantage of low interest and high prospective profits from the rise of prices about to follow.

inadequate, the process is repeated, and thus by continual trial and error the rate approaches the true adjustment.

When a fall of prices begins, the reverse effects appear. Money profits fall. Borrowers cannot afford to pay the old rates of interest. If, through miscalculation, they still attempt to do this, it will cut into their real profits. Discouraged thus for the future, they will then bid lower rates.

Since at the beginning of an upward price movement the rate of interest is too low, and at the beginning of a downward movement it is too high,[35] we can understand, not only that the averages for the whole periods are imperfectly adjusted, but that the delay in the adjustment leaves a relatively low interest at the beginning of an ascent of prices and a relatively high interest at the beginning of a descent. This would explain, in part at least. the association of high and low prices with high and low interest.[36] The fact that the adjustment is more perfect for long periods than for short, seems to be because in short periods the years of non-adjustment at the beginning occupy a larger relative part of the whole period.

§ 13.

What has been said bears directly on the theory of "credit cycles". In the view here presented periods of speculation and depression are the result of *inequality* of foresight. If all persons underestimated a rise of price in the same degree, the non-adjustment of interest would merely produce a transfer of wealth from lender to borrower. It would not influence the volume of loans (except so far.as the diversion of income from one person to another would itself have indirect effects, such

[35] These facts may be verified from the tables in the Appendix.
[36] Cf. § 2.

as bankruptcy). Under such circumstances the rate of interest would be below the normal, but as no one knows it, no borrower borrows more and no lender lends less because of it. In the actual world, however, foresight is very unequally distributed. Only a few persons have the faculty of always "coming out where they look". Now it is precisely these persons who make up the borrowing class. Just because of their superior foresight, society delegates to them the management of capital. It is they who become "captains of industry". Their share consists of profits (or losses), while others lend them capital and receive interest or commuted profits.[37] It therefore happens that when prices are rising, borrowers are more apt to see it than lenders. Hence, while the borrower is willing to pay a higher interest than before for the same loan, lenders are willing to loan the same amount for the same interest. That is, the "demand schedule"[38] will rise, while the "supply schedule" remains comparatively unchanged. This will, of course, raise the rate of interest. But it will also cause an increase of loans and investments.[39] This constitutes part of the stimulation to business which bimetallists so much admire.

When prices fall, borrowers see that they cannot employ "money" productively except on easier terms, but lenders do not see why the terms should be made easier. In consequence, "entrepreneurs" borrow less, enterprise

---

[37] Hadley, "Interest and Profits", *Annals of the American Academy of Political and Social Science,* November, 1893; also "Economics" (New York, 1896), pp. 116, 269.

[38] Marshall, "Principles", Vol. 1 (3rd ed.), p. 171.

[39] That this and the corresponding statement in the next paragraph are borne out by facts appears to be confirmed, so far as bank loans and discounts are concerned, by Sumner, "History of Banking in the United States" (New York, 1896), and Juglar, "Crises commerciales" (Paris, 1889).

languishes, and, though interest falls in consequence of decrease in demand, it does not fall enough to keep the demand from decreasing.[40]

If lenders, as a class, were possessed of greater foresight than borrowers, we should find trade languishing during rising prices and stimulated during falling prices. In the former case lenders would require high interest, for fear, as in 1871-73, they were lending at a loss of real wealth, while borrowers would be afraid of the apparently high rates charged; and in the reverse case lenders would be eager to reap the benefits of an appreciating standard, while borrowers, deceived by the apparently low rates, would rush in to profit by them.

We see, therefore, that while *imperfection* of foresight transfers wealth from creditor to debtor or the reverse, *inequality* of foresight produces over-investment during rising prices and relative stagnation during falling prices. In the former case society is trapped into devoting too much wealth to productive uses and in "long production processes",[41] while in the contrary case under-investment is the rule. It does not seem possible to decide the question which of the two evils is the greater.[42]

---

[40] President Andrews in "An Honest Dollar", p. 3, writes: "Interest is low . . . not because money is abundant as before, but because it is not, its scarcity having induced fall of prices and so paralysis in industry." But it should be added, the cause of the fall of interest is primarily the *expectation* of small profits. *Cf. infra.*

[41] Professor Böhm-Bawerk ("Positive Theory of Capital", p. 335) writes: "Now the constant presence of the agio on present goods is like a self-acting drag on the tendency to extend the production period. Extensions which would be harmful as regards social provision are thus made economically impossible." During rising prices this drag presses too lightly and during falling prices too heavily.

[42] Bimetallists usually claim that falling prices are the greater evil. For arguments on both sides see Professor Marshall's evidence, Report on Depression of Trade. (1886), p. 422.

It is believed that the foregoing theories correspond closely with observed facts as to business stimulation and depression, volume of loans, etc., but it is not proposed here to enter upon a special statement of them.[43]

Nor is this the place to treat fully the reaction on prices themselves. But it can scarcely be doubted that the maladjustment of interest is a central feature in the whole movement. Professor Marshall, who recognizes fully the distinction between money and commodity interest, says :[44] "When we come to discuss the causes of alternating periods of inflation and depression of commercial activity, we shall find that they are intimately connected with those variations in the real rate of interest which are caused by changes in the purchasing power of money. For when prices are likely to rise, business is inflated, and is managed recklessly and wastefully; those working on borrowed capital pay back less real value than they borrowed, and enrich themselves at the expense of the community. When afterwards credit is shaken and prices begin to fall, everyone wants to get rid of commodities and get hold of money, which is rapidly rising in value; this makes prices fall all the faster, and the further fall makes credit shrink even more, and thus for a long time prices fall because prices have fallen."

We would add that these effects of credit could not follow if the interest rate were perfectly adjusted. Interest, rather than credit, appears as the chief independent variable, objectively speaking, though behind it all is imperfection of foresight.

---

[43] See Report on Depression of Trade, 1886; and Report of the Gold and Silver Commission, 1888.

[44] "Principles of Economics", Vol. I (3rd ed., 1895), p. 674.

PART III. APPLICATIONS.

CHAPTER XI.

THE BIMETALLIC CONTROVERSY.

§ 1.

It is not the purpose here to follow all the arguments for and against bimetallism, but merely to outline the bearing of the foregoing theories and facts upon some of those arguments.

We have seen in theory and in practice that the rate of interest has tended to accommodate itself to the changing value of money. It follows that it is quite erroneous to obtain the amount of the debtor's or creditor's loss by merely reckoning the effect of appreciation or depreciation on the *principal* of the debt.

And yet, after all allowances are made, it is true that there remains a net loss alternating between debtors and creditors according to the varying tides of credit and prices. During the last twenty years it has happened that the debtor was on the losing side. We have estimated his average loss at $\frac{2}{3} + \frac{1}{3}\%$ per annum in England and probably less in this country. This loss is not inconsiderable. When looked at in the aggregate, it appears very large indeed. The minimum net indebtedness public and private in the United States is given at 20 billions,[1] on which $\frac{2}{3}\%$ would amount to 130 millions per annum. But when we compare this with the aggre-

---

[1] G. K. Holmes, Bulletin of the Department of Labor, November, 1895, p. 48.

gate principal involved or with the 14 odd billions[2] of
annual product, it does not seem capable of the deep
social harm attributed to it.   In fact, it is always misleading to consider aggregates except in comparison with
each other.   Applied to an ordinary two months' loan of
$1,000, ⅔% amounts to one dollar.   In New York City
the up-town banks often charge a rate more than ⅔%
higher than that of the down-town banks without driving
away customers.

§ 2.

   The ordinary estimates of the debtor's loss are based
on index numbers.   From Sauerbeck's tables it appears
that between 1873 and 1895 money appreciated in terms
of the commodities selected, 79.0%, which is at the rate
of 2.7% per annum.   This is from three to eight times
as much as the estimate we have made.   The error of the
ordinary calculation does not consist simply in neglecting
the matter of interest.   The use of index numbers is itself
subject to fatal objection.[3]   When unchecked by other
statistics they are very misleading.   Not only do we
reach different results according to the number of commodities and the method of averaging,[4] but the very best
methods fail to give a trustworthy measure of ordinary
domestic purchasing power, both because they are based
on wholesale instead of retail prices, and because they
ignore expenditure for house rent and for labor and
domestic service, which, in the family budgets of those
who borrow and lend, must form a very large item.

---

   [2] Edward Atkinson, *Engineering Magazine,* December, 1895.

   [3] The reader is reminded that, though we have used index numbers to determine "commodity interest", we have not employed them
to estimate the debtor's loss.

   [4] See articles by Edgeworth, Sauerbeck and Pierson in the *Economic Journal,* March, June, and September, 1895, and March, 1896.

Moreover, to know the purhasing power of a dollar does not enable us to know the "subjective value" or marginal utility of money. The number of dollars at command (*i. e.,* money incomes) must also be considered. And even were our knowledge complete as to the marginal utility of money, as well as its purchasing power, we should be as far as ever from solving the problem of the debtor's loss. The question is not one of appreciation of gold relatively to commodities, or to labor, or any other standard. It is, as we have seen, exclusively a question of foresight and of the degree of adaptation of the rate of interest.

§ 3.

It scarcely needs to be pointed out that bimetallism can only affect unpaid debts. We should therefore clearly recognize the fact that the most of the loss which debtors have suffered since 1873 has already passed beyond the reach of remedy. Of the residuum the losses vary with the duration of the debt. On debts three years old the loss in England is probably about two per cent., on those six years old about four per cent., and so on. Moreover, on debts contracted before the fall of prices began, the annual rate of loss was greater, being probably, as we have seen, $1 \pm \frac{1}{2}\%$. Most such debts, however, including even national debts, have received part of the benefit of low interest through extensive conversions.

Now bimetallism, if adopted, so far from rectifying gains and losses, would simply increase the inequalities. If it resulted in debasing the standard ten per cent., it might exactly remedy debts fifteen years old, but the correction would be too small for those older and too large for those younger than fifteen years. The latter form the great bulk of existing indebtedness. The average life of a farm mortgage is 4⅔ years,[5] so that the average age of mortgages now in force would be about 2⅓ years. Bank loans run only a few days or months. These and other short time loans make up some sixty per cent. of existing indebtedness.[6] The remainder consists of railway and government loans, and few of them extend back to 1873.[7] The chief and dominant effect of debasement would therefore be to defraud the lender of to-day and yesterday.[8] The older debts, for which the remedy is designed, no longer exist.

§ 4.

But even if bimetallism or any other financial scheme could so scale debts as exactly to counteract the losses connected with the fall of prices, the ethics of such an arrangement ought not to go unmentioned. The fact that debtors have lost does not imply that they have suffered an injustice. If a man insures his house and it burns the next day the insurance company suffers a loss but not an injustice. If the company should ask for legislative relief on the ground that it had not expected so sudden a termination of its policy, that the fire was brought about by causes which it could not possibly foresee or provide against, it would be laughed to scorn. "Keep your contract", would be the reply. It would

---

[5] Eleventh Census, Bulletin 71.

[6] Holmes, *loc. cit.*

[7] Probably much less than one-fourth for American railways. This estimate is made by looking over all the funded indebtedness whose dates of issue are given in the "Official Intelligencer" for 1894.

[8] For effects on "Social Classes", see article by Professor H. W. Farnam, *Yale Review*, August, 1895, p. 183.

make no difference if the fires were universal, and every insurance company lost. Those who assume the risks must take the consequences. A farmer mortgages his farm and agrees to pay $1,000 and 5% interest. By the terms of the agreement he takes all risks as to what the dollar will buy of wheat or anything else. He may lose and all farmers may lose, and the causes may be in India or Australia or in the sun spots, but we can scarcely afford to surrender the ancient principle of the Inviolability of Contracts through sympathy with the misfortunes of any individual man or group of men. That elements of risk exist in every contract and that this risk implies responsibility are too often ignored. President Andrews writes:[9] "Increase in the value of money robs debtors. It forces every one of them to pay more than he covenanted [!]—not more dollars, but more value." But contracts which call for money do not call for "value" any more than contracts to deliver wheat call for money. If a man had agreed a year ago to deliver 10,000 bricks to a builder at a fixed price, he would not be justified in offering only 9,000 on the ground that the price had gone up. A contract to pay "value" would be a legal curiosity, and the court which should attempt to interpret it would hear an interesting assortment of definitions from our leading economists.

Closely associated with the principle of the Inviolability of Contracts is the principle against retro-active laws, and in particular against laws which alter existing contracts. The world has reached these principles through a long and weary struggle and much costly experience with repudiation and the abuses of legal tender. The burden of proof rests on those who would revert

___

[9] "An Honest Dollar", p. 2.

to these experiments for the sake of any benefits from bimetallism.   Surely the practical reasons against such a course are obvious enough.   When once a government has undertaken to "correct" debtor's losses, it will not stop at one attempt.   History teaches that a nation once embarked on such a policy never keeps its most solemn word as to where it shall leave off.[10]   Creditors will fear to lend except at usurious rates, and the debtor of the future will pay dearly for the emancipation of the debtor of the present.[11]

§ 5.

To those who claim that the cause of the aggravation of debts was governmental action in the first instance, and that therefore it is now a fit subject for governmental correction, the obvious answer is that this does not apply to the great mass of existing contracts which have been formed since demonetization.

Finally, it may be objected that the gold standard as such is on the side of creditors as against debtors because it is an appreciating standard, and according to our own statistics the debtor usually wins in rising and loses in falling prices.

Such reasoning, however, is entirely fallacious.   The fallacy is of the same kind as that contained in the face-tious advice to young speculators: "Buy when stocks are low and sell when they are high."   It is easy to prophesy after the event; investors in India silver bonds have lost for twenty years, but this does not prove that the present price of rupee paper is still too high.   If it did, London

---

[10] Shaw, "History of the Currency" (1895) ; also Sumner, "History of American Currency", p. 331.

[11] See the writer's "Would Bimetallism benefit the 'Debtor Class'?" *The Bond Record*, April, 1896.

brokers would be the first to know it and correct it. We cannot therefore say the "present arrangement is all in favor of the creditor and against the debtor". What bimetallist will risk his reputation in predicting the course of prices and interest in the next twenty years. *If* prices rise, we may with great probability predict that the debtor will win. *If* they fall, he will lose. But who knows which is the true "if"?

§ 6.

Legislation to offset the effects of a fall of prices in the past is wrong, because retro-active. Legislation to offset the effects of a fall in the future is absurd, because we cannot know there will be a fall, and if we could, there would be no need of legislation.

There remains to be considered legislation for the purpose of making the monetary unit less variable, that is, not to prevent something which we can foresee, but to prevent something which we cannot foresee. Such a reason for monetary legislation must be recognized at once as thoroughly sound. But it applies equally well to "symmetallism"[12] and other plans[13] for monetary reform.

That bimetallism (as long as it lasted)[14] would be

---

[12] Edgeworth, "Thoughts on monetary reform", *Economic Journal,* September, 1895.

[13] *E. g.,* the multiple standard propounded by Lowe, 1822, and Scrope, 1833, and advocated by Jevons, "Money and the Mechanism of Exchange", p. 328, and "Investigations", p. 123, and by Marshall, Report of the Commission on Depression of Trade, p. 423; also the various forms of double standard suggested by Marshall, *ibid.,* Edgeworth, *ibid.,* Hertzka, "Das internationale Wâhrungsproblem", 1892, and Stokes; "Joint Metallism" (1895); also the various forms of elastic currency suggested by Professor Walras, "Theorie de la Monnaie" (Lausanne, 1886), by Secretary Windom and others.

[14] See the writer's "Mechanics of Bimetallism", *Economic Journal,* September, 1894.

more dependable than monometallism is probable on *a priori* grounds, but the statistics which we have given seem to reveal as great uncertainty in price movements before 1873 as since. It is indeed a large question how far any sort of monetary reform could remedy the matter; for the expansion and contraction of credit might be almost as violent and mischievous as ever. It may be, however, that "the evils . . . are so great that it is worth while to do much in order to diminish them a little".[15] If a more stable and less expensive[16] monetary standard can be found, it will be an inestimable boon to the civilized world. As an improvement on the two single standards now existing, bimetallism, launched at the market ratio, may be worth serious consideration. But the proposal now before the world is bimetallism at 15½ or 16 to 1. Such bimetallism means debasement of the standard of any single country which attempts it. If international, it means debasement in gold standard countries, and a violent contraction and appreciation in silver standard countries. In no other way could the influence of the legal ratio on the market ratio be felt. We should witness not only losses to creditors in the former countries, but losses to debtors in the latter, and these losses would be far in excess of those which we have found to follow from the slow and half foreseen appreciation of the last twenty years.

---

[15] Marshall, "Principles of Economics", Vol. I, 3rd ed. (1895), p. 674.

[16] Jevons, "Investigations", p. 104: " . . . the very scarcity of gold is its recommendation . . . in itself gold digging has ever seemed to me almost a dead loss of labor as regards the world in general." Also Lexis, *Economic Journal*, June, 1895, p. 276.

CHAPTER XII.

§ 1.

The relation existing between interest and appreciation implies that the rate of interest is relative to the standard in which it is expressed. Economists, from Hume and Adam Smith down, seem to have considered the money element entirely eliminated from the rate of interest by the simple fact that, in the last analysis, it is capital, not money, which is loaned and returned. But, as has been seen, we can identify the rate of interest in terms of capital with the rate of interest in terms of money only when the price ratio between money and capital remains constant.

The first thought suggested by this fact is to distinguish between "nominal" and "real" interest in the same way that we distinguish between "nominal" and "real" wages. This seems to be the thought of all the writers who have touched on the subject. Professor Marshall, in fact, uses the words "real" and "nominal".[1] de Haas speaks of the effect of the appreciation of depreciation of money as introducing a "third element"[2] into the rate of interest. This "element" is to be added to or subtracted from the sum of the other two elements, which are a payment for capital (or the rate of interest proper) and a payment for insurance. John Stuart Mill and the eigh-

---

[1] "Principles of Economics", Vol. I, 3rd ed. (1895), p. 674.

[2] *Journal of the Royal Statistical Society*, March, 1889. It will be seen from the formula $1 + j = (1 + i)(1 + a)$ that the "third element" is not a mere additive term.

teenth century pamphleteer[3] were evidently thinking of
a normal rate of interest in coin to which a certain extra
charge is to be added if paper depreciates in reference
to coin. Finally, the article of Professor John B. Clark[4]
is devoted chiefly to a search for an absolute standard to
which we may refer any monetary appreciation or depreciation and in which, therefore, "real" interest could be
expressed. It is not denied that the words "real" and
"nominal" are very convenient terms, and for a rough
and ready expression may serve a useful purpose. But
the mere distinction between "real" and "nominal" is
quite inadequate for a true and accurate statement of
the case.[5]

If we seek to eliminate the money element by expressing the rate of interest in terms of real "capital", we are
immediately confronted with the fact that no two forms
of capital maintain or are expected to maintain a constant
price ratio. There are therefore just as many rates of
interest on capital as there are forms of capital diverging
in value. Even if we could find an ideal index number
for capital in general or for commodities, there are other
kinds of interest which might also claim the title of
"real"; we refer to "labor" and "income"[6] interest. It
cannot even be claimed that relative changes in prices,
wages and incomes are abnormal phenomena, or incident
only to a dynamic society. Even in the most ideal stationary state, the mere changes in seasons would make
interest between summer and winter low in terms of sum-

---

[3] See Chapter I, § 2.

[4] *Political Science Quarterly,* September, 1895.

[5] Professor Edgeworth ("Variations in Value of Monetary Standards", *Report of the British Association for the Advancement of
Science,* 1889, p. 163) exhibits seven kinds of standards for deferred
payments.

[6] See Chapter X, §§ 8, 9.

mer products such as fruit, and high in terms of winter products such as ice. The rate of interest is, as Professor Böhm-Bawerk shows, an agio on present goods exchanged for future goods of the same kind. It is a simple corollary of this theorem, though Professor Böhm-Bawerk does not express it, that this agio may be in theory and must be in practice a different agio for each separate kind of goods.

§ 2.

But, it may be urged, surely there is some invariable standard conceivable in theory if not determinable in practice, which may serve for a base line of appreciation and depreciation for all goods and money, and in terms of which we may express a "real" rate of interest. This brings us to the question of an absolute standard of value. But here we encounter another difficulty. Such an absolute standard will differ with each individual.[7] The fact that a dollar is a smaller unit to a millionaire than to a poor laborer, has as its consequence that as the millionaire grows poorer his dollar grows larger, while as the laborer grows richer his dollar grows smaller. On account of such changes in personal fortunes, the dollar, however defined, will be constantly appreciating and depreciating in different degrees among different men and classes. In fact, the phenomenon of borrowing and lending is to some extent itself a consequence of the different degrees in which money appreciates or depreciates to borrower and lender.

---

[7] Marshall, "Principles", Vol. I (3rd ed.), p. 198, and Royal Commission on Depression of Trade, 1886, p. 423; also the writer's "Mathematical Investigations in the Theory of Value and Prices", *Transactions of the Connecticut Academy* (New Haven, 1892).

§ 3.

In addition to the differences already mentioned, there is a different rate of interest for each period of time considered.   The rate in any given goods for a loan contracted to-day and payable one year hence is the agio of this year's over next year's goods; the rate for a loan to be contracted one year hence and payable two years hence is the agio (reckoned to-day) of next year's goods over the goods of the succeeding year, and so on.   The rate for a loan contracted to-day and payable two years hence is the "actuarial average"[8] of the two previous rates.   There is no reason why these three rates and others constructed in the same manner should not be all different.[9]

§ 4.

We thus reach a *multiple* theory of interest.   Our results are, first, that different standards have in general different rates of interest; secondly, that of the numerous standards thus possible a different one is "absolute" for each individual; thirdly, that in each standard there will be a different rate for different periods of time.[10]

---

[8] See Chapter V, § 4.

[9] Professor Böhm-Bawerk ("Positive Theory", p. 280), in showing how "arbitrage transactions" tend to equalize rates, tacitly assumes that the first two rates above mentioned are equal and only proves that in that case the third will be equal to the first.

[10] Besides these three sorts of variations there are others due to uncertainties of various kinds. In the theory of Part I, we have only considered the case where the relative divergence of two standards is foreknown with certainty. To complete the picture it is necessary to introduce the theory of probabilities as applicable to economics. (See Marshall's "Principles", p. 198, note, and 211, note.) When this is done it will also explain the different terms for call loans, 30 days, 60 days loans, etc., as well as for different degrees of security. Although in the latter case we may distinguish pure interest as the rate for perfect security, yet the surplus above this sum is not simple insurance. It is not a certain sum paid for a contingent loss, but it

In actual business experience none of these three sorts of differences attract attention. The third is usually very slight in amount.[11] The second is not reducible to statistical measurement; while the first escapes notice because of the habit of reckoning always in money. In a few cases, as for Indian and Chinese bonds, London brokers must have occasion to note the fact that 3% in silver is usually not equivalent to 3% in gold, but even in such cases the gold rate is thought of as "the" rate. So also speculative contracts in wheat, land, etc., and ordinary loans, which are really advances of stock, materials, and other forms of capital, are always translated into money and their essential nature as involving independent standards is concealed. But the economist, who so often finds it necessary to forsake the language of money and speaking in terms of the things which money measures, must here also recognize the fact that the rate of interest in terms of money is simply a common representative of multiform rates in other standards.

These rates are mutually connected and our task has been merely to state the law of that connection. We have not attempted the bolder task of explaining the rates themselves. Such an explanation constitutes the "theory of interest" in the more usual sense and forms the subject of Professor Böhm-Bawerk's masterly treatise. The relation between the two branches of the subject may be pictured as somewhat analogous to that between the theory of relative prices and the theory of price levels.

---

is itself contingent; and, what is more important here, it is not a present sum but a series of deferred sums, and as such is itself subject to the principles of pure interest. It follows that we cannot strike out the "insurance element" as a mere additive term with which the theory of interest proper has no concern. A complete theory has yet to be written.

[11] For a supposable case of great variation, see Chapter V, §§ 1, 2.

APPENDIX.

STATISTICAL DATA.

§ I.

The writer has found so much difficulty in securing a long series of yearly averages for rates on "money", that the results are here presented in the hope that they may be of use to others.

	London		Berlin		Paris		New York			Calcutta	Tokyo		Shanghai	
	Market	Bank	Market	Bank	Market	Bank	Call	60 Days	Prime a Name 60 Days	Bank	Market	Bank	Market	Bank
1824	3.5	4.0												
1825	3.9	4.0												
1826	4.5	5.0												
1827	3.3	4.5												
1828	3.0	4.0												
1829	3.4	4.0												
1830	2.8	4.0												
1831	3.7	4.0												
1832	3.1	4.0												
1833	2.7	4.0												
1834	3.4	4.0												
1835	3.7	4.0												
1836	4.2	4.4												
1837	4.5	5.0												
1838	3.0	4.1												
1839	5.1	5.1												
1840	5.0	5.1												
1841	4.9	5.0												
1842	3.3	4.3												
1843	2.2	4.0												
1844	2.1	2.5		4.3		4.0								
1845	3.0	2.7		4.4		4.0								
1846	3.8	3.3		4.7		4.0								
1847	5.9	5.2		4.8		4.9								
1848	3.2	3.7		4.7		4.0								
1849	2.3	2.9		4.0		4.0	4.5	7.8						
1850	2.2	2.5		4.0		4.0	4.8	7.2						
1851	3.1	3.0		4.0		4.0	5.9	8.3						
1852	1.9	2.2		4.0		3.2	5.1	7.3						
1853	3.7	2.7		4.2		3.2	6.9	10.1						
1854	4.9	2.1		4.3		4.3	7.7	12.5		3.9				
1855	4.7	2.9		4.1		4.5	6.6	9.3		9.7				
1856	5.9	6.1		4.9		5.5	7.0	9.9		6.5				
1857	7.1	6.7		5.8		6.1	6.9	10.4		7.0				
1858	3.1	3.2		4.5		3.7	3.8	6.7		6.1				
1859	2.5	3.7		4.0		3.5	5.0	7.2		4.9				
1860	4.1	4.2		4.0		3.6	6.1	8.4	7.7	4.2				
1861	5.5	5.3	3.0	4.0		5.5	5.4	9.0	6.6	4.2				
1862	2.4	2.5	3.0	4.0		3.8	5.6	6.8	5.4	5.1				
1863	4.3	4.4	3.5	4.1		4.6	5.0	6.7	5.8	5.5				
1864	7.4	7.4	5.1	5.3		6.5	7.2	9.3	8.0	8.7				
1865	4.6	4.8	4.6	5.0		3.7	6.1	10.2	8.2	6.9				
1866	6.7	6.9	6.2	6.2		3.7	5.9	7.8	6.3	9.1				13.
1867	2.3	2.6	2.9	4.0		2.7	5.9	8.7	7.2	5.1				11.
1868	1.8	2.1	2.5	4.0		2.5	5.8	8.8	7.3	5.8	15.	18.		12.
1869	3.0	3.2	3.2	4.1		2.5	6.0	10.8	9.1	6.0	18.	18.		12.
1870	3.1	3.1	4.5	4.8		4.0	5.1	8.1	7.2	5.7	14.	18.		11.
1871	2.7	2.9	3.8	4.2		5.1	4.5	6.0	6.1	4.7	14.	18.		12.
1872	3.8	4.1	4.0	4.3	4.2	5.1	5.6	9.0	8.0	5.0	14.	18.		10.
1873	4.5	4.8	4.5	5.0	5.0	5.2	6.3	9.8	10.3	3.9	14.	14		10.
1874	3.5	3.7	3.3	4.4	4.0	4.3	3.9	6.4		6.0	12.	14.		10.
1875	3.0	3.2	3.7	4.7	3.2	4.0				5.7	12.	14.		9.
1876	2.2	2.6	3.1	4.1	2.3	3.4				5.2	12	15.		9.5
1877	2.3	2.9	3.3	4.4	1.8	2.3				5.2	10.	13.		9.5
1878	3.5	3.8	3.4	4.3	2.0	2.2				4.8	11.	15.		9.
1879	1.8	2.5	2.7	3.7	2.2	2.6				5.0	11.	16.		9.
1880	2.2	2.8	3.1	4.2	2.5	2.8				5.2	13.	17.		8.5
1881	2.9	3.5	3.4	4.4	3.7	3.9				5.2	14.	17.		8.
1882	3.4	4.1	3.9	4.5	3.4	3.8				5.7	10	17.		8.
1883	3.0	3.6	3.1	4.1	2.6	3.1				6.8	7.9	11.		
1884	2.6	3.0	2.9	4.0	2.4	3.0				6.4	12.	16.		8.
1885	2.0	2.9	2.9	4.1	2.5	3.0				5.2	13.	11.	4 6	7.
1886	2.1	3.0	2.1	3.3	2.2	3.0				4.1	8.8	9.2	6 1	7.
1887	2.4	3.3	2 3	3.4	2.4	3.0				4.7	9.0	8.8	6.5	7.
1888	2.4	3.3	2.1	3.3	2.8	3.3				5.7	10.	9.7	6.0	7.
1889	2.7	3.6	2.7	3.7	2.6	3.1				4.9	10.	10.	6 2	7.
1890	3.7	4.5	3.7	4.5	2.6	3.0				5.5	11.	11.	7.2	7.
1891	2.5	3.3	3.0	3.9	2.6	3.0				6.0	9.4	9 4	3.5	7.
1892	1.5	2.5	1.8	3.2	1.8	2.7				5.7	8.3	8 4	5 0	7.
1893	2.1	3.1	3.2	4.1	2.2	2.5				4.3	7.8	7.8	6 9	7.
1894	1.0	2.1	1.7	3.1	1.8	2.5				7.1	9.3		3.8	7.
1895	.8	2.0	2.0	3.1	1.6	2.1				4.9	9.6		2.8	6.5

Tokyo column note: Before 1868, 10 to 12 Per Cent.

New York Calcutta Bank 1854–1895: 3.9, 9.7, 6.5, 7.0, 6.1, 4.9, 4.2, 4.2, 5.1, 5.5, 8.7, 6.9, 9.1, 5.1, 5.8, 6.0, 5.7, 4.7, 5.0, 3.9, 6.0, 5.7, 6.8, 8.4, 5.3, 6.3, 4.6, 5.3, 6.6, 6.8, 6.4, 5.4, 6.0, 5.6, 5.5, 7.0, 5.8, 6.0, 3.1, 3.5, 4.9, 5.4, 4.3, 3.4, 3.8

[1] The London, Berlin and Paris market rates are on first class merchants' bills. The

All the rates are entered in the foregoing table as rates of "interest", though the rates for the Banks of England, Germany and France are rates of discount. The two are not quite equivalent, but, for the purposes of the fore-going work, the distinction between them is unnecessary, because, in a continuous series, the error, if any, affects all items nearly alike and thus cancels itself out in the comparisons.

Had it been necessary, some of the tables could have been extended back. Thus the Bank of England rate could be given to 1696, but it was too inflexible to be of use. The Berlin and Paris bank rates could also be ex-tended, and the Paris market rate could be given from 1861 (except for 1870 and 1871) from data in the *Economist*.

---

figures for 1824–58 are from the evidence of D. B. Chapman before the Committee on the Bank Act, 1857, Sess. 2, X, pt. I, p. 463, (also reprinted in *Hunt's Merchants' Magazine*. Vol. 41, (1859) p. 95). The remaining figures are compiled from the *Economist*. For those for 1884–94, the writer is indebted to Professor F. M. Taylor of Michigan University, who had collected them from the *Economist* for a different purpose. The Bank of Eng-land rates for 1824–43 are reduced from Burdett's "Official Intelligencer," (1894), p. 1,771. The remaining ones for England, Germany and France are reduced from those given in the Report of the Royal Commission on the Depression of Trade, 1886, p. 373, and the *Economist*. They represent the Bank "minimum." The New York rates are taken, the first two columns, from a table by E. B. Elliott (afterward government actuary) in the (New York) *Bankers' Magazine*, 1874. The quotations given as "60 days" apparently included single name paper. The third column to 1890 is compiled from a diagram of highest and lowest monthly rates prepared at Yale college by Mr. G. P. Robbins of the class of 1891, and has been completed from the *Financial Review*, by averaging the highest and lowest weekly rates. It has been found impossible to extend the table back beyond 1849, as the rates are not systematically reported. The Calcutta rates are the minimum of the Bank of Bengal and have been kindly furnished by Messrs. Place, Siddons and Gough, brokers, of Calcutta. The market rates of Tokyo are averages of the highest and lowest rates of each year, furnished by Mr. Ichi Hara of the Bank of Japan, Tokyo. The bank rates are for the Tokyo and Yokohama Co-operative Bank and were translated by Mr. Sakata, student at Yale, from a history of Japan by Zenshiro Tsuboya. The tables for Shanghai have been procured through the kindness of Mr. F. W. Williams of the de-partment of Oriental History of Yale University, who obtained them from Mr. J. F. Sea-man of Shanghai. The first column contains the rates ruling in the native market, and the second, those of the Hong Kong and Shanghai bank (under English control) on overdrawn current accounts, a species of demand loans and the ordinary form of lending in Shanghai. Mr. Seaman was told that the market rates cannot be extended back beyond 1885, as the books of the Chinese banks for previous years are burnt.

[2] This rate is only from September when the operation of the Bank Act began. Pre-vious to this the custom of the bank was to have a uniform rate for all loans.

Many of the sources from which the table has been drawn also contain other information, such as the rates for Vienna, Amsterdam and other money centers, the weekly or monthly rates, the variation with the seasons, the number of changes of the Bank Minimum, etc.

§ 2.

Of sources not mentioned in the above note, the chief which the writer has encountered are:

Adolf Soetbeer, "Materiallen zur Währungsfrage (Berlin, 1886), p. 78.
> Covers 1851-85 for Banks of England, France and Germany, and market rates of Hamburg and Vienna.

Austrian Government, "Tabellen zur Währungsfrage" (Vienna, 1892), pp. 204-6. (A second edition has just appeared, 1896.)
> Covers 1861-91 for banks of Italy, England, France, Germany, Austria, Belgium and Holland, and market rates in Vienna, 1869-91.

W. Stanley Jevons, "Investigations in Currency and Finance" (London, 1884).
> Contains diagram for prices of consols and 3 per cent. stock from 1731, and minimum rate of interest in London from 1824; also monthly variations in rate of interest, p. 10. The diagram for the price of consols shows that during the middle and first half of the eighteenth century the interest realized was almost as low as in the present generation. This was a period of falling prices.

Eleventh Census of the United States, Bulletin 71 (on real estate mortgages, 1880-89).
> This is probably the most elaborate series of interest averages ever constructed. If these averages be compared with the course of prices during the average term of the contracts (five years), it will be found in nearly every case that interest is high or low according to the degree of the rise or fall in prices.

Viscomte G. D'Avenel, "Histoire économique de la propriété, des Salaires, des Denrées et de tous les Prix en général depuis l'an 1200 jusqu'en l'an 1800" (Paris, 1894), vol. II, p. 882.
> This work contains also tables of the purchasing power of money, but neither the interest nor price statistics are sufficiently exact or detailed for use in the foregoing study.

Tooke, "History of Prices", and
Tooke and Newmarch, "History of Prices from 1793 to 1856".
G. Winter, "Zur Geschichte des Zinsfusses in Mittelalter," *Zeitschrift für Social und Wirtschaftsgeschichte* (Weimar, 1895), IV, 2.
Arthur Crump, "English Manual of Banking" (4th ed., London, 1879), pp. 141-4.
> Gives Bank of England rates for 1694-1876.

Alph. Courtois fils, "Histoire des Banques en France" (Paris, 1881).
Gives rate of interest at the Bank of France, 1800-1880.

Wilhelm von Lucam, "Die Oesterreichische Nationalbank während der Dauer des dritten Privilegiums" (Vienna, 1876), p. 121.
Gives rates for Bank of Austria, 1817-75.

"Jahrbücher für Nationalökonomie und Statistik", February, 1896, pp. 282-83.
Gives bank and market rates for London, Paris, Berlin, Amsterdam, Brussels, Vienna and St. Petersburg, 1841-80 by decades, and 1881-95 by years.

"Handwörterbuch der Staatswissenschaften", Article "Banken".
Gives rates for Bank of Prussia and Germany, 1847-89; also for Bank of Austria, 1878-89; Switzerland, 1883-88.

A. N. Kiaer, "Om seddelbanker" (Kristiania, 1877).
Contains diagram of bank rates at Kristiania, Stockholm and Kjobenhavn, 1853-76.

M. G. Mullhall, "Dictionary of Statistics" (London, 1892), pp. 76, 607.
Gives rates for countries of Europe by five and ten year periods since 1850.

William Farr, "On the valuation of railroads, telegraphs", etc., *Journal of the Royal Statistical Society,* September, 1876, pp. 464-530.

"Report of the New England Mutual Life Ins. Co.", Boston, 1890.
Gives rates realized by twenty representative insurance companies for 1869-88, and for Massachusetts savings banks for 1877-89, and bank dividends in Boston, New York and Philadelphia. The rates realized by the insurance companies for the twenty years, 1869-88, inclusive, were 6.0, 5.9, 6.1, 6.2, 6.5, 6.2, 6.5, 6.1, 5.6, 5.1, 5.0, 4.7, 4.8, 5.1, 5.1, 4.7, 4.7, 4.9, 4.7, 4.6, respectively. These represent (if the writer mistakes not) the average rate earned on the par value of investments of all ages, some old, some new, some terminable soon, and others having many years to run. For this reason they are of little or no use for the foregoing study.

Robert Giffen, "Essay in Finance", second series (London, 1886), p. 37.
Seasonal variations of interest in connection with bank reserves. etc.

F. M. Taylor, "Do we want an Elastic Currency?" *Political Science Quarterly,* March, 1896, pp. 133-157.
Gives diagram showing the relation of surplus reserves and rates of discount; also seasonal variation of rate of discount.

R. H. Inglis Palgrave, "Analysis of the Transactions of the Bank of England" (London, 1874).
Gives rates, 1844-72, and seasonal variation, 1844-56 and 1857-72. Shows dependence of rate on ratio of reserve to liabilities.

R. H. Inglis Palgrave, "Bank-rate in England, France, and Germany, 1844-78; with remarks on the causes which influence the rate of interest charged; and an analysis of the accounts of the Bank of England" (London, 1880).

R. H. Inglis Palgrave, (London) *Bankers' Magazine,* March, April, May, 1878.
Number of changes in bank rates of England, France, and Germany.

Theodor Hertzka, "Währung und Handel" (Vienna, 1876).
  Gives the number of weeks each rate lasted for the Banks of England,
France, Germany, and Austria during 1844-73.

George Clare, "Money Market Primer" (London, 1891).
  Diagrams for seasonal variations of interest, bank reserves, etc.

Commercial and Financial Statistics of British India. Second issue
  (Government Printing Office, Calcutta, 1894), pp. 354-64.
    Monthly Discount, Bank of Bengal, 1861-94, and average quotations of
    government securities held in London.

Report of the Secretary of the Treasury, 1893, p. 401.

Report of the Comptroller of Currency, 1894, p. 179.

H. W. Farnam, "Some Effects of Falling Prices", *Yale Review,*
  August, 1895.
    The last three references contain statistics of rates of interest realized on
    some United States Government bonds.

R. A. Bayley, "National Loans of the United States" (Government
  Printing Office, Washington, 1882).
    Gives rates of interest and price of issue of all United States loans from
    July 4, 1776, to June 30, 1880.

"Dictionaire des Finances", Article "Interêt".
    Gives rates at which France has borrowed.

§ 3.

The following tables of index numbers are appended
in order that the reader may verify the periods of rising
and falling prices which have been discussed in Chapter
X and for the reason that many of the tables, notably
those for India, Japan and China, have not hitherto been
accessible to most readers.

INDEX NUMBERS IN SEVEN COUNTRIES.[1]

	England		Germany	France	United States		India	Japan	China
	Prices	Wages	Prices	Prices	Prices	Wages	Prices	Prices	Prices
1824 . .	105	. . .	. . . .	. . . .	. . . .	. . .	. . . .	. . . .	. . . .
1825 . .	124	. . .	. . . .	. . . .	. . . .	. . .	. . . .	. . . .	. . . .
1826 . .	108	. . .	. . . .	. . . .	. . . .	. . .	. . . .	. . . .	. . . .
1827 . .	108	. . .	. . . .	. . . .	. . . .	. . .	. . . .	. . . .	. . . .
1828 . .	97	. .	. . . .	. . . .	. . . .	. . .	. . . .	. . . .	. . . .
1829 . .	95	. . .	. . . .	. . . .	. . . .	. .	. . . .	. . . .	. . . .
1830 . .	97	. . .	. . . .	. . . .	. . . .	. . .	. . . .	. . . .	. . . .
1831 . .	98	. . .	. . . .	. . . .	. . . .	. . .	. . . .	. . . .	. . . .
1832 . .	93	. . .	. . . .	. . . .	. . . .	. . .	. . . .	. . . .	. . . .
1833 . .	90	. . .	. . . .	. . . .	. . . .	. . .	. . . .	. . . .	. . . .
1834 . .	93	. . .	. . . .	. . . .	. . . .	. . .	. . . .	. . . .	. . . .
1835 . .	96	. . .	. . . .	. . . .	. . . .	. . .	. . . .	. . . .	. . . .
1836 . .	103	. . .	. . . .	. . . .	. . . .	. . .	. . . .	. . . .	. . . .
1837 . .	101	. . .	. . . .	. . . .	. . . .	. . .	. . . .	. . . .	. . . .
1838 . .	101	. . .	. . . .	. . . .	. . .	. . .	. . . .	. . . .	. . . .
1839 . .	110	. . .	. . . .	. . . .	. .	. . .	. . . .	. . . .	. . . .
1840 . .	104	. . .	. . . .	. . . .	98	83	. . . .	. . . .	. . . .
1841 . .	102	. . .	. . . .	. . . .	98	80	. . . .	. . . .	. . . .
1842 . .	90	. . .	. . . .	. . . .	90	84	. . . .	. . . .	. . . .
1843 . .	85	. . .	. . . .	. . . .	84	83	. . . .	. . . .	. . . .
1844 . .	83	. . .	. . . .	. . . .	85	83	. . . .	. . . .	. . . .
1845 . .	89	. . .	. . . .	. . . .	88	86	. . . .	. . . .	. . . .
1846 . .	89	. . .	. . . .	. . . .	95	89	. . . .	. . . .	. . . .
1847 . .	94	. . .	. . . .	. . . .	95	91	. . . .	. . . .	. . . .
1848 . .	82	. . .	. . . .	. . . .	88	92	. . . .	. . . .	. . . .
1849 . .	77	. . .	. . . .	. . . .	83	91	. . . .	. . . .	. . . .
1850 . .	77	. . .	. . . .	. . . .	89	91	. . . .	. . . .	. . . .
1851 . .	79	. . .	100	. . . .	99	91	. . . .	. . . .	. . . .
1852 . .	78¹	. . .	102	. . . .	98	92	. . . .	. . . .	. . . .
1853 . .	95	. . .	114	. . . .	105	93	. . . .	. . . .	. . . .
1854 . .	102	. . .	121	. . . .	105	96	. . . .	. . . .	. . . .
1855 . .	101	. . .	124	. . . .	109	97	. . . .	. . . .	. . . .
1856 . .	101	. . .	123	. . . .	112	98	. . . .	. . . .	. . . .
1857 . .	105	. . .	130	. . . .	114	99	. . . .	. . . .	. . . .
1858 . .	91	. . .	114	. . . .	113	98	. . . .	. . . .	. . . .
1859 . .	94	. . .	116	. . . .	103	100	. . . .	. . . .	. . . .
1860 . .	99	100	121	. . . .	100	100	. . . .	. . . .	. . . .
1861 . .	98	. . .	118	100	94	101	. . . .	. . . .	. . . .
1862 . .	101	. . .	123	118	104	104	. . . .	. . . .	. . . .
1863 . .	103	. . .	125	127	132	119	. . . .	. . . .	. . . .
1864 . .	105	. . .	129	129	172	134	. . . .	. . . .	. . . .
1865 . .	101	. . .	123	112	232	149	. . . .	. . . .	. . . .
1866 . .	102	113	126	115	188	156	. . . .	. . . .	. . . .
1867 . .	100	. . .	124	100	166	164	. . . .	. . . .	. . . .
1868 . .	99	. . .	122	95	174	165	. . . .	. . . .	. . . .
1869 . .	98	. . .	123	97	152	167	. . . .	. . . .	. . . .
1870 . .	96	111	123	94	144	167	. . . .	. . . .	. . . .
1871 . .	100	. . .	127	94	136	166	. . . .	. . . .	. . . .
1872 . .	109	. . .	136	105	132	167	. . . .	. . . .	. . . .
1873 . .	111	. . .	138	103	129	166	100	104	. . . .
1874 . .	102	134	136	94	130	162	98	104	100
1875 . .	96	. . .	130	87	129	158	95	105	103
1876 . .	95	. . .	128	85	123	151	99	102	111
1877 . .	94	129	128	82	114	144	121	105	101
1878 . .	87	. . .	121	78	105	141	125	114	106
1879 . .	83	. . .	117	76	95	139	119	145	111
1880 . .	88	120	122	79	105	143	112	160	105
1881 . .	85	. . .	121	76	108	151	99	175	110
1882 . .	84	. . .	122	73	109	153	98	159	108
1883 . .	82	124	122	73	107	159	96	130	103
1884 . ·	76	. . .	114	72	103	155	97	116	104
1885 . .	72	. . .	109	70	93	156	95	116	105
1886 . .	69	121	104	69	93	156	99	107	107
1887 . .	68	. . .	102	71	94	157	101	109	105
1888 . .	70	. . .	102	74	96	158	104	112	100
1889 . .	72	. . .	106	89	98	163	107	116	105
1890 . .	72	. . .	108	84	94	168	103	124	104
1891 . .	72	135	109¹	79	94	169	104	123	104
1892 . .	68	. . .	106	. . . .	. . . .	. . .	115	124	108
1893 . .	68	. . .	102	. . . .	. . . .	. . .	119	129	109
1894 . .	63	. . .	92	. . . .	. . . .	. . .	. . . .	. . . .	. . . .
1895 . .	62	. . .	91	. . . .	. . . .	. . .	. . . .	. . . .	. . . .

[1] For England, the figures for prices are from Jevons and Sauerbeck. Those from

Sauerbeck begin in 1852. They are taken from the Aldrich report (I, 247) and from the *Journal of the Royal Statistical Society*, March, 1896. Those from Jevons are from 1824 1852 inclusive, and are taken from his "Investigations in Currency and Finance." In order to make the tables of Jevons and Sauerbeck continuous, Jevons' number for 1852 is called 78 (*i. e.*, Sauerbeck's for that year) instead of 65 as given in the "Investigations," and all the other numbers are raised in the ratio 78 : 65. Jevons' figures are for forty commodities; Sauerbeck's for forty-five. The index numbers for English wages are from the article by Bowley in the *journal of the Royal Statistical Society*, June, 1895.

The German numbers are from Soetbeer, Heinz and Conrad. Those for 1851-91 inclusive, are from Soetbeer, continued by Heinz, and given in the Aldrich report (I, 294); those for 1891-95 inclusive, are from Conrad, as given in his *Jahrbücher*, 1894-6, but all are magnified in the ratio 109 : 98 in order to make the series continuous, since Heinz's figure for 1891 is 109, and Conrad's 98. The statistics of Soetbeer and Heinz cover 114 commodities.

The French numbers are from the Aldrich report (I, 335) founded on the figures of the *Commission permanente des valeurs*. They cover only sixteen articles.

The figures for the United States are those of Professor Falkner in the Aldrich report (I, 9, 13), the weighted averages (last method) being employed.

Those for India, Japan and China are from the Japanese Report of the Commission for investigation of monetary systems, 1895. The writer is under great obligations to Mr. Ichi Hara, of Tokyo, for a copy of the report, and to Mr. Sakata of Yale University, for translating the tables.

That for India is an average of three tables which cover respectively twenty–one articles of export, sixteen articles of export priced at Calcutta and Bombay, and eight grains at Bombay. That for Japan is an average of three tables, of forty-two articles at Tokyo, sixteen at Osaka and thirty-one articles of export. That for China is an average of three tables, of twenty inland commodities, seventeen articles of export and fifteen foodstuffs in Shanghai.

The tables for India were based on official statistics, those from Japan on information from guilds and merchants, and those for China on the reports of the consuls of Japan and England (Mr. Jameson) in China.

In the Japanese report the prices for Japan are reduced to a silver basis. As silver was at a premium up to 1885 it has been necessary in constructing the above table to reconvert into currency by applying the premium for 1873–85, viz. : 4, 4, 3, 1, 3, 10, 32, 48, 70, 57. 26, 9, 5 per cent. respectively.